D1388542

Praise for The Thousand Dollar Dinner:

"That long-ago dinner at Parkinson's Restaurant [is] engagingly resurrected, deconstructed and served up for modern readers by food historian Becky Libourel Diamond . . . a prudent and careful chronicler of one of the most deliciously over-the-top dinners ever served in America."
—**Aram Bakshian Jr.**, *The Wall Street Journal*

"This richly detailed chronicle showcases the fantastic dining experience concocted in 1851 by Philadelphia chef James W. Parkinson in response to a challenge from 15 wealthy New Yorkers who claimed their city produced the best meals. Diamond dishes out more than the menu of this remarkable meal, deconstructing each course with details of the class mores, cultural habits, and food preferences of elite nineteenth-century Americans. This tale of a Gilded Age mega-meal will delight culinary historians and anyone wanting a peek at over-the-top consumption."
—*Publishers Weekly*

"A mouthwatering tale of one luxurious 1851 dinner."
—*Entertainment Weekly*

"This long-forgotten meal is deliciously dissected . . . . Chefs like Parkinson did their part to highlight the most artful aspects of the profession, setting the groundwork for the popularity of today's celebrity chef competitive-cooking TV series."
—**Drew Lazor**, *The Philadelphia Inquirer*

"Drenched in Champagne and Cognac, *The Thousand Dollar Dinner* is a delicious taste of our country's first restaurant revolution. An equally light and luxurious read, this book will leave every food fanatic and history buff hungry for more."
—**Maureen Petrosky, author of** *The Wine Club* **and NBC** *Today Show* **Lifestyle Expert**

"[Diamond's] sensible and sensitive detailed analyses of each of the dozens of dishes virtually materialize them for the reader's sight, smell, taste, and touch." Although the age of this sort of sumptuous banqueting has passed, contemporary tasting menus from acclaimed chefs owe much to the precedents of feasts such as this one."
—*Booklist*

"The story of the genesis of this type of rich living is fascinating, her details complete and vivid. . . . a delightful book to read by the fire."
—*Bookreporter*

"From the first chapter to the last, *The Thousand Dollar Dinner* captivates readers with a sumptuous feast that would top any modern-day event. In this well-researched book, Diamond shows how American cuisine was sophisticated, elegant, and show stopping."
—**Walter Staib, proprietor of Philadelphia's City Tavern Restaurant and Emmy Award-winning host of PBS's *A Taste of History***

"Diamond's brilliantly-researched and well-turned tome is a time machine for food geeks. Working through Chef Parkinson's menu course-by-course, Diamond elegantly serves up richly detailed historical context for each dish in such vivid and engaging detail—from the sourcing of ingredients, to course preparation, to dining etiquette—that you feel like you were actually at the dinner. *The Thousand Dollar Dinner* is the Downton Abbey for dining devotees."
—*PhilaFoodie*, **former restaurant critic for the** *City Paper*

"Allotting one chapter per course, Diamond guides the reader dish by dish through the menu. The history, regional significance, and preparation techniques of each ingredient make for dozens of entertaining digressions. An appetizing read."
—*Library Journal*

"From the first through the seventeenth course, *The Thousand Dollar Dinner* paints an astonishing picture of food history and customs. Enlightening and entertaining, the story of this fascinating culinary event is not to be missed. A great read."
—**Diane Richardson, Executive Director, Ebenezer Maxwell Mansion**

THE THOUSAND DOLLAR DINNER

AMERICA'S FIRST GREAT COOKERY CHALLENGE

BECKY LIBOUREL DIAMOND

Leabharlanna Poiblí Chathair Baile Átha Cliat'
Dublin City Public Libraries

WESTHOLME
Yardley

First Westholme Paperback 2016

© 2015 Becky Libourel Diamond

All rights reserved under International and Pan-American Copyright
Conventions. No part of this book may be reproduced in any form or by any
electronic or mechanical means, including information storage and retrieval systems, without permission in writing from the publisher, except by a reviewer
who may quote brief passages in a review.

Westholme Publishing, LLC
904 Edgewood Road
Yardley, Pennsylvania 19067
Visit our Web site at www.westholmepublishing.com

10 9 8 7 6 5 4 3 2
ISBN: 978-1-59416-260-2
Also available as an eBook.

Printed in the United States of America.

"Not all our food history is set down in cookbooks."
—James Beard, *American Cookery*

CONTENTS

AN INVITATION

A cool spring breeze swept over the Camden and Philadelphia Steamboat ferry as it chugged its way across the Delaware River toward the city of Philadelphia. In the distance, squat steamboats lined the wharfs, intermingled with tall swaying ships, their white sails flapping in the wind. Behind the ships stood rows of worn red brick buildings, housing residences, shops, hotels, and taverns. The steeple of Christ Church, a well-known landmark, loomed above them all, piercing the early evening sky. Just beyond, the American flag flew from the castle-like garret of the ten-story Jayne Building, the nation's first skyscraper.[1]

That evening in April 1851, many of the ferry passengers were on the final leg of their journey from New York City. To make the trip to Philadelphia, they had taken a steamboat down the Raritan River to Amboy, and then boarded a train that crossed through New Jersey to Camden. Among those who had made this excursion were fifteen impeccably dressed New York gentlemen. They had accepted an invitation to dine at an exclusive Philadelphia restaurant called Parkinson's.

After the boat docked at the Walnut Street wharf, the men collected their leather travel cases and stepped off the ferry, making their way to the nearby Bloodgood's Hotel, which also served as a waiting area for Camden and Amboy Railroad passengers.[2]

Entering through the heavy glass-paneled door, they stepped into its plush parlor. While several of the recently disembarked passengers were already in line at the hotel desk trying to get a room or hire a hackney coach or cab, the fifteen New Yorkers had been told a driver would be waiting there to meet them. As they scanned the room, a young man walked over and asked them if they were due at Parkinson's. They replied yes, and the young man bowed and pointed to a spot on the street outside where three black carriages were parked.

The drivers helped the men into the carriages, secured their bags, and then set off, the horses' feet clip-clopping on the cobblestones. As the carriages reached Eighth Street, they turned south and stopped in front of number 38, a three-story brick building displaying a large sign with "PARKINSONS" in block lettering. Gleaming white marble steps led up to the restaurant's front door, which was surrounded on either side by a storefront made completely out of clear glass, with etched detailing at the top. The second floor featured a small balcony, its three doors open to the mild spring evening, revealing hints of the luxurious dining room inside.

The drivers retrieved the gentlemen's bags and carried them to the entryway. The New Yorkers followed, and as they made their way up the stairs, a handsomely dressed waiter came out to meet them. Introducing himself as Parkinson's headwaiter, he ushered them inside, remarking that he hoped their journey to Philadelphia had been a pleasant one. More waitstaff came to take the men's coats and belongings, stowing them in a large closet off the entryway, while the headwaiter led them into one of the restaurant's richly furnished front salons. Decorated in deep shades of burgundy, the room featured Wilton carpets, marble-topped tables, and ornately curved mahogany furniture.

Waiting to greet the New Yorkers were their Philadelphia friends. They shook hands warmly and made light conversation. While they were chatting, several waiters approached with aperitifs on silver trays—cognac and wine bitters, with Madeira and sherry—designed to stimulate the appetite.[3] Unknown to the guests, this was the first taste of a meal they would remember for a lifetime. The men conversed for several minutes, enjoying the invigorating liquors, much appreciated by the New Yorkers after their lengthy trip.

We know for sure only two names of the men at the dinner—R. B. Valentine, a well-known insurance agent from New York, and Joshua Price, a wealthy gentleman from an old Philadelphia Quaker family. However, one source described the fifteen Philadelphians as "merchant princes," so we can speculate that the guests would have been among Philadelphia's wealthiest at the time, which would have included men such as broker Francis Drexel, dry goods merchant Richard Ashhurst, flour merchant Thomas Ridgway, and physicians J. Rhea Barton and James Rush, both married to heiresses of the Ridgway estate. Other likely guests could have been book publisher Theophilus B. Peterson, *Philadelphia Sun* editor and publisher Colonel James Wallace, and General George Cadwalader, all of whom were known to have ties to James Parkinson. We can also guess the fifteen New Yorkers were among the wealthiest and most connected in New York City at the time. Some possible guests could have been Henry J. Raymond, cofounder of the *New York Times*, Samuel Cutler Ward, author and noted epicure who was the husband of Emily Astor, and dry goods merchant Alexander Turney Stewart. All were known to have been frequent Delmonico's customers.[4]

Soon a staff member approached the headwaiter and gave him the signal that the table was ready. The waiter politely waited for a lull in the conversation and then requested that the group follow him upstairs to the large second-floor banquet room. The gentlemen ascended the slightly curved stairway. The polished mahogany railing was intricately carved, and the walls were lined with gold-framed mirrors, still-life paintings, and landscapes. Overhead, a sparkling gas chandelier gave a soft, sustained light.

At the top of the stairs the headwaiter directed them to the left, leading them into the banquet room where they would be dining.

Spacious and airy, it was indeed the room the men had seen when they arrived—the three large doors that led to the balcony were now just partly open, in anticipation of the cool evening air.

Thirty place settings of the finest china, silver, and crystal were situated around the enormous mahogany table, covered with a cloth of freshly starched white linen. A table fork and a fish fork were placed to the left side of each plate, and to the right lay a table knife, a silver fish knife, a soup spoon, and a small fork for oysters. Small individual saltcellars were above each plate on the right side.[5] To the left of each plate a silver stand held the bill of fare, a large booklet beautifully printed in gold and decorative colors. Mounted pieces of ornamental confectionery, statuettes, and striking flower arrangements were artfully displayed down the center of the table. The light of dozens of candelabras mixed with the glow from three gas chandeliers. Tall, exquisitely decorated cakes, meringues, and colorful confectionery were arranged on the massive carved sideboard. The long buffet held rows of wine and liquor bottles, ice buckets of champagne, and pitchers of water.

As the gentlemen took in the opulent scene, the restaurant's owner, James W. Parkinson, appeared and greeted them, shaking hands all around. A handsome young man in his early thirties with a head of abundant curly black hair, he was wearing his chef's hat and apron. Although pleasant and cordial, he seemed subdued, almost shy, making the New Yorkers wonder about his expertise in the kitchen.

Inviting the gentlemen to make their way over to the table, Parkinson told them how pleased he was that they could come, and that he hoped that they would enjoy the dinner he had the honor of preparing. As they found their place cards, a group of waiters came over to help seat them. The waitstaff wore formal evening wear—black pantaloons, swallowtail coat, white vest, tie, and spotless white kid gloves. The waiters then took their positions—one behind each gentleman. The time was precisely 6 P.M. These thirty men were about to experience a meal of extraordinary proportions.

It was 1851, a time of significant progress and change. That year, Britain's Great Exhibition—the first of its kind—displayed the marvels of industry and manufacturing from around the world, including the latest kitchen appliances, steel-making displays, textile looms, and firearms. The specialty grocery store, Fortnum and Mason, debuted their famous ready-prepared hampers packed with exotic foods, spices, and drinks to the delight of exhibition visitors. In America, the restaurant industry was experiencing rapid growth, where some of the foods displayed at the Great Exhibition could now be found on menus.

Places to eat, drink, and socialize in America had been around since the colonial period in the form of taverns, inns, boarding-houses, and coffee houses. However, the food was typically simple and rustic, more of a necessary sustenance. Customers often didn't even have a choice of what to eat; the cook dictated what was on the menu for the evening. A few places were more refined, such as New York's Fraunces Tavern and the City Tavern in Philadelphia—a favorite meeting place of the Founding Fathers. But for the most part, haute cuisine was reserved for dinner parties at the residences of upper-class society.

The modern restaurant had its beginnings in eighteenth-century Paris. Originally the term *restaurant* referred to a restorative, or fortifying, light soup. But when a bouillon establishment promoted the sale of "divine restaurants" in 1765, the Parisian caterer's guild took the owner to court. His crime—offering not only soup, but also a sheep's foot *ragout*—considered more substantial than a simple broth. He won the case and the term stuck as a way to refer to eateries where one could get a meal using special ingredients and preparations, often associated with a particular chef.[6]

The idea spread to America, and by the mid-nineteenth century, restaurants were popping up by the dozens in cities throughout the United States, where demand was the highest. In 1850, Philadelphia had 254 restaurants, and New York City went from having about one hundred restaurants in 1847 to over five thousand by the 1860s.[7]

A number of factors contributed to the rise of the restaurant. People were flocking to cities in droves. For example, the population of Philadelphia doubled between 1840 and 1860. Many were immigrants, trying to escape the potato famine in Ireland and political unrest in Europe;[8] others were young men seeking jobs. Both groups often resided in boardinghouses or hotels, taking their meals there and in other eateries. In addition, merchants, bankers, and other businessmen began to commute to the cities from suburban locations. These men needed a place to have lunch since they were no longer eating their midday meal at home.[9]

In addition, class structures were being redefined as the rapidly growing American middle class exerted more influence and strived to match the higher standards of the upper class. The middle class realized how they dressed, behaved, decorated their houses, and dined was a powerful tool that could be used to set them apart from those they considered to have a less significant social standing.[10] Sophisticated and stylish establishments such as Parkinson's catered to the wealthy as well as this growing middle class.

Both Philadelphia and New York were leaders in this restaurant revolution and developed a culinary rivalry. Upper-class residents of each city felt their metropolis had the best chefs and superior restaurants. This competitiveness was the driving force in bringing these fifteen wealthy New York gentlemen to dine at Parkinson's.

This culinary duel began a few months earlier, when the New Yorkers wanted to show a group of Philadelphia friends just how impressive a meal could be had in their city. These two "clubs of good-livers" apparently "spent one day in every year and all their spare cash in trying to rival each other's banquets." To pull off this feat, they went to Delmonico's, New York's finest restaurant, and requested the services of its host, Lorenzo Delmonico. Delmonico's did not introduce the concept of the free-standing restaurant to the United States, but they helped revolutionize and perfect the idea.[11] They told him they wanted to "astonish our Quaker City friends with the sumptuousness of our feast," assuring him that money was no object and instructing him to do "his level best" as their honor and the honor of New York were at stake.

Lorenzo Delmonico agreed, and he treated the New Yorkers and their fifteen invited Philadelphians to a magnificent banquet at his restaurant on South William Street, much enjoyed by all. However, not to be outdone, the Philadelphia men politely invited the New Yorkers "to drop in upon *them* some evening and take pot-luck with them."[12] They then contacted their best caterer and restaurateur, James W. Parkinson, and asked him to create a similar dinner.

They settled the date for April 19, which made things rather tricky for Parkinson, as it was between seasons. As noted by R. B. Valentine, an avid epicure, the timing "took the caterer greatly at a disadvantage as to both game and vegetables. He could only obtain what he did by special use of both telegraph and express." But Parkinson successfully rose to the challenge, creating a seventeen-course feast famously referred to by Philadelphia newspapers as the "Thousand Dollar Dinner" (since it reputedly cost the Philadelphians $1,000, an enormous sum equivalent to perhaps thirty-two times that amount today).[13] The guests sat down at 6 P.M. and did not rise from their chairs until 6 A.M. the next morning. A gastronomic turning point, this luxurious meal helped launch the era of grand banquets in nineteenth-century America.[14]

Parkinson's dinner paired different rare wines and liquors with each of the courses, which included such delicacies as fresh salmon and baked rockfish, braised pigeon, turtle steaks, spring lamb, out-of-season fruits and vegetables, and several dessert courses showcasing rich pastries, ice cream, cakes, and puddings. Each of Parkinson's courses was designed to meld familiar dishes with novel presentations. Special praise went to an artful and luscious sorbet that he created using an expensive Hungarian Tokaj wine.

The dinner was typical of the multifaceted affairs popular during the Victorian era. According to Valentine, "not only the general appearance, but every detail and minutia showed the hand of a master." A wine cooler filled with ice was positioned in front of each of the thirty guests; a personal waiter stood behind every chair.

It was a transformative time in the culinary world, including the way courses were presented. For centuries, formal dinners were served using the technique known as *à la française* (French style), where the meal was divided into just two or three courses and the food was attractively laid out on the table for the diners to see. However, in the early nineteenth century a new way of formal dining was introduced, known as *à la russe* (Russian style),[15] where courses were brought out by servants individually in succession, each a separate presentation in itself. This new style gradually began to merge with the old and by the end of the century, the idea of crowded tables had gone away and serving individual courses had become standard. Parkinson embraced and incorporated this new style for his Thousand Dollar Dinner, bringing out each course one at a time, while still mixing a bit of the French style in terms of the order the dishes were served.[16]

The eighteen-page menu, titled "Empire and Keystone," was a work of art, printed in gold and bright colors, with a beautiful picture of each course on individual consecutive pages.[17] A printed menu was an expected feature at formal dinners at this time. While menus written on stone tablets date back to ancient Greece and Rome, for centuries the most common method of communicating the various dishes to be served at a banquet was assigning a person—either the host or a servant—to announce the menu. An explanation of the different preparations was often included, specifying the freshness of the ingredients and age of the wines. This is familiar to restaurant goers today when a waitperson recites the day's specials. This was especially helpful when dining à la française was popular, since this style was all about presentation. A verbal description of the artistic display of dishes added to the meal's performance. But when à la russe style became customary, and dishes were no longer displayed, diners appreciated receiving a written list of what they could expect to be served during each course. When guests entered the dining room at a banquet, they would find a written menu at each place at the table, similar to a theater program.[18] As *Gaskell's Compendium of Forms* (1881) clarifies in its section on "Etiquette of dinner parties": "On each plate a bill of fare is placed so that the guests may see what will be handed around, and may be prepared to select, or wait for, whatever dishes they may prefer."[19] Throughout the nineteenth century, written menus were introduced in restaurants as a way to list the various food dishes that were available to the customer. Both Parkinson's and Delmonico's had extensive menus, complete with prices for each item.

The thirty New York and Philadelphia diners were not the only ones to enjoy Parkinson's special meal. A group of Philadelphia's best caterers had gathered in a small room off the banquet hall to witness this bit of history (and probably also learn a thing or two). Hidden from view of the thirty patrons, they were able to watch the dinner festivities and see their contemporary and competitor performing his behind-the-scenes gastronomic magic. Joseph Head, proprietor of the Mansion House Hotel on Market Street, was among the observers. Like Parkinson, Head was a culinary master, well known for entertaining Philadelphia's upper-class society. He praised Parkinson's achievement, declaring, "Neither in England nor in America have I ever seen so superb a banquet, and I never expect to see, nor do I think any of *you* will ever see, such another."[20]

The meal was astonishing, unlike anything the New Yorkers had ever experienced. Soon, they realized any doubt they had about the shy young chef's expertise was ill placed, and they gracefully admitted defeat. Three different times during the meal the New Yorkers stood in appreciation, not only to acknowledge that the Philadelphians had "conquered them triumphantly," but also to unanimously declare that the meal "far surpassed any similar entertainment which had ever been given in this country."[21] This was not a light compliment. Delmonico's set the tone for nineteenth-century fine dining in New York City, and the rest of America as well.

A partnership of two brothers from the Italian-speaking part of Switzerland, Delmonico's began in the mid-1820s as a wine shop/confectionery at 23 William Street in the Battery section of New York. As a former ship's captain, Giovanni Del-Monico knew wines, and his brother Pietro was a trained pastry chef.[22] The business was highly successful, and in 1831 the brothers were able to open a proper Parisian-style restaurant in the adjoining building. They hired a French chef and soon brought in their young nephew Lorenzo to take over management duties. Lorenzo learned quickly, turning Delmonico's into a unique dining experience, with fresh, innovative cuisine, impeccable service, and lavish furnishings and décor, down to the elegant crystal, silver, and porcelain that graced the tables.[23]

Soon Delmonico's began to take Manhattan by storm, opening another restaurant at Beaver and William streets in 1837, directly across from the stock exchange. With this location they incorporated not only European-style fine dining and wines, but some artifacts from the Old World as well; the imposing marble pillars used to support the portico and entrance were imported from Pompeii, giving the restaurant its nickname, "The Citadel."[24] With its prime position in the middle of the rapidly expanding financial district, Delmonico's developed a large client base of businessmen and merchants, who began taking time out from their busy day to enjoy a luxurious lunch while doing a little deal making at the same time. By the mid-1860s, the family had two restaurants near Wall Street, another one on Lower Broadway, and one on Fourteenth Street. During the ninety-six years of their reign, they operated a total of eleven different Delmonico locations in New York as well as a lodging house and a hotel.[25]

A parade of famous people dined at Delmonico's over the years, including Charles Dickens, Mark Twain, and Oscar Wilde, every U.S. president from James Monroe to Franklin Delano Roosevelt, the future Edward VII, actress and singer Lillian Russell and her companion "Diamond Jim" Brady, as well as society families such as the Vanderbilts, Astors, and Belmonts. Many were given special banquets in their honor, and others were regulars doted on by the attentive staff.[26]

Delmonico's employed a number of outstanding culinary professionals, most famously Charles Ranhofer, who joined as principal chef in 1862 and presided over the restaurant's kitchens for thirty-four years. Born into a French family of chefs, Ranhofer began his cooking apprenticeship at the age of twelve and by age sixteen he was chef to an Alsatian prince. In 1856 he made his way to America and after stints in Washington, D.C. and New Orleans, was hired by Lorenzo Delmonico. The timing couldn't have been better for both Ranhofer and Delmonico's. It was the dawn of what Mark Twain would later dub, the "Gilded Age," and Delmonico's clients fully embraced Ranhofer's passion for French cuisine, delighted by the chef's seven-page menu (with dishes listed in both French and English) and fully stocked wine cellar.[27]

With Ranhofer in the kitchen and Lorenzo as host, Delmonico's thrived, providing unrivaled service. The various locations were staffed with hundreds of skilled chefs, all with specific areas of expertise. Behind the scenes, butchers made sure customers received the choicest cuts, dozens of line cooks worked the stoves and plated meals artistically, and pastry chefs created elaborate confectionery. Ranhofer was famous for honoring special events and Delmonico guests by creating dishes in their honor, such as lobster Newburg (after sea captain Ben Wenburg), eggs Benedict (for a Mrs. LeGrand Benedict), and baked Alaska (to commemorate the U.S. purchase of Alaska from Russia). His opus was *The Epicurean*, one of the most thorough and instructive cookbooks ever written, a tome of over 1,000 pages and more than 3,500 recipes.[28]

While Delmonico's remains a well-known brand name, Parkinson's is now forgotten to all but the most assiduous food historians. Originally from England and Scotland, George Parkinson and his wife Eleanor began their restaurant careers in

Philadelphia by operating the Burns Tavern on Strawberry Alley in the early 1800s. In 1818 (the same year their son and future protégé James was born) they opened another tavern, the Pennsylvania Arms, often referred to as "The Green House," due to the building's bright green color. George managed the tavern, which offered wine, whiskey, and lemonade, as well as typical pub fare such as savory pies, bread, and cheese. Adjoining the tavern was a confectionery run by Eleanor, featuring pies, cakes, creams, fruits, colorful jellies, and richly flavored cordials. The location also catered to private gatherings. An ad placed by George Parkinson in 1819 proclaimed: "Snug parties are accommodated here, with dinners, suppers and all kind of cheer. Of all my patrons' wishes most obedient, I am their faithful, most observant servant."[29]

But it was Eleanor's confectionery business that captured the public's attention, causing George to abandon tavern keeping and partner with his wife. This savvy move launched a culinary presence that continued for several decades. Exquisitely flavored ice cream was their specialty, and by 1830 they had opened an ice cream saloon and confectionery store on Philadelphia's fashionable Chestnut Street.[30] In addition to rich ice cream, the store sold refreshments such as water ice, Turkish sherbets, cakes, candies, and bonbons. Fine fruits such as grapes, pears, and peaches were also available, many procured from local gardens and hothouses. The Parkinsons also provided wedding and ornamental cakes, both in the Parisian style and their own designs.[31]

As their business grew during the 1830s, the couple were grooming young James to follow in their footsteps. George had planned for his son to travel to France and apprentice under a celebrated Parisian confectioner, but James fell ill and could not make the voyage. So George invited the Frenchman to come to Philadelphia. Over the next few years, he hired other well-known confectioners from England, France, Germany, Italy, and even China to share their expertise with James, giving each of them two-year stints in his establishment. In addition to this comprehensive training, James also shadowed his mother, which effectively made him into a top-ranked confectioner. The family's hard work and preparation paid off. When George retired in 1838, James joined the business with his mother and eventually took it over himself.[32]

By this time, the Parkinson name was nationally known for their ice cream and confectionery, and in 1844 Eleanor capitalized on their fame by publishing the popular recipes they served in a cookbook called *The Complete Confectioner*. But it was James who made their name gastronomically, establishing fine dining at their 180 Chestnut Street location and several others over the next few decades, including the restaurant on South Eighth Street in 1846 (with financial backing from General George Cadwalader).[33] This new restaurant provided innovative, seasonal fare in addition to his family's famous confections. James Parkinson also developed a lucrative catering business, supplying the city's high-society parties, soirees, weddings, and picnics. As noted by the *Philadelphia Inquirer* in 1849, Parkinson was "at the head of his profession as a supper party purveyor. His taste in the arrangement of the tables alone is admirable."[34]

Parkinson had the reputation of serving the best food that could be obtained at a decent price, and was well known for his ability to procure items that were out of season. He was also an early proponent for American foods and cookery, often incorporating them into his menus, including canvasback ducks, terrapin, soft-shell crabs, oysters, and of course the rich ice cream his family made famous.[35] He was so adamant that these foods were prepared in the proper "American-style" that he would not let Leon, his celebrated Italian chef, touch them. Instead, he left them in the hands of Martha, an African American cook from Maryland who was well versed in local cookery and was known to fry up the most plump, tender, and juicy oysters.[36]

James had a creative, innovative way with food, such as the invention of Champagne frappe à la glacé (a semi-frozen froth made with the sparkling wine) and the creation of elaborate ice cream sculptures, such as the dramatic nightingale suspended from a harp he designed specifically for Jenny Lind, the world-renowned Swedish soprano who embarked on an American tour in 1850 at the request of P. T. Barnum.[37] For an exhibition at the Franklin Institute, he created a colossal, beautifully decorated cake that contained a whopping 1,440 eggs, 150 pounds of butter, 150 pounds of flour, 150 pounds of sugar, and 500 pounds of fruit, and weighed about 1,200 pounds.[38]

He also had quite a flair for marketing. During a time when most shops and eating places were rather unwelcoming to children, he embraced the fact that children adored his confectionery and ice cream, making the shop very child-friendly, with delightful displays of candies and trinkets in a wide range of prices. In fact, his store was the first in America to feature visits with Santa Claus at Christmastime as a way to attract children to his winter wonderland of festive sweets and toys. His holiday display was one of the "sights of the town," featuring a life-size Kris Kringle, reindeer, and sleigh.[39]

By the time of the Thousand Dollar Dinner in 1851, Parkinson had closed his smaller location on 180 Chestnut, but he launched a grander restaurant, café, and confectionery on the northwest corner of Tenth and Chestnut streets in 1852. The imposing three-story brick mansion had been built in 1819 by a wealthy philanthropist named Frederick Kohn. The main entrance featured white marble steps and a large curved window above the doorway, topped by a marquee displaying the Parkinson name in large block letters. Trim grassy areas bordered either side of the door, kept tidy behind an intricate wrought-iron fence. The adjoining ice cream saloon and confectionery store had its own equally grand entrance, with a separate sign, elaborately carved masonry, and Grecian-style stone columns.[40]

Parkinson completely remodeled the interior, hiring artists to paint the walls with colorful frescoes and expanding the mansion's east wing to provide an expansive space for the ice cream saloon. Other rooms were lavishly furnished as cozy gathering spots, perfect for private parties and small groups, including a large ladies' salon, the main attraction on the first floor. The décor throughout was elegant and tasteful, with sumptuous carpets, expensive curtains, gilded mirrors, sparkling chandeliers, plush velvet furniture, and rosewood and marble-topped tables.[41]

Behind the restaurant was a lush garden area featuring exotic plants, blooming trees, shrubbery and flowers, paved walkways, gas lampposts, and a magnificent fountain in the center. Tucked in a corner was a large building designated as a gentlemen's smoking and reading room, stocked with the most current books, journals, magazines, and newspapers of the day. The gardens were illuminated every evening, enticing dozens of Philadelphians on hot summer nights to the cool, refreshing spot in order to escape the heat and view the light show. Parkinson's also featured other live entertainments such as music, fireworks, and balloon launches, all free of charge. One of the most famous of these balloon ascensions occurred in August 1856 when a Frenchman named E. Godard launched a balloon carrying a live donkey.[42]

This location was strategically placed, as Chestnut Street with its many stores, offices, theaters, museums, hotels, and public buildings was the lively "Broadway" of Philadelphia during the nineteenth century. The road and sidewalks bustled with strollers, shoppers, sightseers, carts, and omnibuses. The section from Fourth to Tenth streets served as a promenade for young men and women to display the latest fashions, largest moustaches, and most stylish bonnets. The designs worn by Philadelphia ladies were considered even more colorful and unique than those in New York. The attractiveness of the women was also said to be unrivaled. As George G. Foster noted in the *New York Tribune* in 1848, "the average standard of female beauty in Chestnut Street is decidedly higher than in any other city or any other street in America, and of course the world."[43]

In addition to their fashions, Philadelphians loved entertainment. They could peruse the Arcade (the first indoor shopping area in the United States) or take in a show at one of the many theaters. Parkinson's was at the heart of all this activity, drawing theatergoers and other entertainment-seekers inside its welcoming interior or verdant gardens for the most delicious pre- or post-performance meals and confections. The area's large hotels also attracted throngs of visitors, adding to the restaurant's customer base. The Girard House with its magnificent ironwork balcony and accommodations for a thousand guests was located just a few doors down from Parkinson's. The even larger Continental Hotel opened across the street in 1860, complete with a newfangled elevator.[44]

So, at the same time Delmonico's was firmly entrenching itself as *the* place for elegant dining in New York, Parkinson's was establishing a similar presence in Philadelphia. It was no surprise then that this group of fifteen wealthy Philadelphians would choose Parkinson's restaurant to host their banquet. They knew James W. Parkinson had the culinary prowess to win over their New York friends. As described by Louis N. Megargee in the *Philadelphia Times*, Parkinson was "a gastronomic savant" who possessed "the air of a prince among confectioners. . . . There was nothing worth knowing about good eating that he could not talk instructively about."[45]

And on a seasonable April evening in 1851, the history of American cooking would be changed forever.

LA CARTE

OYSTERS

Morris River Cove, on shell

"It has become quite fashionable to serve raw oysters as one of the preliminaries to a dinner party; sometimes on small plates, sometimes on the half-shell. They are seasoned by each guest according to his own taste."

—Marion Harland, *Common Sense in the Household*, 1873

It is not at all surprising that James Parkinson began his Thousand Dollar Dinner with oysters. Throughout the Victorian era, a sumptuous meal always featured oysters as a first course, and the feast planned and hosted by Parkinson was the ultimate in extravagance. These men would have *expected* oysters. The dinner took place in Philadelphia, after all, with invited guests from New York—both cities central to the oyster craze.

Oysters were such an integral part of New York's dining scene that until the end of the nineteenth century every formal dinner started with them. The menus of Delmonico chef Charles Ranhofer always listed oysters as a first course, and the restaurant's legendary patron Diamond Jim Brady was said to pop them in his mouth like candy before he even thought about choosing an appetizer.[1]

So beginning this culinary challenge with oysters was a given—quite possibly Parkinson's easiest menu choice—and he chose one of North America's finest, Morris River Cove.

N orth American oysters have been in high demand since the Europeans began landing on its shores and joined the Native Americans in gathering and devouring the seemingly unlimited supply. The English, French, and Dutch were already huge oyster lovers—they must have thought they struck gold. They soon found these oysters were much larger and had a different flavor than the metallic-tasting European flat oysters they were used to.

The size and lusciousness of the oysters as well as all the other bountiful food available in the Americas pleased and astounded visitors to the wild, unblemished land they initially encountered. In his mid-seventeenth-century *Description of the New Netherlands*, Dutchman Adriaen van der Donck describes the area now known as New York as producing such large-scale flora and wildlife as pears larger than a fist, wild turkeys weighing forty pounds, six-foot long lobsters, and oysters measuring a foot. Oysters were said to have been particularly abundant around Staten Island, with some beds large enough to capsize ships.[2]

New York harbor and the lower Hudson River were once home to 350 square miles of fertile oyster beds, supplying more than half the world's oysters. A 1730 map of New York harbor shows the entire Jersey shore section of the harbor to be "one gigantic oyster reef." European colonists named the tiny island in the harbor Little Oyster Island, while its larger neighbor was dubbed Great Oyster Island.[3]

The Delaware Bay—the triangular waterway wedged in between the states now known as Delaware and New Jersey—was also a treasure trove of seafood delicacies. Native Swede Thomas

Campanius Holm writes about the region's "various kinds of shell-fish, including oysters, lobsters, sea and land turtles, cockles and muscles" in his 1702 *Description of the Province of New Sweden*.[4] In describing Delaware Bay oysters Holm says they "are so very large that the meat alone is of the size of our oysters, shell and all."[5] By the 1750s, Delaware Bay oysters were being shipped to Philadelphia and New York, and throughout the nineteenth century they were renowned for their unique taste and high meat quality.[6]

Pehr Kalm (1716–1779) was another Scandinavian who commented on the substantial wildlife in the New World. Kalm was a diligent Finnish botanist and agricultural economist who was sent by the Royal Swedish Academy of Sciences to search for seeds and plants that could be profitable in Europe. He made his way to America in 1748 and established his base in the Swedish-Finnish community of Raccoon (now Swedesboro) in southern New Jersey (formerly New Sweden). While visiting New York he sampled colossal oysters: "About New York they find innumerable quantities of excellent oysters, and there are few places which have oysters of such an exquisite taste and of so great a size." He describes how they were pickled and sent to the West Indies and other places, which kept them well-preserved for years and allowed them to be sent to the farthest corners of the world.[7]

What these folks didn't realize at the time was how lucky they were to have such a seemingly endless supply of rich delicacies to feast on. As America's population grew, many of the items they ate regularly began to thin out. Fish and other seafood such as turtles became smaller in size since they were caught before they had a chance to fully mature. Oysters were plucked from their natural beds and sold directly to market. It soon became obvious that unless limits were established, this rapid harvesting and consumption would deplete the supply that had once seemed nearly endless.

In the mid-1800s, it was discovered that if young oysters were carefully picked from their natural beds and relocated to saltier waters, they grew more quickly, bringing the oysters to market size much sooner.

Thus began the concept of using these "seeds" to sow plots of oysters. Staten Island brought in seed oysters from Virginia, and New Jersey planted oysters from its own waters and neighboring states along the shores of Delaware Bay's Maurice "Morris" River Cove. Just like vegetables in a garden, the clusters of oysters were eventually thinned out and separated in order to accelerate growth and produce a better product.[8] Throughout the nineteenth century and most of the twentieth, the majority of oysters in this region were replanted and grown in saltier waters instead of being harvested directly from the natural seed beds and sent directly to market.[9]

These farmed oysters revitalized the industry, evidenced by the popularity of the oyster bars that sprung up throughout nineteenth-century New York, Philadelphia, and other coastal cities, and their reasonable prices—with such advertising as "all you can eat for just six cents!"[10] And on an 1884 menu from James Parkinson's restaurant, oysters and other shellfish including crabs and even lobsters are similarly priced (some are even less expensive) than the featured egg dishes such as omelets.[11]

The "star" of the shellfish world, the oyster has seesawed between serving as a sustenance food and a delicacy—sometimes balancing both roles at the same time. This was the case in nineteenth-century America when oysters were the focal point of fancy dinners yet also served up for working people by street vendors and in oyster bars, often situated in tucked away basement locations. These were not forbidden or illegal like alcohol-serving speakeasies during Prohibition, but the underground locales gave them a somewhat illicit and enticing feel. Not surprising for a food that is considered the most desirable of all things edible from the sea and has often had aphrodisiac qualities attached to it. In fact, the late nineteenth century produced two scandalous pornographic magazines, *The Oyster* and *The Pearl.*

The oyster has been so important to American gastronomy that poems, songs, and even entire books have been written about the popular shellfish. Restaurants and oyster bars were created just to feature and serve its lusciousness. In the Philadelphia area, social gatherings with menus that revolved around oysters became extremely popular in the nineteenth century. These included oyster roasts at the Jersey shore, with oysters nestled inside covered pans and placed in the coals of huge fires built out of driftwood. Oyster roasts also took place indoors, with hosts simply popping trays of whole oysters still in the shell into the oven.[12]

According to nineteenth-century domestic expert Eliza Leslie, an oyster supper party typically featured a wide variety of oyster preparations—fried, stewed, broiled, roasted, raw, and in patties. Roasted oysters in the shell were brought in piping hot throughout the meal, since they were usually gobbled down as quickly as they were served. Because the men were responsible for opening oysters for the ladies at the table, a thick folded towel and an oyster knife were placed to the right side of their plate, and a small bucket (usually of maple or stained wood, with brass hoops) was strategically positioned near their chairs for the empty shells.[13]

Oyster suppers must have been doubly special for women—not only did they get to have their oysters opened for them, but the fact that they were invited to these events was significant. A supper party most often referred to a "gentlemen's supper"—an all-male evening social event analogous to a ladies' luncheon. As Miss Leslie says, "*Except* at an oyster supper, it is not very customary for ladies to appear at these entertainments." Supper parties were held in either private homes or public establishments. Terrapin, canvasback duck, game, and French dishes were standard fare, although oysters may have been included on the menu. For example, a ten-course "Gentlemen's Fish Supper" in *Practical Cooking, and Dinner Giving* (1878) by Mary F. Henderson features "Raw oysters served in a block of ice" as the first course (the ice has a pretty effect in the gaslight, she says).[14]

Banquet dinners also had menus of multiple courses, each featuring a different oyster preparation. In reminiscing about one such feast that took place in Lower Merion in 1934, Philadelphia writer and Germantown resident Cornelius Weygandt said: "We had to eat: first, five raw oysters, extraordinarily good, and second, oyster stew, extraordinarily good. There were of course, sours in plenty on the table, the dill pickle and horse-radish prominent among them. The third course was turkey with scalloped oysters. The turkey was neatly folded around an egg-shaped mass of (oyster) filling as big as a goose egg. The fourth course was fried oysters—as big as the palm of your hand. It was single-dipped, bless it, and tasty as could be."[15]

This brings up yet another factor—how an oyster is prepared. While some insist the oyster is best simply served up raw on a half shell (how Parkinson presented them for his Thousand Dollar Dinner), clever chefs have delighted in coming up with numerous ways to showcase oysters over the years—fried, baked, frittered, cooked in soups, bisques, and gumbo, swimming in a rich sauce such as oysters Rockefeller, oysters à la Foch—even as flavorings for items ranging from a dressing for poultry (still a highlight on many Thanksgiving tables) and even catchup.[16] Many nineteenth-century cookbooks devoted pages and pages to oyster recipes.

Even with all these delicious and interesting preparations, raw oysters were still the favorite, with presentation and accompaniments as important as the oysters themselves. Serving them in blocks or boats of ice was extremely fashionable, especially later in the nineteenth century as refrigeration methods improved, but this presentation was still no easy task—from obtaining huge blocks of ice, to shaping it, and then keeping it cold.

Catherine Stuart, author of *The Complete Cook-book* (1882), preferred "raw oysters in a boat of ice" as the most effective serving technique. She recommended starting with a crystal-clear block of ice, using a flat iron to melt a large enough space at the top to hold the oysters, and then chipping the sides away until it was shaped like a boat. Oysters seasoned with salt and pepper were placed on top of this artistic ice sculpture, which then needed to be stored where it wouldn't melt. Just before dinner was served, the boat was arranged on a bed of geranium leaves and garnished with intertwined delicate green vines and bright crimson geraniums.[17]

And according to the 1880s publication *Caterer and Household Magazine* (of which James Parkinson was the editor for two years), raw oysters were often placed in blocks of ice hollowed out for this purpose, or frozen in the shape of a salad bowl or other attractive dish, "so as to contain them."[18] Alternatively, they could be served on the half shell or in a shallow plate, swimming in their own juice.[19]

The French style was to leave the upper shell on when serving, according to the celebrated Pierre Blot, a French chef, cookbook writer, and cooking school instructor who immigrated to the United States in 1855.[20] According to his instructions, when the oysters are "well washed, open them, detaching the upper shell, then detach them from the under shell, but leave them on it; place on a dish, and leave the upper shell on every oyster, and serve thus."[21]

Blot suggested serving raw oysters alongside a separate dish of shallots, chopped fine and gently bruised in a coarse towel, but solely at a gentlemen-only table, undoubtedly so as not to offend the ladies. Parkinson's recommended accompaniments included lemon, pepper, vinegar, and horseradish, or a relish consisting of chopped onion (placed in a towel and then dipped into cold water to remove the rank juice), parsley, lemon juice, cayenne pepper, salt, and vinegar. Both Blot and Parkinson also endorsed mayonnaise-based dressings such as tartar sauce.[22]

Philadelphians also adored oyster fritters—a specialty introduced by Italian-born restaurateur Minico Finelli. Visitors to Philadelphia flocked to his restaurant to enjoy a taste of this famous dish. Finelli fried the oysters in the olive oil of his native Italy, and used a light hand in coating them, producing a delicious delicacy that was not at all heavy or greasy.[23]

Finelli often paired the oysters with his chicken salad, which became a well-known combination in and around Philadelphia, featured not only in his restaurant but also as a luncheon staple at private gentlemen's clubs. "His preparing of the luscious bivalves and delicious salads is alone worth a visit to our restaurant—the most charming space in the city for light luncheons," bragged a 1906 advertisement in the *Philadelphia Inquirer* for the Blum Restaurant on Tenth and Market streets. The ad announced the reopening of their fourth-floor Café Parisien, touting Finelli as an important addition to the culinary staff.[24]

Restaurants in other locations (especially New York) tried to duplicate Finelli's technique, but none could. In fact, apparently Charles Delmonico sent a chef to Finelli's in Philadelphia to see if he could master the method and bring it back to his New York restaurants. The man ate plate after plate of the plump juicy treats trying to solve the secret of the magical batter. This is the procedure he tried to replicate: "heat the olive oil in an intensely red-hot pan, quickly drop the oysters in and then spear them right away." Unfortunately for him (and Delmonico's), the first day he served the oysters at the Broadway restaurant he lost his job. He had absolutely failed.[25]

For those who fancy all things oyster—where do the tastiest, juiciest, biggest oysters come from? Oyster-producing areas around the world have all proclaimed that their oysters are "the best," and continue to vie for this claim. With his special affinity for American oysters, Parkinson was not immune to this boasting. In his 1874 essay, *American Dishes at the Centennial*, Parkinson refers to American oysters as "not the peanut, copperish caricature of France or England, but the large, sweet, delectable, and glorious American oyster—the envy of the world."[26]

Where and how an oyster is grown makes all the difference—not unlike fine wine. Water temperature, salinity, and mineral content, as well as the oyster's diet, all affect its flavor. For example, although Atlantic coast oysters are all from the same family, they vary in size, shape, color, and taste. Since oysters grow faster in warmer water, they tend to be larger in size in more temperate locations, particularly if left alone to grow. Conversely, colder water tends to produce oysters that enthusiasts call more flavorful and critics label as too briny. As a result, Northerners feel southern oysters are large and flavorless and Southerners think northern varieties are small and harsh.[27]

This strong bias toward local oysters has provided friendly banter up and down the East Coast for hundreds for years. Of all the American oysters, M. F. K. Fisher gave those from Long Island Sound the highest marks, although she also gave Chincoteagues and Delaware Bay oysters a rating of "very good." She felt oysters from the southern U.S. waters were "less interesting served in the shell, and almost cry out for such delicacies as horseradish or even cooking."[28]

And as stated in an 1877 article in *Scribner's* magazine, oyster dealers in Washington, D.C. and Baltimore "admitted" that it was possible to find good oysters outside of the Chesapeake Bay; but if seeking a perfect oyster, it was useless to look elsewhere. For Philadelphia residents, the Delaware Bay was the ideal oyster's only home—a concept inconceivable to New Yorkers, who insisted the only first-rate oysters were caught in their waters. But as the article points out, these people were all quite lucky—anyone living between the parallels of 36 and 40 degrees north would have access to tasty oysters.[29]

At the time of Parkinson's Thousand Dollar Dinner, if you were from the New York area you probably would have cited Blue Point oysters from the Long Island coast as the finest on the market,[30] but if you were from Philadelphia, it would have been Morris River Coves from the Delaware Bay. They probably didn't taste all that different since the two cities are only about a hundred miles apart—although the Blue Points may have been saltier since Morris River Coves typically came from more brackish water. Yet these strong regional preferences prevailed throughout the nineteenth century.

When the Philadelphia gentlemen's club "The State in Schuylkill"[31] celebrated the centennial of its founding in 1832 with an elaborate dinner in their Fairmont clubhouse, the menu specified Morris Cove oysters—a copious five hundred to be exact.[32] Twenty years later, James Parkinson also chose Morris River Cove oysters to kick off his Thousand Dollar Dinner. Particularly sought after for their smaller and plumper size, they were perfect for serving raw in the shell. Parkinson's decision was a smart one—showcasing Philadelphia's premium oysters to his New York guests.

Although spelled "Maurice" today, the river's name is still pronounced "Morris." It trickles its way down through Cumberland County, New Jersey, like a thick squiggly line until it reaches the upper northwest part of the Delaware Bay, feeding into the Maurice River Cove and creating a brackish mix of fresh and seawater. This curved, sheltered estuary lined with broad salt marshes is an oyster's paradise, as they thrive in shallow water where the salinity is not too high.

It is likely the oysters Parkinson secured for his dinner in 1851 were shipped up the Delaware River by boat, since this was the most common transportation method in the nineteenth century. The holding areas of ships had special bins that would allow the saltwater to flow through.[33]

Oysters also traveled to Gloucester and Camden, New Jersey, by relay teams on blocks of ice.[34] But when the railroad came to the Maurice River area in 1876, the industry boomed. In 1880, 2.4 million oysters were harvested, and within ten years a constant stream of railcars flowed out of the region each day, each conveying burlap bags bursting with oysters. The recipients of this bounty were not only Philadelphia and New York, but other parts of the U.S. as well, including the Midwest and even the Western states. In addition to the railroad, faster ships allowed huge numbers of oysters to be sent across the Atlantic to eager European epicures, allowing oysters to become the number one fishery product in the United States.[35]

The thriving Maurice River oyster industry spawned a number of small towns whose income and livelihood revolved around the popular delicacies—notably Port Norris, Maurice River, and Mauricetown, as well as the aptly named Shellpile and Bivalve. The residents of these places were oyster planters, shell stock shippers, ship smith and dredge makers, wholesale shippers, shuckers, and oyster boat captains.

The oyster business was so lucrative that fortunes and dynasties were built on this unassuming asymmetrical shellfish in a relatively short time. In the oyster industry's heyday at the turn of the twentieth century, there were more millionaires per capita in Port Norris than anywhere in the world, and oystermen were said to roll up their tobacco using hundred dollar bills to celebrate a good catch.[36]

In addition to being coveted for their superior taste, Morris River Cove oysters were prized for shipping due to their hard shell and ability to stay fresh during these long journeys. According to an 1870 *Philadelphia Inquirer* article, Morris River Cove and Delaware Bay oysters would keep longer and could be shipped farther than any other variety. A barrel of Morris River Coves would also yield more meat compared to other types since the shells were small but the meat encased within was generous, making the freight cost more economical.[37]

The advent of pasteurization in the twentieth century made it possible for shucked oysters to be shipped in cans, and in 1922 the first oyster-shucking house was established in the area, allowing the industry to grow even more. Prior to this, most of the oysters were shipped in the shell.[38]

All of these innovations allowed the finest restaurants throughout America to feature Delaware Bay oysters on their menus until the late 1950s, when a deadly parasite called MSX wiped out much of the population in a very short period of time.[39] As a result, the region's oyster industry collapsed almost overnight. By the end of 1959, over 90 percent of the planted oysters and more than half of the seed oysters had died. In 1956, the total harvest was 711,000 bushels, but by 1960 it had declined to only 49,000.[40] Then in 1990 another parasitic disease called Dermo spread through much of the eastern Delaware Bay, destroying many planted and seed oysters.[41]

As New Jersey's oyster industry floundered in the 1990s, a series of changes were set in motion. In 1996, an old strategy was revived for the first time in 150 years—putting a cap on the number of oysters than can be harvested each season to help the stocks replenish and grow. With this direct-marketed technique, there are now only about fifteen active oystering boats in the Delaware Bay (compared to 365 in 1883). Each has a limit on the number of oysters they can collect (usually 1,000–3,000 bushels per season), helping to alleviate overharvesting.[42]

Since 2000, the average Delaware Bay oyster harvest has been approximately 75,000 bushels per year, a drastic reduction from the one to two million taken in every year between 1880 and 1930, although undoubtedly still better than the low haul of 1960. The oyster seed research, new regulations, and aquaculture development seem to be working, but everyone working within the industry continues to keep on top of present and future challenges.[43]

WINES

Sauternes, vintage of 1846, especially selected from the stock of
WASHINGTON MORTON, *at Bordeaux*

A sweet full-bodied white wine with medium to high acidity, Sauternes is often considered a dessert wine and might seem like a rather odd choice to complement the briny tang of oysters. But the wine's high acidity perfectly balances its creamy, honey-like layers, enabling savory combinations. Pairing a luscious taste of rich Sauternes with a bite of plump and salty goodness like an oyster can create an outpouring of flavor.[44]

Sauternes is rich, lush, and expensive—as with all his menu selections, Parkinson knew what he was doing. Plus, this pairing probably wouldn't have seemed so odd to his guests in 1851. Americans used to drink Sauternes as an aperitif (and the French still do—often serving it with fresh foie gras or fish at the start of a meal). Today, however, Americans often view tastes differently and are apt to save a sweet wine for the dessert course.[45]

Sauternes was a favorite of Thomas Jefferson and George Washington, particularly those from Château d'Yquem, which many wine enthusiasts feel is the only Sauternes. Jefferson visited the chateau while he was minister to France and later ordered Yquem for himself and Washington during the time he was secretary of state. The late food and wine expert and cookbook author Richard Olney recommended drinking "a relatively young" Sauternes with oysters, which correlates with the 1846 vintage served at Parkinson's Thousand Dollar Dinner in 1851.[46]

Tucked inside the Graves section of France's Bordeaux wine region is tiny Sauternes, one of the few areas in the world devoted to producing sweet wines. Just five villages are allowed to make and label their wines Sauternes—Preignac, Fargues, Sauternes, Barsac, and Bommes.

Rich, luscious Sauternes wine is created using sémillon, sauvignon blanc, and muscadelle grapes. The misty conditions along the Garonne River in the farthest southern reaches of Bordeaux help foster a "noble rot"—*Botrytis cinerea* (a type of fungus). This rot occurs when the grapes are left on the vine well into the autumn, allowing the fungus to "infect" them. With its thin skin and high sugar content, the sémillon grape is particularly vulnerable and a perfect candidate for this process.[47]

Noble rot sucks the liquid out of the grapes, turning them brown, rotten, shriveled, and moldy, but also concentrates the sugar and acidity, giving them an intense, honeyed flavor, with a deep brown color. Although it seems bizarre that rotten grapes could produce such a superior product (or really anything drinkable), what was probably a chance result turned out to be a hugely important discovery. The first written evidence was in the mid-1600s when fear of an invasion by the approaching Turkish army forced a Hungarian priest/winemaker to delay the wine harvest for two months. The rotten grapes were harvested anyway and made into wine. Soon the technique of making sweet wine from noble rot-infected grapes spread to Germany and France.[48]

Even after years of practice, this method of encouraging the fungus to take hold is still not a perfect science, since so much is in the hands of Mother Nature. The correct amount of humidity and warmth must exist and the rot must be the precise extent. This usually doesn't happen to all the grapes at the same time, requiring several harvests throughout the fall where only the most affected grapes are picked, often individually by hand—a painstaking, expensive process. As a result, during years where the weather was uncooperative, rather than producing an inferior product, a top chateau in Sauternes might decide to not make any sweet wine at all.[49]

Although Parkinson chose Sauternes, any number of other wine varieties have been paired with oysters over the years, typically light, unoaked wines. Dry white Bordeaux, Chablis, Graves, and Chambertin were common nineteenth-century recommendations. It was important for wines to "enhance the taste of the oyster and assist digestion." And it didn't hurt to have an attractive table— *The Complete Cook-book* author Catherine Stuart suggested a colorful mélange of raw oysters served alongside chilled Moselle in green- or yellow-tinted glasses.[50]

The most versatile of all wines, Champagne has long been considered a classic complement for oysters. Its fizzy bubbles and high acidity refreshingly cleanse and scrub the palate, allowing each bite to taste like the first. This lively combination acts like a refreshing squeeze of lemon on raw oysters. And its variety of sweetness levels allows oyster–Champagne pairings to be tweaked accordingly.[51] In addition to the traditional sparkling wine, iced or still Champagne was also offered with oysters in the nineteenth century.[52]

Beer and hard liquor such as gin, Schiedam, and Irish and Scotch whisky were also consumed with oysters in the 1800s, although this may have been due to social class as much as preference. As noted by British citizen Charles Mackay while visiting America in 1857, "the rich consume oysters and champaigne; the poorer classes consume oysters and lager bier, and that is one of the principal social differences between the two sections of the community."[53]

SOUPS

Green Turtle • Potage, à la reine

"Green turtle is the epicurean soup, par excellence."
—Eunice C. Corbett, *Good Housekeeping*, March 1894

"Potage à la reine is the richest and most delicate potage that can be made and served at a well-ordered table."
—Pierre Blot, *The Galaxy*, 1868

Soup had a rather showy place at nineteenth-century dinner parties, usually brought to the table in elaborate soup tureens and placed directly in front of the lady of the house. If there were two soups, a tureen was situated at each end of the table. The serving process was slow and deliberate—the wait-servant would hold each guest's soup plate close to the tureen, passing one ladle full to each person. Rules of etiquette dictated that "soup should be eaten from the side, not the point, of the spoon, and there should be no noise when sipping." Apparently asking for seconds was considered rude and strictly impermissible.[1]

In Victorian America, the class and quality of the soup course at a fine meal was often seen as a predictor of the dinner to follow. James Parkinson was well aware that his culinary abilities would be judged and defined by the soup he served at his Thousand Dollar Dinner. His menu choice would set the tone for the rest of the meal. His decision to serve not just one, but two soups—green turtle and potage à la reine—was not unusual, as two choices were typically offered at large dinner parties during this timeframe: one clear and one puree.[2]

The history of soups can be traced back over five thousand years to the Bronze and Iron ages and the invention of leak-free containers that could withstand boiling over an open fire for lengthy periods of time. No doubt the first soups were a rudimentary mix of whatever edibles were on hand—roots, bits of meat, vegetables, and grains. Some of the earliest recorded soup recipes and descriptions include those for meat and vegetable broth from Babylonia, and lentil and barley from ancient Rome.[3]

The flavor and variety of soups evolved with technological advances such as improved farming practices, higher quality vegetables and herbs, and more sophisticated cooking pots. By the Middle Ages, farmers frequently ate simple soups as breakfast or lunch, while the upper class enjoyed more complex versions as a separate course at banquets. Most of the time, these "soups" were actually rich sauced meat dishes, later considered entrees in the seventeenth and eighteenth centuries. Examples of other soups included pea soup, oyle (onion-ale) soup, and tredure (broth thickened with eggs and bread crumbs).[4]

Soup courses were included at feasts throughout the medieval period, but the timing of when they were served during a celebratory dinner moved around a bit. Sometimes soup was offered as a first course, and sometimes after the entrée or "table platter" that started the meal (what we think of as French hors d'oeuvres or Italian antipasto), and before the various roast courses and the "finish" (dessert course) that ended the meal.[5]

The Renaissance ushered in soups that were increasingly varied and sophisticated, with Italian, French, and other European cooks creating recipes for consommés, broths, potages, and soups.[6] A 1662 French menu based on Pierre de Lune, *Le Nouveau et Parfait Maistr d'hostel royal,* features three different soups: chicken soup with peas, squab soup, and gosling soup with asparagus.[7] Along with the more refined soup types, the use of spoons to consume them began to increase during this timeframe, particularly among the European upper classes. Prior to this, soups were sipped from a cup or bowl like a beverage, which continued for another hundred years or so until spoons became widely available.[8]

Throughout the seventeenth and eighteenth centuries soups often appeared as part of a special course preceding the entrees, and by the early nineteenth century, they were firmly entrenched as a first course, although it appears that oysters pushed soups back to the second course when they began to be served as the standard starter at dinner parties. The variety and number of recipes for soups continued to increase throughout the nineteenth century, which is reflected in the cookbooks of the time.

In the latter part of the century, Mary Lincoln of the Boston Cooking School described soup as water or milk based, served thin and clear, or thickened with vegetables or cereals. Ingredients included meat, fish, and vegetables, with seasonings ranging from sweet herbs, spices, curry powder, catchups, aromatic sauces, and even fruit.[9]

Clear soups such as consommés became standard dinner party fare, revered for their elegant look and rich taste. Producing a perfect consommé was considered quite an art, involving slow, gentle simmering of meat juices and the bone gelatin, and requiring time and patience to remove every drop of grease that rose to the surface. British cookbook writer Isabella Beeton stressed the fact that "clear soups must be perfectly transparent . . . it is requisite to continue skimming the liquor until there is not a particle of scum remaining."[10]

This focus on presentation was important, apparent by the use of attractive soup tureens and numerous "floating garnishes for soup" such as quenelles (a mixture of creamed fish, chicken, or meat, sometimes combined with breadcrumbs, with a light egg binding), timbales (creamy mixtures of minced foods encased in a small pastry shell), or herbs. According to Catherine Owen in *Choice Cookery* (1889), "garnishes that are merely ornamental need not be so expensively made as those intended for eating. Foremost among fashionable floating garnishes for soup are the colored custards known as pate royale; they are perfectly easy to make, yet very effective served in clear bouillon."[11] And Mary F. Henderson recommended the French custom of serving little squares of thick slices of buttered brown bread with soup at fancy dinners in her *Practical Cooking, and Dinner Giving* (1878).[12]

Soup tureens not only kept the soup warm, but also functioned as a pretty and practical way to transport the steaming liquid to the table. By the 1840s they were frequently made of ironstone or earthenware; silver was reserved solely for special occasions. Many times they were quite the conversation piece, especially in the Victorian era when visual puns were all the rage. For example, a beef consommé or stew might be served in a tureen that featured an elaborately carved cow on the top of the lid and/or handles. And due to the widespread popularity of turtle soup, the use of decorative turtle-shaped tureens became a distinctive way to showcase this delicacy at the table.[13]

It might sound unusual today, but turtle was one of the most popular and fashionable foods in Europe and America from the 1600s through the early twentieth century. The green sea turtle was the most prized of all. Turtle gourmands described its meat as having a unique, rich flavor, comparable to lobster or veal. In his handbook *The Market Assistant* (1867), Thomas Farrington De Voe asserts, "This fine turtle is well known to the epicure for its delicious steaks and the savory soup which it affords. The flesh appears to be of three colors, and it is said to combine the taste of fish, flesh, and fowl."[14]

Like oysters, green sea turtles were once plentiful enough to serve as a sustenance food, consumed by Caribbean, Hawaiian, and Polynesian islanders as well as European explorers and pirates as they made their way around the globe. As noted by *The Edinburgh Encyclopedia* (1832), the flesh of the turtle was considered extremely nutritious and an excellent restorative in cases of debility and emaciation. These creatures of tropical and subtropical waters soon became a highly sought-after delicacy when sailing merchants began to ship them from the West Indies to England and America. Their extreme popularity caused them to become overfished fairly quickly, with quantities beginning to show a decline as early as 1700.[15]

As a result they became increasingly expensive, but were still available through the eighteenth and nineteenth centuries, and period cookbooks provided detailed instructions on how to butcher and prepare sea turtle, no easy task for a home cook since these reptiles could be five feet long and weigh fifty to over three hundred pounds. "Dressing the turtle" was a gory process that required room to work, since the directions involved killing the turtle, hanging it upside down by its hind fins, and cutting off its head. The turtle was then left to bleed for at least two hours before cutting it up.[16] Louis Eustache Ude gives a slightly easier method in his 1822 cookbook, *The French Cook*: "If you wish to make turtle soup with less difficulty, cut off the head the preceding day. In the morning open the turtle; this is done by leaning heavy with your knife on the shell of the animal's back, whilst you cut it off all round. Turn it upright on its end, that all the water, etc. may run out."[17]

After all the blood was drained away, the turtle was placed on a table with several containers of cold water, and a big pot of boiling water was situated nearby for the different parts, such as the fins, belly (called the calipee), organs, and any eggs. The shell was pried off and intestines and gall bladder were carefully removed and discarded. The green fat from the upper shell (known as the calipash) was most valued. This piece was placed in the pot of boiling water until soft and easily removed from the shell and then left to cool; sometimes the liquor in which it was cooked was saved and incorporated into the soup and other dishes. The coarser pieces of meat and bone were transferred to the soup vessel along with a pound of ham, eight large calves' feet (or two knuckles of veal), onions, and some herbs and spices. After simmering slowly for five hours in a beef or veal broth, it was skimmed and strained, and the best meat (including some of the green fat and liver) was added. It was then put back to boil along with veal forcemeat balls and the turtle's eggs or hard-boiled egg yolks. A pint of Madeira and two sliced lemons were added at the end, about fifteen minutes prior to serving.[18]

As a large port city, Philadelphia received regular shipments of turtles from the Caribbean, sometimes up to three times a week. They were sent to the city's High Street Market and kept alive in large carts, fed with cabbage leaves and beet-tops, or auctioned right from the docks to caterers and tavern owners. Although some private households followed the complicated steps to dress and prepare turtle, it was much more likely to take place in the kitchens of taverns and catering establishments due to the expense and lengthy procedure.[19]

Turtle soup became a Philadelphia specialty. As just one turtle could feed quite a crowd, turtle soup was frequently the featured dish at large feasts or festivals, often sponsored by open-air inns, where patrons could enjoy outdoor seating. Demand for turtle was so high that hosts would advertise these upcoming events in the city's newspapers and sometimes even sell tickets in advance. Turtle soup also served as an early form of "takeout," offered for sale by various places throughout the city so that it could be brought home, saving the lady of the house the trouble and mess of making it herself.[20]

As sea turtles became more and more scarce, ingenious alternatives soon emerged so Philadelphians could satisfy their turtle soup cravings, including the use of terrapins (smaller turtles found in the Chesapeake and Delaware bays and Egg Harbor in New

Jersey). Although much smaller in size than sea turtles (weighing in at about four pounds), they were local, abundant, and produced a similar tasting soup—even referred to as exquisite.

Clever cooks came up with another substitute when sea turtles were unavailable or too expensive—mock turtle soup. "Mock" dishes actually go back to the Middle Ages as creative workarounds for the original versions. In this case, a calf's head and/or feet stood in for the turtle, with the first published recipe appearing in a 1758 cookbook—the fifth edition of *The Art of Cookery Made Plain and Easy* by Hannah Glasse. Mock turtle soup soon became as ubiquitous as authentic turtle soup—even on fine dining tables—as its ingredients were more economical and much easier to obtain. The idea to use calf as a substitute stemmed from the fact that the flavor of turtle was often compared to veal—even real turtle soup called for calf hooves and veal broth.[21]

Once canning was perfected as a way to keep food from spoiling, tinned turtle meat was used to make soup, although one can imagine it was not nearly as rich tasting as a soup infused with the slow simmering of turtle meat, bone, and shell. Then even the various types of turtle soups themselves were sold in cans by the latter part of the nineteenth century: green turtle, terrapin, and mock turtle. They were marketed to the public as convenience foods, particularly helpful when needing to serve unexpected guests.[22]

Eventually terrapin numbers also began dwindling due to over-fishing, but resourceful Philadelphians came up with yet one more alternative—snapping turtles. Today, snapper soup is the variety of turtle soup available for purchase in the Philadelphia region since both sea turtles and terrapins are considered endangered or threatened in most locations. Freshwater snapping turtles are now the only turtle species allowed to be harvested in Pennsylvania, and many area restaurants still offer the specialty—from local diners to the Sansom Street Oyster House. Like a richer, more complex cousin to Maryland's crab soup, snapper soup is a deep reddish color, thick with vegetables, potatoes, hard-boiled egg, and lots of tender turtle meat. It is customary for a tiny pitcher of sherry to be sent to the table with the soup so the patron can add a splash just before eating.[23]

The other soup chosen by Parkinson (potage à la reine) may not have been a Philadelphia specialty, but like turtle soup, it has had an extensive legacy of gracing fine dining tables. In the Middle Ages, the French used the word *potage* to describe anything cooked in a pot—this could range from thick soup with a liquid base to a stew or roast. "The richest potages are made with *consommé* and some other compounds; such as bread, Italian pastas, vegetables, etc.," declared nineteenth-century French chef Pierre Blot. Today, a potage can signify either cream or broth soup, and a consommé is a pure, completely clear stock.[24]

Translated into English as "in the queen's style," the phrase "à la reine" has come to indicate a recipe with chicken as its main ingredient, just as dishes with "à la king" in the title represent chicken dishes in America. Described as one of the oldest and most delicate of soups, potage à la reine is a creamy white soup made with chicken and almonds that originated as a sort of a savory blancmange. The dish was given the title "potage à la reine" during the Renaissance era, although there are conflicting reports about which queen is the soup's namesake.[25]

Although attribution has been given to both Mary Queen of Scots and England's Queen Victoria, the most commonly held legend links the dish to Queen Marguerite, wife of Henry IV of France. Potage à la reine was "Thursday's soup" at the court of the Valois, and the name is said to derive from the fact that Queen Marguerite was extremely fond of it. Pierre Blot supports this theory by maintaining that French dishes were modest and rather rustic until Marguerite's mother Catherine de Medici brought Italian cooking to France when she married the future Henry II in 1533. Catherine eventually became queen consort when he was crowned king in 1547, and although he never gave her any political control, she was able to parlay her appreciation for fine cooking by arranging a contest to see who could invent the most superior French dishes. This inspired her son-in-law Henry IV to develop consommé à la reine (chickens simmered in a beef broth), and also coin the phrase "poule au pot" (chicken in a pot), expressing his desire that all of his subjects would be able to afford to eat this dish every Sunday.[26]

French chef François Pierre de la Varenne is generally considered the first to publish a recipe for potage à la reine in his 1651 culinary masterpiece that helped lay the foundations of classic French cuisine, *Le cuisinier François*.[27] Although chicken has always been the main ingredient, this is not the salty canned "cream of chicken" soup that is incorporated into many casserole recipes by busy cooks today. A multilayered soup with a distinctive look and taste, potage à la reine cleverly fused a meat stock derived from poultry (and sometimes veal or beef) with rich almond milk. In order to obtain the consistency of a smooth, velvety puree, the chicken was roasted or boiled, then pounded in a mortar until smooth, and diluted with milk or cream of almonds.

In medieval cookery, almonds were often used as a thickener in soups, stews, and sauces, particularly as almond milk, made by steeping ground almonds in water, broth, or wine.[28] The almonds also give the potage its characteristic whitish color—the use of dairy products or rice to provide a creamy look and feel were substituted much later. In addition to adding depth, texture, and flavor, the light color was also a mark of status. On royal tables, the queen was always given the choicest, most tender white meat of the chicken since foods that were light or white in color were considered superior.[29]

The popularity of potage à la reine soon spread throughout Europe and eventually the New World as well. Although its basic concept as a creamy chicken soup largely carried over, variations emerged as it made its way around the globe, based on the tastes and availability of foods in each region. Rice, cream, egg yolks, and hard-boiled egg were all used as thickeners—sometimes in place of almonds, sometimes in addition to them. Sarah Josepha Hale's 1857 cookbook directs:

Stew 2 or 3 young fowls for about an hour in good freshmade veal broth: then take them out, skin them and pound the breast, or only the white meat, in a mortar until it becomes quite smooth. That done, mash the yolks of 3 or 4 hardboiled eggs with the crumb of a French roll, soaked either in broth or in milk, and mix this with the pounded meat to form a paste, which must be afterwards passed through a sieve.[30]

Today most recipes for "soup à la reine" substitute cream for almond milk, and often incorporate some of the shredded chicken and vegetables used to make the soup's broth as garnishes to make it more substantial. However, the idea to serve a pureed version at the beginning of a fine meal as Parkinson did in 1851 is still considered chic. According to modern-day French chef Jacques Pepin, the chicken can be reserved and used for another source such as chicken salad, and the creamy soup—now a veloute of chicken— is a nice first course for a dinner party.[31]

WINES

Snider's Imperial Cognac (in pint bottles)

What wine is the best match for soup? Even though soup is food, it is liquid. Some might find it strange to both eat and drink a liquid at the same time. But wine is actually an ingredient in many soups, which adds dimension to the flavor. Sipping a wine of the same varietal alongside the soup can serve to complement the experience, which the French have perfected through the tradition called *faire chabrol*, where a bit of wine they are drinking is poured into the soup.[32]

The turtle soup served by James Parkinson is a perfect example, since Madeira or sherry has always been an ingredient—from the earliest turtle soup recipes through the present day. These two warming, fortified wines were the varieties typically paired with the soup course at nineteenth-century formal dinners, and are still the wines that most often accompany soups at grand occasions today.

Why then did Parkinson pair his soup course with cognac, a beverage we often think of as an after-dinner drink—a luxurious experience ideal for sipping by itself or maybe enjoying with dessert or cheese? Well, cognac is elegant, sumptuous, and full bodied, and so were the two soups Parkinson offered. Even though cognac has a higher alcohol content than most beverages typically served with food, its high acidity and aromatic fruit nuances are well balanced. Savory dinner foods that are rich, fatty, and fully textured such as duck confit, pate, fois gras, roast meats, and whole milk cheeses help soften and neutralize cognac's alcohol and crisp acidity. This cuts through the dish's lush flavors, brightening and enhancing both the food and the cognac. So perhaps this is what Parkinson was striving for, or maybe he simply wanted to share the imperial cognac he was able to procure with his guests.[33]

A type of brandy, cognac is made from grapes, but unlike wine, it is distilled, which makes it more concentrated and results in a higher alcohol content (40 percent, or 80 proof). Egyptians were the first to devise the distilling process back in 3000 B.C., but they used their stills to make perfumes. The Germans were the first to use a distiller to create alcoholic beverages by boiling soaked grain. However, these mixtures were harsh and fiery, primarily used for medicinal purposes. It wasn't until the Dutch tried distilling wine in the 1600s in order to prevent it from going bad during long sea voyages that brandy was created. The concept soon caught on and the French began making high-quality brandy in the country's Cognac region.

Cognac is actually distilled twice (unlike most other brandies), which allows it to retain some of the wine's original qualities. A cloudy liquid that is about 30 percent alcohol is the result of the first distillation. When it is distilled a second time, a clear cognac that is 70 percent alcohol is produced. It is then transferred to oak barrels where it is aged for years. The water in the brandy eventually evaporates (between 2 and 5 percent a year) until it is brought down to the required 80 proof level for bottling. During the aging process oxygen causes the brandy to soften and become more fragrant, and the amber liquid absorbs the rich vanilla and caramel flavors from the oak, creating an experience that is complex, smooth, and velvety on the palate.[34]

FISH

Fresh Salmon, lobster sauce • Baked Rock, à la Chambord

"In choosing fresh fish, select only those that are thick and firm, with bright scales and stiff fins; the gills a very lively red, and the eyes full and prominent."

—Eliza Leslie, *Directions for Cookery*, 1844

When Europeans first began arriving in America, they were thrilled to find the Atlantic coastline, bays, and other waterways teeming with fish—many of them of an immense size. Fish were said to be so plentiful that the Native American Lenape people had only to reach into the water and scoop out fish with their bare hands when they wanted to eat.[1] In 1621 Plymouth colonist Edward Winslow wrote that the cod were so abundant that it was "but coarse meate with us."[2]

In his descriptive tribute to American cookery, *American Dishes at the Centennial* (1874), James Parkinson sings the praises of the numerous varieties of American fish—some so revered and specialized that they were named after the region they hailed from, including Delaware shad, Burlington herring, and sturgeon (sometimes called "Albany beef"). He mentions many that are still popular today, such as rockfish (striped bass), codfish, halibut, pike, bluefish, grouper, trout, and salmon. Others on his list are perhaps not as commonly served on modern tables: sheep's head, frost fish, silver eel, mascalonge, and pompano.[3]

As per the typical order of a multicourse nineteenth-century dinner, Parkinson chose fish as his first relevé. (This French term means "remove," signifying a dish which "comes to remove"—in other words, follow—another, usually the soup.) In this case, the fish was fresh salmon with lobster sauce and "Baked Rock, à la Chambord" (striped bass that was larded, stuffed, and elegantly garnished). It was customary after the soup to transition into more substantial dishes, starting with fish, seguing into poultry and then meats. As explained by French chef Pierre Blot, "*Relevés* of fish, and then of meat follow the soup course. . . . A fish served whole is always a *relevé.*"[4] Eliza Leslie echoed this idea of serving fish at the beginning of a meal, stating, "it is customary to eat fish only at the commencement of the dinner."[5]

It was common to offer two types of fish at a large dinner party—typically one baked and presented whole, and the other cut into fillets and boiled, accompanied by a sauce such as tomato or Spanish (a savory brown gravy), or a shellfish-based one such as oyster, shrimp, or lobster.[6] Parkinson's choices stayed true to this tradition: The rockfish would have been baked whole, as per the à la Chambord method, and the salmon was likely filleted and boiled before being served with a rich lobster sauce.

Shad was probably the most common fish of the Philadelphia region, and although the females were (and still are) especially valued for their roe, shad meat is rather oily and studded with numerous small bones, making them difficult to fillet. Regardless, many people still found shad very tasty, and since they were so abundant, cooks came up with creative ways of preparing them. Parkinson himself raved about shad, especially served planked—a popular presentation. He claimed an ocean steamer captain declared planked shad was so delicious, "it was well worth the round trip from England and back, to eat one dinner of it." Parkinson's dinner took place in April, which would have been during the spring shad run (their yearly upstream migration), so shad would have been easy to procure, and a natural choice to showcase Philadelphia's bounty.[7]

However, Parkinson didn't go with the local specialty this time, instead deciding on two other fish favorites: salmon and rockfish. Salmon have been a globally popular fish throughout history. With their scarlet-colored meat and rich, distinctive flavor, salmon were often considered "red-blooded"—a "royal fish" served to those of noble status. Salmon were also much enjoyed by both Native Americans and early colonists, which resulted in overfishing of the once prolific wild Atlantic salmon, known as the "king of fish." Formerly extremely plentiful in the rivers along the Atlantic seaboard north of the Potomac (including the Delaware and the Hudson), salmon populations were further depleted by dams built in the eighteenth and nineteenth centuries, which made it impossible for them to reach their spawning grounds, driving them further north. Steamships and factory manufacturing also drove them away, and by 1850, Maine and Massachusetts were the only Atlantic states recording salmon catches. Spotting a wild Atlantic salmon is now a rare occurrence.[8]

Parkinson specifies "fresh salmon" on his Thousand Dollar Dinner menu, and it was indeed very fresh, as apparently it had been swimming in Maine's Kennebec River the night before.[9] In *The Market Assistant* (1867), Thomas Farrington De Voe refers to salmon as the choicest, most savory, and nutritive of all fish, with the eastern salmon from the Kennebec River considered the best. In the 1830s schooners sailing along the Atlantic coast began to regularly supply New York City with Kennebec salmon packed in ice. By the 1880s, the fish were arriving in New York and Philadelphia markets by steamship from March through

September, commanding high market prices due to their dwindling numbers and the distance traveled, not to mention the difficulty of keeping them fresh.[10]

Nineteenth-century cookbooks are chock-full of salmon recipes, ranging from more basic methods such as baked, boiled, broiled, pickled, roasted, and fried salmon cutlets, to fancier presentations including Salmon en Papillotes, Salmon Colbert, Salmon rolled à l'Irlandaise, and the elegantly garnished Salmon à la Genoise and Salmon à la Regence. Many of the methods involved boiling salmon—some called for boiling the fish whole, some as larger cuts, and others as fillets. Although a whole salmon was occasionally served at a large dinner party, it is more likely that Parkinson cooked the middle portion, which was considered the most exquisite, then served it sliced into fillets for his guests.

In *One Hundred Ways of Cooking Fish* (1892), Alexander Filippini recommended boiling the salmon in a fish kettle at a moderately fast simmer, for six to eight minutes per pound, depending on the thickness. When done, he says to place the salmon on a fish-drainer and immediately cover it with hot cloths. For the lobster sauce, he instructs making a rich fish stock from the lobster shell, then simmering this with butter and flour to create a thick white sauce. Chopped lobster is added at the end, along with some minced coral (the roe or egg sac found only in female lobsters) for color, if desired. To serve, he suggests plating the salmon on a neatly folded napkin and garnishing it with coral.[11]

P arkinson's other choice for the third course was rockfish, also known as American striped bass, a favorite game and food fish found in brackish, marine, and fresh waters along the Atlantic coast from the St. Lawrence River in Canada to the Gulf of Mexico.[12] He apparently pulled out every stop to obtain fresh rockfish for his Thousand Dollar Dinner, sending privately hired anglers to Virginia to catch the fish he needed and bring them back to Philadelphia.[13]

Like salmon, rockfish were also prepared in various ways. Eliza Leslie was partial to boiling them (with the heads and tails left on) and serving them with egg sauce (hard-boiled eggs chopped and mixed with melted or drawn butter) seasoned with a little cayenne, or simply cutting hard-boiled eggs into halves and placing them in a row along the back of the fish.[14]

However, Parkinson chose the much more stylish à la Chambord method, which involved stuffing the fish with forcemeat, larding it with bacon, and braising it with white wine and seasonings, then finishing it off with decorative skewers of fish quenelles and cooked crawfish and a rich Chambord and Espagnole sauce. This method was actually created for carp at the chateau of Chambord in France, and although other large fish such as salmon, pike, trout, and bass have been used as substitutes, "Carpe à la Chambord" is the most famous presentation. James Beard referred to it as "one of the most elaborate dishes in all of cookery."[15]

Once again we have Catherine de Medici to thank for this highly celebrated dish. Her Italian cooks introduced fricandeau (larded veal roasted and glazed in its own juices) at Chambord in the 1500s, and in a stroke of genius, one thought to apply the concept to the carp that swam in the ponds surrounding the castle in order to make the muddy fish more palatable. This larding technique of dressing carp (where long strips of fat are woven through the fish with a needle) soon took off throughout France, became a staple in French kitchens, and is now regarded all over the world as one of the greatest French artistic accomplishments. In typical French fashion, the presentation was just as extravagant, and it became standard to elegantly garnish the carp with truffles, crayfish and crayfish tails, quenelles of whiting, and generous amounts of carp roe.[16]

So why did Parkinson choose to give rockfish the à la Chambord treatment instead of carp? Well, carp was not introduced to North America as a food fish until the 1870s, so he improvised, swapping striped bass for carp. Although Bass à la Chambord does show up on some nineteenth- and early twentieth-century menus, it was difficult to find a recipe for this dish. However, yet again the extensive *One Hundred Ways of Cooking Fish* by Alexander Filippini came through.

Filippini was a Delmonico chef who worked his way to the top of the famous restaurant firm, eventually becoming manager of the lower Broadway location. He used the knowledge he gained at Delmonico's to make the transition to a successful cookbook writer and advisor to railroad and steamship lines when that branch closed in the 1880s. Not only did he compile recipes for fish (which he claimed were the "best" recipes he served during his twenty-five years at the famous eatery), but his other cookbooks included *One Hundred Ways of Cooking Eggs, The International Cook Book: Over 3,300 Recipes Gathered from All Over the World*, and *The Delmonico Cook Book: How to Buy Food, How to Cook It, and How to Serve It* (which he dedicated to the Delmonico family). Although the recipes in his cookbooks are in brief paragraph form, the information is comprehensive and the recipes methodically organized.[17]

Filippini's recipe for Bass à la Chambord says to lard a three-pound bass and place it in a buttered baking pan, then add some white wine, sliced carrot and onion, and a bouquet of parsley, soup-celery, bay leaf, thyme, and two cloves. The fish is then seasoned with salt and pepper, covered with buttered paper, and baked for thirty minutes, basting frequently. When done, the fish is removed to a plate, and the cooking liquid is strained into a saucepan, along with half a pint of Espagnole and half a pint of Chambord garnishing (truffle, thinly sliced mushrooms, Espagnole sauce, bouillon, fish quenelles, and oysters), and reduced for five minutes. To serve, the fish is embellished with clusters of the garnish and three decorated fish quenelles.[18]

Although Filippini's Chambord garnishing recipe sounds luxurious (in both taste and look), another Delmonico chef, Charles Ranhofer, provides an even more over-the-top description in his famous 1893 cookbook, *The Epicurean*. The garnishes in his version include: eighteen truffles trimmed into the shape of garlic cloves, cooked in Madeira wine and rolled in a fish glaze and fine butter; eighteen crawfish tails from which the shells have been removed and the bodies glazed; eighteen heads of fluted mushrooms cooked in a little water, butter, and lemon juice; ten pieces of fish quenelles decorated with truffles; eighteen small pieces of milt à la Villeroi (fish roe) or fillets of striped bass. For his sauce he suggests a Spanish sauce reduced with Madeira and white wine, or a lean velouté (white) sauce reduced with fish broth, mushrooms, and Champagne, and buttered at the last moment. To serve, he says to dress the truffles, the mushroom heads, and the crawfish in alternate clusters and cover them with the sauce, then arrange the quenelles decorated with truffles, the Villeroi milts, or fillets of striped bass around this garnishing and send some of the sauce to the table in a separate sauce-boat.[19]

As cooking techniques often have the tendency to do, the à la Chambord method changed a bit over time. When it was first introduced, applying the larding component to the fish was what made it so special, but as its popularity grew, it seems more emphasis was placed on the sauces and garnishes. This is not so surprising, as sauces are the heart and soul of French cuisine. Mastering the art of sauce making is considered so crucial to French cookery that sauce recipes and descriptions are usually listed at the beginning of French cookbooks.[20]

So, à la Chambord was borrowed from the Italians but the French made it their own. Then the Americans and other cultural groups further tweaked the recipe according to their preferences and whatever fish and garnishes were available. As noted by French chef Louis Eustache Ude in his book *The French Cook* (1822), the Chambord technique was rarely served in Britain, since the English nobility typically preferred sea-fish to freshwater fish. When the dish occasionally was presented, British cooks included essence of anchovies, cayenne, and lemon juice in the marinade, and added lamb sweetbread, cockscombs, and squab (small pigeons) to the traditional garnishes of truffles, mushrooms, and quenelles.[21]

WINES

Extra Cabinet. Steinberg—Vintage of 1834
Especially selected from the cellars of the Duke of Nassau

In Germany's Rheingau wine district, a long, continuous chain of steep hills rise majestically over the Rhine River. These picturesque, south-facing slopes perfectly capture the sun's rays, allowing tidy rows of Riesling grapes to prosper in the varied soil rich with gravel, clay, shale, chalk, and limestone. Stacked terraces built into the steeper hills prevent the soil from eroding, and the dense forests of the Taunus Mountains nestled just beyond the vineyards help form a protective barrier.

Although many people consider France as the country that produces the world's most elegant white wines, the majority of wine experts agree that it is actually Germany—a status based mainly on the lush, aromatic Rieslings that have been produced in the Rheingau for centuries. As wine expert Tom Stevenson has noted, "Classic German Riesling is incomparable. No other wine can offer in a single sip as much finesse, purity of fruit, intensity of flavor, and thrilling acidity as a fine Riesling."[22]

Johannisberg (named for Saint John the Baptist) is the most famous of the Rheningau vineyard estates, but Steinberg has been considered a close second, with a fine reputation for producing high-quality wines. In fact, in the mid-nineteenth century there was a great rivalry between the two, with Steinberg wines fetching much higher prices than Johannisberg in some years.[23]

Steinberg was founded in 1135 by Cistercian monks as the Kloster Eberbach monastery and was one of the most innovative and successful wine estates of the Middle Ages. The monks originally planted red grapes as they had in the Burgundy region of France. However, they soon realized that red varieties did not ripen as well in the German climate, so they eventually converted to white grapes and in the 1760s built a high protective wall around their sixty-two-acre vineyard.[24]

Johannisberg and Steinberg were held in such high regard because their proprietors devoted a great deal of time, energy, and patience to their vineyards, meticulously selecting only perfect grapes for their wines. Milder weather in the eighteenth century allowed them to experiment with keeping grapes on the vine until early November, which brought them to the point of overripeness bordering upon decay. The grapes were more dried up than full, with uncommonly rich juice, which produced less wine, but more strength and aroma. After they were picked, the grapes were moderately pressed in order to prevent expressing any crude flavor from the skin or seeds. This wine was put into fresh casks, sulfurized, and left until it began to ferment. It was then poured into other casks and the process continued until the wine had entirely ceased to effervesce, usually in about five years. At this point it was immediately bottled and considered its best after another two years of storage in the bottle.[25]

This approach led to the creation of the "Cabinet cellar"—a place where the most superior wines were kept, and subsequently the wines stored there were called Cabinet (or Kabinett) wines. These wines were consistently categorized as the most valuable of their time. It is not known for sure which estate coined the term and if it meant cabinet in the sense of a place to keep fine goods, or if the wines were reserved for those in power (like a political cabinet).[26]

The Duke of Nassau attained ownership of the Steinberg estate in 1803 when the monastery was secularized. He and his family worked hard to maintain the vineyard's fine reputation and level of care. In 1806, they began conducting wine auctions, with many clients from European nobility.[27] Cabinet wines were usually sold in smaller quantities by private arrangement, although they were also periodically offered for sale by public auction, leading wine connoisseurs to worry that these bottles were an inferior product, blended with cheaper wines.[28]

The Steinberg served at the Thousand Dollar Dinner was "especially selected from the cellars of the Duke of Nassau" and considered one of the best Rhine wine vintages (1834) of that century due to temperate weather conditions.[29] It would have been seventeen years old when opened at the dinner, and likely very mature and full-bodied, yet delicate; a perfect match for the two fish dishes served by Parkinson.

BOILED

Turkey, celery and oyster sauce • *Chicken and egg sauce* • *Beef tongues*

"All meats are best cooked, whether by steam or immersion, by
being slowly or gently boiled; consequently the fire must be properly attended to, and a vigilant eye kept upon the state of the pot."
—Richard Dolby, *The Cook's Dictionary and
Housekeeper's Directory*, 1830

Today we take the simple act of boiling water for granted—
whether it is making pasta, cooking vegetables, or simply
heating water in a teakettle for a comforting cup of tea. The discovery of fire was a huge development for ancient people, giving
them the ability to cook their food, but it wasn't until the invention of cooking vessels (such as clay pots) thousands of years later
that they could effectively boil water. Once they figured out this
cooking method, the possibilities were endless.

Fast forward to nineteenth-century America—all kinds of foods
were boiled, including meat, fish, eggs, vegetables, and even puddings. Meat and vegetables were often conveniently combined to
make a one-pot meal, such as the now-traditional New England

boiled dinner, which pairs corned beef with potatoes, carrots, and cabbage. This St. Patrick's Day favorite likely originated from a hearty recipe called "Boiled-Dish—Meat," which showed up in the 1844 cookbook *The New England Economical Housekeeper, and Family Receipt Book.* This version added even more winter vegetables to the pot, including parsnips, beets, and turnips.[1]

But the "boiled dishes" course at fancy dinners was meat—most often ham, beef tongue, and poultry, typically served after the fish and before the roasts and entrees. These meat courses served as the *relevés* that "removed" the fish and the soup. Boiled meats preceded those that were roasted or grilled because these moister cuts were considered less filling, and quicker and easier to digest. This theory was shared by French, English, and Italian cooks, and eventually made its way to multicourse American dinners as well.[2]

Boiling meat seems like a pretty basic task—just place it in a pot and let the heat of the water cook the food until it is done. But as with other cookery techniques, art and science combine to produce the most flavorful dishes. Nineteenth-century cookbooks are full of specific rules and instructions for the proper way of boiling meat, sending the message that mastery of this skill was not to be underestimated.

Just as modern cooks have their favorite types of pots and pans, there were also differing opinions throughout the nineteenth century about what kind of pot was best. Sturdy, heavy-duty cast iron was standard for open hearth cooking, and most cooks had a nest of iron pots in various sizes for this purpose. But as cook stoves took over throughout the mid-1800s, some cookbooks advised using copper vessels, especially for large joints such as beef rump roast and ham, because they regulated the heat better. However, copper had a disadvantage, as pots made out of this material needed to have a durable tin lining in order to prevent lead from leaching into the food. For this reason, Eliza Leslie did not recommend copper, and adamantly stated: "If copper vessels *are* used in a kitchen, they should be well tinned on the inside; and they will require new tinning at least once a year, or still more frequently if the tin appears to be in the least wearing off."[3]

The style of cooking utensils Miss Leslie *did* recommend were those lined with porcelain. Even though she warned that the lining could crack and flake off if used over too high a heat, she still felt they were "more wholesome and more easily kept clean than any other cooking utensils" and would last for many years with the proper care.[4] But pots and pans made out of tin were probably the most popular, especially in smaller households, as this material was often deemed the lightest, safest, and most economical—a brand-new tin saucepan was about the same price as tinning a copper one.[5]

The water was also important—boiling meat in hard water was considered unwise. Using soft water was of such great importance that one cookbook even declared, "where soft water is not to be procured, the cook cannot be expected to do justice to her reputation, even with the greatest attention to her business."[6] The cook also had to make sure the percentage of water to meat was correct—using more water than necessary made the meat less savory and weakened the broth. The suggested ratio was about a quart of water to every pound of meat, so that the meat was just barely covered during the boiling process. It was advised to replenish the water as needed since some would be lost to evaporation.[7] Matching the size of the pot to the meat's proportions was also key, as larger vessels took up more space on the stove and required a larger quantity of water to boil.[8]

Most cookbooks advocated gradually heating the water and meat at the same time, rather than placing meat in water that was already boiling, which could make it hard and tough. Once the water was boiling, maintaining a slow, gentle simmer was essential—an approach mentioned over and over as rendering the most evenly cooked, tender, and flavorful meats. A rolling boil was thought to be wasteful, since much of the water ended up needlessly evaporating. It also extracted the savory juices to a greater extent, depriving the meat of its flavor and nutritional value.[9]

This "poaching" method was very popular in the nineteenth century and led to the invention of the fish kettle. This was an oblong covered boiler with a removable perforated insert, perfect for cooking delicate fish, but it could also be used to cook large cuts of meats, such as a filet of beef. The insert (or trivet) was placed on the bottom of the boiling pot, raising the meat about an inch and a half from the bottom, allowing for more even cooking. The insert could be lifted out when the fish or meat was done, carefully drained then transferred directly to the table.[10]

The concept of a moderate boil is very similar to the process of rendering stock and making soup. Inventor and fireplace expert Sir Benjamin Thompson (also known as Count Rumford) compared the fragrant aroma of the steam rising from pots containing slowly boiling meat to the strong flavor and superior quality of soups cooked over a gentle fire for a long time.[11] And as in the preparation of soup, careful and constant skimming was required, otherwise the scum that rose to the surface would attach to the meat, making it appear dirty and unappetizing. In order to prevent this from happening, sometimes cooks would wrap the meat in a cloth prior to cooking. Tips to help poultry retain a clean delicate look and enhance its white color included rubbing lemon juice all over it or adding milk to the pot. But most cookbooks felt these methods suppressed the meat's flavor, and instead promoted skimming to ensure plump, pure, and succulent boiled dishes.[12]

Nineteenth-century cooks who wanted to produce even more tender and flavorful cuts of meat than those boiled in an open pot could try a Papin's digester. Invented by French physicist and mathematician Denis Papin in 1679, this contraption was a cast-iron boiler whose cover (fastened down with screws) shut so tightly that no steam could escape—a precursor to the pressure cooker. As the food heated in its cooking liquid, pressure was created, allowing very hot steam to cook the food more quickly than other cooking methods available at the time.[13]

The cooks that used them had to be somewhat daring, however, since there were some drawbacks to the novel technology.

Although Papin thought to include a valve in his design as a way to release steam, there was the possibility the digester would explode if the pressure and cooking temperature were not properly monitored. In addition, high levels of pressure over time would lead the vessel to eventually crack along its seams, forcing the contents to erupt like hot lava from a volcano.[14]

Even though Papin never saw his concept and invention reach its full potential, he at least introduced the idea of cooking under pressure. Over time, the pressure cooker evolved, with cast-aluminum models introduced in the 1920s and the eventual standardization of safety valves and gauges.[15]

Tasty, often spicy sauces always accompanied boiled dishes as a contrast to the simplicity of the plain boiled meat. This flavor-enhancing concept is popular among many cultures: English leg of mutton with lobster sauce, Italian bollito misto with salsa verde, and German Tafelspitz (boiled beef) with horseradish sauce, for example. Sauces were also used to enhance the color of the meat—white sauce poured over white meat such as poultry made it appear lighter, and brown sauces complemented darker cuts like beef. The sauce also dressed up the dish, making it look prettier and helping cover any imperfections.[16] The pairings Parkinson chose were quite common for the time and the two most often found on his menus as part of the boiled dishes course—turkey with oyster sauce and chicken with egg sauce.

Although boiled turkey was considered an elegant and fashionable dish for a mid-nineteenth-century fancy dinner, some thought that much of the flavor boiled away during the cooking process, making it rather bland. In her book *Practical Cooking and Dinner Giving* (1881), Mary Foote Henderson claimed a boiled turkey could be quite tasteless unless it is "well managed." She recommended using a hen turkey, and making sure it was well trussed and tied, or the "legs and wings of a boiled fowl will be found pointing to all the directions of the compass." Instead of gradually boiling the water and turkey together, as many cookbooks instructed, she advised placing it in water that was already boiling. To serve, she suggested plating the turkey on a bed of rice, topped with a spoonful or two of oyster, caper, cauliflower, parsley, or Hollandaise sauce.[17]

Stuffing the turkey was optional according to Mrs. Henderson's recipe, but others insisted it was a necessary step in boiling a turkey, probably because it kept the meat tender and added flavor. The stuffing could range from a simple breadcrumb mixture to a more elaborate blend with seasonings such as chopped oysters, sausage, ham or suet, chestnuts, mushrooms, truffles, parsley, pepper, salt, and ground nutmeg, as well as egg and milk for moistness. Some cooks also tucked the turkey liver under one wing and the gizzard under the other for additional richness.[18]

But one of the most interesting preparations is credited to the famous Victorian-era French chef Alexis Soyer.[19] Often referred to as the first "celebrity chef," Soyer was extremely vocal and passionate about food. For example, his view on boiled turkey: "This is a dish I rarely have, as I never could relish it boiled as it generally is, by putting it into that pure and chaste element water, into which has been thrown some salt, the quantity of which differs as much as the individuals that throw it in."[20]

Because Soyer thought boiled turkey was so bland, he made sure his version was highly seasoned and served with a savory sauce or other accompaniment. His method of trussing the turkey was rather complicated, including cutting off the legs and tucking them under the apron of the turkey, slipping the liver and gizzard under the wings, and then lacing the turkey every which way until it was a tightly wound package. He would then stuff the breast cavity, adding chopped oysters to the mixture only if the turkey was to be served with oyster sauce. To boil it, instead of using plain water, he added an aromatic mixture of butter, salt, onions, celery, carrots, turnips, a large bouquet of parsley, two bay leaves, and two sprigs of thyme to the pot before setting it on the fire. Since the water was constantly skimmed during the boiling process, he was effectively creating a delicious broth, which he recommended using to make soup the next day. In lieu of oyster sauce, he suggested celery, Jerusalem artichoke, tomato, mushroom, or parsley and butter. Bacon could also be added to the cook pot, and then served with the turkey over some greens or Brussels sprouts dressed with salt, pepper, and butter.[21]

Even though Soyer's method was a sure way to enhance the flavor of boiled turkey, he still much preferred the taste of roasted turkey, claiming, "The flavour of a roasted turkey, hot or cold, is as superior to the boiled as it is possible to be. I think if you try it, you will never again resort to that bubbling system of salt and water."[22] Soyer was not so far off—boiled turkey gradually began to lose favor throughout the later part of the nineteenth century, eventually eclipsed by other preparations, most notably roasting and braising. Indeed, ask most cooks today how they prepare turkey and they will almost certainly say roasted, or maybe grilled or even the recent fad of using a deep fat-fryer—not boiled.

The turkey is one of the most quintessential American foods, through its association with Thanksgiving and its reputation as one of the bounteous foods that Europeans encountered in the New World. Indigenous to the Western Hemisphere, the turkey's ancestors have ranged through most of North and Central America for millions of years, with evidence of the modern wild turkey emerging about 50,000 years ago. When explorers began arriving in the Americas, they found wild turkeys had already been domesticated by native peoples of Mexico and parts of Central America and were living in vast regions of what is now the United States.[23]

The Spanish brought some of these domesticated turkeys back to Spain around 1520 where they quickly proliferated throughout Europe. So when European colonists began arriving and settling North America, they were already familiar with the impressive bird. Wild turkey became an extremely important food source for them, as they were large, abundant, and rather easy to hunt. Then, in an ironic twist, soon after the formation of the British colonies, domesticated turkeys were imported back into America from England. This was timely, as wild turkeys had started becoming scarce in parts of North America due to overhunting.[24]

These domesticated turkeys began to mate with wild turkeys, creating new varieties. Nineteenth-century farmers saw the benefit of this blending and began to breed turkeys on purpose to produce particular characteristics, such as larger birds and more breast meat, a trend that continues today. However, it appears that taste was compromised in these experiments. According to James Beard, domesticated turkeys have never come close to rivaling the delicious flavor of a wild turkey, which has been described as darker in color, more juicy, and possessing a slight gamy taste. The French epicure Jean Anthelme Brillat-Savarin declared, "The flesh of the wild turkey has more colour and more flavour than that of the domestic turkey."[25] Delmonico chef Charles Ranhofer also thought the meat of a wild turkey was "far more delicate and succulent than that of a domestic turkey," and featured it on his menus in different ways, including roasted, stuffed, and pureed as a soup.[26]

Although wild turkeys may have a richer taste, most folks were eating domesticated turkeys by the mid-nineteenth century, especially if they lived in a large city like New York or Philadelphia. The commercialization of the turkey was taking off and the meat was increasingly blander, but luckily there were a large number of interesting turkey recipes other than just boiling and roasting. For example, deviled turkey was a turkey leg that was cross hatched with a knife, rubbed all over with a mix of mustard and flour so that the flavorings soaked into the meat, then broiled. And scalloped turkey was an excellent way to use leftovers, as it called for dicing cooked turkey into small pieces and layering it in a dish with breadcrumbs, beaten egg and milk, seasonings, and "any stuffing, gravy or scraps left from the turkey."[27]

Today when many Americans think about having turkey, it is often as a Thanksgiving dinner showpiece, when it makes a grand entrance served on a platter, nicely browned, roasted, and stuffed.

But our modern feast actually bears little resemblance to the 1621 Pilgrim harvest celebration commonly known as the "first Thanksgiving," or the Puritan tradition of observing holy days of thanksgiving.[28]

Days of thanksgiving were common in many colonial American communities throughout the seventeenth and eighteenth centuries, typically declared by ministers or governors in response to specific occasions, such as a military victory, a plentiful harvest, or beneficial rainfall, but no specific Thanksgiving Day was celebrated on a yearly basis. For both the Pilgrims and Puritans, days of fasting and thanksgiving, like the Sabbath, were serious occasions marked by long sermons, prayer, and time off from work and play.[29]

Eventually the idea of feasting as part of a day of thanksgiving evolved as an alternative to the fall harvest festivals that were part of the British culture, particularly in the New England area where many people missed these traditions from their homeland. Turkeys (along with other food and drink) were included in these celebrations. The gathering of extended family as part of these events became more significant during the late eighteenth century, and the foods associated with the New World, such as turkey, pumpkin, sweet potatoes, and cranberries were increasingly integrated.[30] Thanksgiving as we now know it began to emerge.

The relationship between Pilgrims and Thanksgiving can be linked back to Rev. Alexander Young's *Chronicles of the Pilgrim Fathers*, published in 1841. In the book, Young included a copy of a letter dated December 11, 1621, from Edward Winslow, one of the Plymouth colony leaders, describing a three-day feast enjoyed by the colonists and a large group of Native American guests held after the crops were harvested. Winslow did not specifically mention wild turkey in his letter—only that four men went hunting and brought back large amounts of fowl, which could have been any type of bird, such as ducks, geese, or even swans. On his own accord, Reverend Young added a footnote stating, "This was the first Thanksgiving, the harvest festival of New England. On this occasion they no doubt feasted on the wild turkey as well as venison." In order to substantiate his turkey reference, Young cited Governor William Bradford's 1650 manuscript, "Of Plymouth Plantation," which states that in the fall of 1621 "a great store of wild turkeys" was available at the colony.[31] So while it was a real possibility that turkey was one of the birds served at this feast, it was essentially Young's statement that secured a place for turkey on the Thanksgiving menu.

By the 1850s, almost every state and territory celebrated Thanksgiving, but it didn't become a national holiday until President Abraham Lincoln issued a proclamation in 1863, the result of a seventeen-year campaign by *Godey's Lady's Book* editor Sarah Josepha Hale. She was able to convince President Lincoln that a national Thanksgiving might help heal the nation after the devastating Civil War. Soon after, with the Victorian era and all its opulence, Thanksgiving dinner became one of the most carefully planned meals of the year for most families (along with Christmas), and roast turkey was a highlight of both menus.[32]

WINES

Champagne—Sparkling, of Peuvrel a Avize

SPECIALLY ON TABLE

Medoc—Haut Brion, 1841 • Burgundy—Cote Roti, 1839

Our fascination with fanciful, bubbly Champagne is actually a fairly recent phenomenon. It wasn't until the nineteenth century that the sparkling wine really began to make an impact, becoming the fashionable, celebratory beverage that it is today.

True Champagne is a product solely of the Champagne region of France, which lies about ninety miles northeast of Paris. One of the coolest wine-producing areas in the world, the soil here is rich with chalk and minerals. Winemakers in the region found that these cold temperatures would often force the yeasts into a state of hibernation over the winter, halting fermentation before all the sugar in the grapes was turned to alcohol. The arrival of spring and warmer weather would "wake up" the yeasts, causing them to froth and bubble, and creating sediment in the bottle. The Champenois found this unnerving, especially since their region's wines were the only ones with this effervescent quality. They struggled to eliminate the bubbles and improve the taste, which could be weak and rather sour, but still the results were often muddy, gritty, and foamy.[33]

In the seventeenth century the region's wine producers eventually gave up on trying to do away with the unique bubbles and instead worked on procedures to capitalize on them. These developments included *remuage*, or riddling, which removed the yeasts in one fell swoop, leaving behind a wine that was clear, sparkling, and golden. The flavor also improved over time, so less and less sugar needed to be added to hide a tart taste. People began to pay attention, and Champagne soon became a hot commodity, especially among the wealthy. At the end of the eighteenth century, fewer than 300,000 bottles of sparkling wine were being made annually in the region, but by 1900, production had increased to 30 million.[34]

Not surprisingly, Parkinson chose Champagne from Avize, one of the premier sparkling wine-making villages at the time, and today considered home to the most prestigious wines of Champagne: Blanc de blancs (made exclusively from white Chardonnay grapes). Located in the Côte des Blancs district, Avize has a long-respected reputation for its unblended wine. It was originally thought of as a poor-quality wine producer, but when the public started to discover and enjoy sparkling wine in the seventeenth and eighteenth centuries, Avize was increasingly acknowledged for its top-notch bubbly. Today the wines produced from the Côte des Blancs region have become the most coveted of all Champagnes.[35]

The most versatile of all wines, Champagne's high acidity level and refreshing effervescence help cleanse the palate, making it a perfect accompaniment to meals. In addition, the wide range of mouth feel (from light to full) and sweetness levels (from quite sweet—*doux*—to very, very dry—*extra brut*) enables all types of food pairings. However, this concept would have been different in 1851, because until this time, virtually all sparkling wine was sweet. It wasn't until 1848 that sparkling wine was bottled without the addition of sugar. Drier Champagnes gradually became more popular, particularly with wine collectors,[36] but it is pretty safe to assume that the wine served by Parkinson was sweeter than we are used to today. In nineteenth-century America, it was typical to serve Champagne with the *removes* or solid joints-meat courses. The refreshing bubbles likely helped balance the richness of the meat and creamy accompanying sauces.

MÉDOC—HAUT BRION, 1841

For centuries, English merchants imported the majority of their wine from the Bordeaux region of France. Small growers sold their wines to merchants who then blended the different wines for bulk resale. Some were good, some not so good, depending on the freshness, season, and reliability of the traders. There was no way to tell ahead of time since the wines were purchased in casks—the English just "got what they got" each time. But in the seventeenth century, Haut Brion changed the game for Bordeaux wines. It is here that the concept of *terroir* developed and the specialization of extraordinary Bordeaux wines began.[37]

Situated on the arid, gravelly soil of the Graves region in the southern portion of Bordeaux, Château Haut-Brion was owned by the Pontac family. In addition to his role as heir to this winemaking estate, Arnaud III de Pontac was a powerful local politician who enjoyed a lavish lifestyle, which included a splendid town house as his city residence. Turns out he was also a savvy businessman. He was adamant that the red wine from Haut-Brion was unique, and through a clever promotional campaign specifically aimed at the established London market, was able to convince wine drinkers that his product was indeed something special.[38]

In 1660 de Pontac started marketing his estate's Haut-Brion wine as a distinct brand at a price much higher than other Bordeaux wines. Today this would be an advertiser's nightmare—trying to sell an unknown wine at a premium price. But de Pontac was passionate about his vineyard and its terroir, and it became clear that a single Bordeaux from just one vineyard really did have distinctive qualities. In 1663 Samuel Pepys enjoyed some of de Pontac's wine and noted in his famous diary that he "drank a sort of French wine, called Ho Bryan, that hath a good and most particular taste that I ever met with." It was the first wine from Bordeaux to be given the name of the estate where it was made. By the 1700s, the concept of making individual wines from particular locations had spread throughout the Bordeaux region.[39]

So what did the 1841 Haut-Brion that Parkinson served taste like almost two hundred years after Pepys's revelatory discovery? There's no way to know for sure since winemaking factors change over time, but the distinctiveness of Haut-Brion wines have been pondered for years, particularly the fact that the grapes do so well in such sandy, gravelly soil. Even today, its taste stands apart from neighboring vineyards. British critic Clive Coates describes Haut-Brion's wines as possessing "warm brick, aromatic flavors, roundness and spice," whereas nearby La Mission is "more minerally, austere and tannic."[40] Taking the vintage into consideration, it is interesting to note that according to a late nineteenth-century book on Bordeaux and its wines, 1841 was considered an "excellent year," even though the wines took some time to mature, possessing "a certain hardness at first; in development however, they become firm, bodied, fruity and coloured." As a result, prices started out moderate and then rose steadily to very high levels.[41]

BURGUNDY—COTE ROTI, 1839

The English translation for *côte rôtie* is "roasted hillside," an appropriate name for a wine born from vineyards planted on the steep, south-facing terraced slopes of the northern Rhône region of France. Having access to full sun causes the grapes to richly ripen, and the high altitude and light breezes temper the process, producing deeply perfumed, bold, spicy wines made mostly from syrah grapes. By French law, up to 20 percent of white wine can be blended in, largely because viognier vines are intertwined with the syrah in some places. Although the creamy viognier can add softness and intensify the exotic aroma of Côte rôtie, most of the region's wine producers choose to include less than 5 percent.[42]

Dating back to Roman times, Côte rôtie was historically a small yield region, with its wines not becoming as well known as other reds such as Bordeaux and Burgundy until the 1700s, when England developed an increasing taste for Rhône wines. These wines must have been something special since it was quite a distance to transport them to Great Britain from this far corner of France. U.S. wine drinkers also discovered the taste, with Thomas Jefferson paying the region a visit in the late eighteenth century. He apparently admired the wine enough to have some bottled and shipped to his home in Paris. "There is a quality which keeps well, bears transportation and that cannot be drunk under four years," he wrote in his diary. A nineteenth-century wine guide describes the character of this region's wines as possessing the body and color of a Burgundy and the elegance of a claret (Bordeaux). The wine Parkinson served was actually labeled a Burgundy, perhaps because the vintage he chose favored the higher tannins and delicate flavors of a Burgundy.[43]

COLD DISHES

Galantine de Dinde à la Gelée • Jambon Décoré
Salade à la Russe en bordure de Gelée • Aspic aux huîtres
Bœuf à la mode • Mayonnaise of lobster
Salade de Volaille, à la Mode Anglaise • Aspic de Volaille aux truffes

"The cold service is the most elegant and artistic one of the culinary art."—Charles Ranhofer, *The Epicurean*, 1893

Tenderloin of beef garnished with vegetables, boned turkey and capon, ham stuffed with pistachio nuts and truffles, aspics, pâtés and terrines of all kinds, foie gras, smoked tongue well glazed and dressed in pyramid form, chicken mayonnaise, ducks' livers à la Toulouse, young rabbit à la mode de Rouen, and salad à la russe. These were just a few of the many elegant items suitable for serving as the "cold dishes" course in the nineteenth century—also referred to as the cold service, cold entrées, or cold meats.

European chef Willi Bode surmises that cold dishes were "possibly a throwback to the times when man ate his food cold (but not necessarily uncooked)."[1] In any case, over time cold dishes developed into elaborate gastronomic masterworks designed to show-case a chef's ornamentation skills. Proper execution of this course required an artistic and creative eye. Cooks would mold and model food into intricate shapes and forms, and then embellish these objets d'art with fashionable garnishings, much like we think of a modern pâtissier working with confectionery and pastry dough to create sumptuous desserts.

In the nineteenth century the term *pâtisserie* actually more often referred to savory items, not sweets. These dishes were meant to add grace and beauty to a well-adorned table or sideboard, but it was of equal importance that they also tasted delicious. Those who could master this delicate balance and come up with the most unique and inventive ideas developed the finest reputations. As chef A. Tavenet asks in *L'Art culinaire*, "Is it not an incontestable fact that a cook cannot become celebrated unless he has an exact knowledge of pâtisserie and has acquired the rudiments of the art as a young man?"[2]

Much thought went into the planning of this course. It was an initiation in culinary creativity for young cook's apprentices, who were expected to sculpt the basic objects, while the master chef would create and decorate the shapes, finishing them off with alluring colors and embellishments.[3] As noted by Delmonico chef Charles Ranhofer, "The pieces must be well defined and designed before beginning; prepare all the needed materials beforehand so that when the work has once begun there will be nothing to delay the progress." Because of all the intricacies involved, Ranhofer also advised that preparation of the cold dishes should be done well in advance, not rushed or finished at the last minute.[4]

Although it was clear that this course was all about grandeur and innovation, there was quite a bit of disagreement among chefs as to where it belonged on the menu. Most nineteenth-century cookbooks advised serving the cold dishes toward the end of a multicourse dinner, usually after the roast (considered the high point of the meal), and before the dessert. "The best place to locate the cold meats is at the end of all the other meats; if entrées are the last let cold meats follow them, if game appears after the entrées let cold meat come after the game," explained chef Jessup Whitehead in *The Steward's Handbook and Guide to Party Catering*.[5]

Ranhofer also recommended serving cold dishes following the roast and before the hot dessert, further clarifying, "in the French service these cold dishes are classified as the last entrée."[6] In the *service français* approach, cold meats, aspics, and pâtés were typically served during the third service, after the roast.[7]

It is interesting then that Parkinson decided to feature the cold dishes three places *before* the roast—although apparently it was not unheard of. In *La Cuisine classique* (1856), French chefs Urbain Dubois and Émile Bernard maintained that (nineteenth-century) customs had not rigidly defined the right moment for cold dishes. Their research on upper-class menus found that rules were flexible and could be modified depending on the circumstances. "Serving a cold selection before fish, immediately after the relevés, instead of after the soup or the hors d'oeuvres, is simply a matter of preferences with no great influence on the order or outcome of a dinner as long as one is aware of it," they wrote.[8]

Even Whitehead gives a few examples of menus where the cold dishes are higher up in a multicourse menu, but he is clearly not in favor of the placement, cautioning, "They do not look so well up there dividing the hot meats."[9] Parkinson's decision was most likely the result of his desire to show he was on top of the latest trends. The Thousand Dollar Dinner occurred in the middle of the nineteenth century, a time when many changes were occurring to the order and flow of the way courses were served. The *service français* technique was slowly being replaced or integrated with the *service russe*, or Russian style, which often listed the cold entrée *before* the roast.[10]

And evidently this order of courses was not unusual for Parkinson, since some of his other menus from this timeframe also place this course in a similar position. His method makes sense: Impress the diners early in the meal with these elegant displays—

keeping them engaged and whetting their appetite for what was to come.

So how were Parkinson and other chefs able to form the different foods into such intricate shapes? Today when we think of a molded salad it usually brings to mind a colorful and quivering mass studded with fruit and maybe nuts, made sweet with multiple boxes of Jell-O. However, before these gelatin salads became a staple at potluck dinners and picnics, a similar concept was used to make cold dishes "set" into elaborate forms and glisten when they were displayed on elegant stands. But instead of a sweet, fruity jelly, a savory, transparent one was used.

Referred to as aspic jellies, the technique was based on medieval gellys (jellies), but really took off in the nineteenth century when French chef Marie-Antoine (Antonin) Carême (1784–1833) took haute cuisine to new levels of extravagance, presenting these *chaud-froid* dishes (prepared hot but served cold) in stunning arrangements.[11] "Jellies should be tasty, limpid and transparent," explained Charles Ranhofer in *The Epicurean.* "If they be defective, then the handsomest pieces are open to criticism."[12]

The jelly was created via a lengthy process that involved making a thick, gelatinous stock from animal products rich in natural gelatin such as veal knuckle, calves feet, bacon hock and rind, poultry bones, and fish trimmings. Once the meat was thoroughly cooked, the broth was strained, then alternately boiled, skimmed, and simmered until it was perfectly clear. The stock was then clarified to ensure the aspic turned out transparent and sparkling. Ironically this involved first making the liquid cloudy by boiling it with frothed egg white and crushed eggshell. When boiled, the congealing properties of the egg trapped fat particles and impurities, which rose to the surface. The broth was then strained through a jelly bag or cheesecloth, leaving the foamy scum behind. Finally, the aspic jelly was left to cool and then set on ice until needed.[13]

Decorative molds made from all kinds of cold cooked foods were set in aspic, including fish, poultry, meat, and vegetables. These dishes were brightly hued and molded into all kinds of shapes, such as a serpent, the namesake some believe the word aspic derived from (the asp), with its icy coldness and jeweled colors. The jelly encased around the cooked meat not only looked pretty, but it prevented air and bacteria from reaching the meat and turning it rancid, therefore enabling the display of these fancy dishes, like museum pieces under glass.

However, Carême warned against using too many colors in order to show off the embellishment to the best advantage. "For instance, the top of a circle of aspic jelly may be ornamented with a wreath, the leaves of which are of the pieces off the breasts of poultry, and the small buds of truffles; you may make the leaves of truffles or girkins, and the buds of meat or truffles, and the leaves of red tongue; but still never use more than two colours at a time," he advised.[14]

The success of these culinary sculptures hinged on a number of factors, from the temperature of the ingredients to the sharp eye, patience, and precision of the cook. As stated by Jules Gouffé in *The Royal Cookery Book: (Le Livre de Cuisine)* (1869), "The jelly should not be moulded until it is quite cold. . . . Should it retain any degree of heat, it would be liable to loosen the ornaments laid in the moulds. On the other hand, avoid using the jelly too cold. . . . if beginning to set, it would fill with air bubbles, and give the *aspic* a dull and misty appearance." Gouffé also advises pouring each layer of jelly into the mold as soon as the preceding one is set to prevent the layers from sticking to each other, causing the aspic to break when unmolded.[15]

Aspic jellies were also used to create galantines—dishes made from poultry, pork, game, veal, or rabbit, stuffed with forcemeat and pressed into a symmetrical shape. Galantine of turkey was perhaps the most celebrated. The technique involved the complex process of boning a turkey, which one recipe cautioned was "very complicated and difficult, better to be left to professional skill." A home cook who wanted to attempt this dish needed to have a strong stomach and advanced knife skills, as it required separating the flesh from the bone by taking a very sharp blade and scraping it loose rather than cutting it. But there was a reward to the time-consuming process, since after all the flesh was separated from the bones; the whole skeleton would come out "as easily as you draw your hand out of a glove." The turkey was then stuffed with rich forcemeat and its wings and legs tightly wrapped and skin sewed up to create a smooth, even surface. To cook the turkey, it was either simmered in water or baked in the oven. When done, the galantine would be placed to cool in a large dish with melted aspic jelly drizzled over it. The jelly formed a transparent coating as the turkey cooled, and was either presented to the table just like that, or loosened with hot water and the fragments placed attractively around the turkey along with a sprig or two of parsley.[16]

As a precursor to the "Turducken" dish that is sometimes seen today,[17] this process could be taken even further by placing a boned chicken stuffed with sausage meat or lean ham inside the boned turkey, "with the rump of the chicken toward the neck of the turkey" so the white meat was not all in the same place. (This idea of stuffing boned fowl and layering one inside the other actually dates back to the Renaissance.) As can be imagined, this poultry combination would have to be cooked for a very long time. Philadelphia Cooking School instructor Sarah Tyson Rorer advised simmering the galantine in a soup kettle for four hours, letting it cool in its own cooking liquor, then placing it on a flat dish with a meat board on top weighted down with two flat irons and left to stand overnight, which helped press it so it could be sliced thin. It was then brushed with beaten egg and dusted with breadcrumbs and parsley before browning in a hot oven, then cooled again and garnished with aspic jelly before serving.[18]

Hatelets (or attelets) were also used to enhance the appearance of cold dishes. These small decorative skewers were threaded with juicy tidbits such as truffles, cockscomb,[19] kidneys, sweetbreads, shrimp, or mushrooms and inserted into the different dishes to create stunning displays. They featured unique handles in animal shapes such as fish, hare, and boar, as well as more elaborate designs including dragons, crowns, and epergnes (flower vases).

The Epicurean has a whole section on preparing cold hatelets, including instructions for stacking rounds of cooked beef tongue, chicken, and truffles into special hatelet molds and filling them with aspic jelly. When set, they were unmolded and placed on a hatelet with a black truffle as a final garnish. Fragments of transparent jelly were made into small square croutons for use as hatelet decorations. Aspic jelly was also used as a type of glue. Made sticky by chopping on a wet cloth and sprinkling with water, the jelly helped the hatelets adhere to the cold dishes and cover the surfaces used as supports.[20]

The most elegant dishes were literally put on a pedestal, referred to as socles or stands. Raising the dishes gave them prominence and artistic balance and allowed more room for fancy garnishes. Like the other items in the cold dishes range, socles were made out of food ingredients—anything edible that could be molded into a base strong enough to serve as a support. Rice, semolina, and mutton fat were the most common.[21]

Socles for large cold dishes were made by melting mutton-kidney suet, mixing it with clean white lard, then straining and whipping it with a whisk until it was cold and smooth. A block of wood in the shape of the socle served as a template. It was placed on a baking sheet and the whipped fat was plastered around the block, and when one layer was dry another was added. When the socle was completely dry, it was heated briefly so that it easily separated from the block of wood and then decorated with colored paste, flowers made of colored fat or real flowers. Gouffé preferred constructing socles out of rice as he felt those made from fat imparted a "disagreeable fatty taste" to the preparations set upon them. This method involved pounding cooked rice in a mortar and then molding it into the required shape. The rice was then lacquered with Montpellier or lobster sauce or plain butter for a smooth appearance.[22]

The popularity of serving elaborate cold dishes as a separate course slowly began to fade as the Russian style of dining took over and merged with the French. It was no longer necessary to focus so much time and energy on food decoration and artistic display since it had become preferable for dishes to arrive at the table already carved or sliced. There was also the view that some chefs had taken the ornamentation of food to extremes, decorating and beautifying everything on the menu. Others developed the habit of using inappropriate ingredients, thus "reproducing clumsy and ridiculous imitations," in the words of Gouffé. However, this change was a disappointment for chefs who believed that a certain degree of style and elegance was necessary to produce true culinary achievements. They feared cooks would become careless and the quality of their craft would begin to suffer.[23]

But decorative molded dishes did find a place during the Victorian era—they just moved into the dessert category. Jelly desserts were fashioned out of molds ranging from basic forms such as oval, round, or cylindrical, to intricate designs in the shape of nobility, pets, and even famous locations in London. Some were filled with Bavarian cream or fruit, others featured a vertical rainbow of colors. Special molds were available to produce layers within layers.[24] There was also blancmange—a sweet, vanilla-flavored milk-based pudding-jelly combination. The invention of powdered gelatins in the mid-1800s allowed these dishes to be easily reproduced in home kitchens, and impressive molded desserts became an expression of status, wealth, and culinary skill.[25]

And the idea of savory cold dishes did not vanish completely. On contemporary multicourse menus, it has been replaced by the salad section, which consists of a cold salad arranged with the main item, or some other delicate cold experience tucked into a sequence of mostly hot dishes, such as chicken mousse with truffles, pâté, or fish terrine. Sometimes an entire meal of these elegantly designed cold dishes was (and still is) served for special occasions such as a christening, luncheon, or ball, or as a special table featured at a holiday celebration. Referred to as *les buffets froids* (cold buffet), this type of buffet might also be served as a special highlight or complement to a prix fixe or à la carte menu.[26]

WINES

RARE OLD CASK

Amontillado—Pale Sherry
Specially selected from the private stock of Thomas Osborne, Esq.,
of the house of Duff, Gordon & Co., Port Andalusia, Spain

Tucked into the southwest corner of Spain within the Andalusia Province lie a land of informal open-air cafes serving excellent food and drink, including fresh, abundant shellfish plucked from the nearby Atlantic Ocean. This is Jerez, the country's warmest wine-producing region, home to the unique fortified wine that is sherry. Although it boasts a mostly Mediterranean climate, influences from the neighboring Atlantic come into play, including the *poniente*—the westerly breeze that transports the ocean's moisture through the Straits of Gibraltar and across the Mediterranean. This wind helps balance its cousin, the easterly *levante*, which blows hot and arid air.[27]

The finest sherries are produced from grapes grown in the brilliant white soil known as the *albarizas*. Rich in lime deposits, the soil soaks up water like a wet sponge, helping feed the grapevines just the right amount of moisture. And its startling brightness functions as a reflector on the vines' lower branches, assisting the ripening process.[28]

The location is so unique that it is the only region in the world that has been able to produce good quality sherry, also known as Jerez or Xeres. The yeast bloom called "flor" that develops on some batches of sherry wines as it ferments is the most important factor. Unlike other wines, sherry is stored in barrels that are partially filled, which allows oxygen to get inside. But the flor consumes oxygen, preventing the wine from turning to vinegar. The *Saccharomyces* yeast that produces the flor is apparently extremely tied to the region, as winemakers have been unable to replicate this specific strain elsewhere. In addition, the flor is unpredictable—present in some batches, but not others. In the past, this meant much was left to chance in terms of what type of sherry would emerge, but winemakers (wine cellars or wine-producing companies called *bodegas*) have learned to manipulate the process a bit.[29]

Time and patience are also key to producing fine sherry. A blending system called a solera is used to mature the wine in oak barrels. The wine in the solera is split into equal units of volume but different stages of maturation. Like a mill's rotating waterwheel, each year's release is taken from the oldest barrels, which are in turn topped up with wine from the next oldest barrels, and so on down the line until the youngest barrels are filled with the current vintage. The idea is to mix very small amounts of the same wine from several different years, which gives the wine complex layers of flavors that are consistent over time. So a bottle of sherry will contain a tiny bit of the first wine introduced to the solera, which could be a hundred or more years old, depending on the producer.[30]

It is estimated that sherry was once made from as many as one hundred different grape varieties—an 1868 Jerez wine region brochure listed forty-two in use at that time. Today, however, sherry is made from just three grapes: palomino, Pedro Ximenez (PX), and muscat of Alexandria. Sherry starts as a white wine that is fermented until it is dry. There are two main categories—the crisp, pale, and dry fino, and the complex, full-bodied oloroso, with seven specific styles falling under each. Depending on the type of sherry being produced, neutral spirits are then added to increase the alcohol level to 15 to 22 percent.[31]

The sherry that Parkinson served was an Amontillado—an aged fino that is fortified to achieve higher alcohol content than a regular fino. It goes through a different cask aging process where it loses its flor protection, resulting in a wine that is deeper in color and has a rich nutty aroma.[32] However, huge variations can exist from bodega to bodega, ranging from very dry to significantly sweeter. Arthur de Capell Brooke refers to this puzzling unpredictability in his 1831 book *Sketches in Spain and Morocco*, calling Amontillado "something like a phenomenon in wine-making, for no cultivator can be certain that the grape will produce it." He describes this type of sherry as "a pale, very delicate, and extremely dry kind of wine . . . very rare, and in high estimation in Spain."[33]

Some food historians have suggested that tapas—the Spanish "grazing" concept of sampling many small plates of different foods—likely had its origins in Jerez, where drinking sherry warranted nibbling to balance the higher alcohol content. In nineteenth-century America, Amontillado sherry was most commonly served with the hors d'oeuvres or soup course, and Jessup Whitehead described Amontillado as "a popular brand of Sherry, served with fish."[34] But Parkinson decided to serve it with the cold dishes, reasoning that the Amontillado's dry yet nutty complex flavors were a perfect balance for the combination of succulent meats and delicate jellies.

ENTRÉE NO. 1

Filet de Bœuf, aux Champignons • *Vol-au-vent à la Financière*
Riz de Veau, Sauce Tomate • *Côtelettes de Mouton*
Croquettes de Volaille

"Entrées are the middle dishes of the feast, and not the principal course, as many suppose; they are a series of dainty side dishes, in the preparation of which the cook demonstrates the extent of her capabilities."
—Thomas Jefferson Murrey, *The Book of Entrées*, 1866

E ntrées have had a rather confused and complicated history. To most Americans, the entrée is the main course—the main dish following the appetizer, soup, and/or salad— which is rather odd, considering the literal translation of the French word is "entrance" or "beginning." For most of recorded culinary history, entrées were designed to be not the meal's main attraction, but rather an expression of the artistry and skill of the chef.

As Louis Eustache Ude explained in *The French Cook* (1822), an entrée is "any dish of meat, fowl, game, or fish, dressed and cooked for the first course," further noting that "the word has no equivalent in English."[1] Almost a century later, Charles Herman Senn gives a slightly clearer interpretation in *The Menu Book* (1908), stating that "the dishes served under this heading are considered by the epicure as the first of the essential dishes of a correct dinner . . . there may be dinners without hors-d'oeuvre, and even without soup, or without a remove or relevé, but there can be no proper dinner without an entrée course."[2]

The word's culinary usage can be traced back to the 1500s, when a meal began with a platter or "course" of entrées. The medley of offerings included juicy fruits such as oranges, apricots, peaches, grapes, melon, and Damascus plums, as well as meat dishes prepared with fruit or pastry—beef palate with gooseberries, wood pigeons with pomegranate, capon breast in pastry shell, and hot venison pies, for example.[3]

Then between the sixteenth and seventeenth centuries entrées and soups switched places, with soups served first and entrées second.[4] However, entrées were still part of the first course (which also included soups, hors d'oeuvres, and relevés) in the classical *à la française* style of dining that evolved from these earlier medieval and Renaissance models. Considered "entries to the meal proper"—entrées were substantial hot "made" meat dishes, usually with a sauce, such as cheek of veal, cutlets, tongue, vol-au-vent, sole, chicken, sweetbreads,[5] and eels. These dishes would have all been served together, then taken away when the second course (roasts and salads) was brought out. Eventually, as the French style of dining was eclipsed by the Russian, the entrée slid into third position—after the opening soup and fish courses, and before the meal's main attraction, the roast.[6]

Although the menu slot for the entrée course had shifted slightly, the type of dishes served had not. Up to ten dishes were commonly offered, showcasing a variety of different meats and sauces. Each dish was made with high-quality ingredients and attractively presented as individual portions. A typical entrée course was likely to include three meats (beef, veal, and mutton), one or two offal (organ meat) dishes, two types of poultry, one type of fish, and one type of game. Certain presentations were fairly standard, such as sweetbreads and vol-au-vent or another type of savory pastry.[7]

Even though the dishes served during the entrée course were rich, meat-focused, and plentiful, the portions were not big. Like Spanish tapas or Turkish meze, each was designed to provide just a taste. As explained by Chef Willi Bode, "probably the most important yardstick and best definition of an entrée is that the meat, game, poultry or offal for this course must always be cut or portioned or prepared prior to cooking." Meats cooked whole or as a large joint and carved after cooking were reserved for the relevé and roast courses.[8]

Another important characteristic of an entrée was that it had to be a complete, distinct presentation, served with its own sauce and/or garnish, which upped the skill required of chefs. The preparation and cooking time for these dishes had to be exactly right, since nothing could be added in case one element was slightly off. And as an added challenge, variety in all details was expected for the entrée course. A dish containing a solid cut of meat or fish was contrasted with one featuring a puree or chopped ingredient; a grilled dish was juxtaposed with one that was poached or fried. It was important that the sauces were complementary and none was used more than once. The use of different colors was also encouraged, such as the palate of sauces listed on one nineteenth-century menu—one each of white, brown, red, and pink.[9]

The shift to the modern classification of entrées occurred in the twentieth century. Previously, entrées appeared after or in conjunction with the fish and roast courses. But in time, these courses began to slowly disappear from American menus, leaving the entrée as the main course, hence the definition of entrée in the United States today. However, in France and many other countries, entrées still retain the literal French meaning as a menu starter—what Americans would call an appetizer. This is due to a change in the type of dishes served under the entrée heading that occurred in France in the 1930s—a switch from a filling meat course to a light course of eggs or seafood. So both countries retained portions of the word's original meaning—the "first course" classification (the French), and the serving of substantial meat dishes (the Americans).[10]

F ew dishes present as pretty a picture as vol-au-vent—a perfect-ly round puff pastry with a savory filling of plump mush-rooms, veal, chicken, sweetbreads, fish, seafood, or game in a fla-vorful sauce and topped with a petite pastry lid. This is a true nine-teenth-century invention, created by Marie-Antoine Carême in the early 1800s. Carême's idea was to fashion a puff pastry case so light that "it flew away in the wind [s'envola au vent] on coming out of the oven." The dish was such a hit that it became standard fare at fancy dinners in both Europe and America, where almost every entrée course included a version of vol-au-vent. Parkinson's Thousand Dollar Dinner was no exception.[11]

Parkinson chose to serve vol-au-vent à la financière, considered by *Larousse Gastronomique* to be one of the most popular and clas-sic presentations. It was the epitome of the nineteenth-century entrée—an attractive, luscious dish that required an experienced hand. In culinary terms, financière is the French name for a rich garnish served with meat or poultry—typically veal or poultry quenelles, olives, truffles, cockscombs, sweetbreads, and mush-rooms. So the literal translation of vol-au-vent à la financière is "a rich flight on the wind."[12]

The success of any vol-au-vent begins with creating a puff pas-try case that is light and delicate, yet sturdy enough to ensure that its savory contents do not leak out. Even Carême admitted that the preparation of puff paste might seem simple, but warned of its extraordinary ability to double in size. His very specific instruc-tions called for gradually mixing flour with butter, salt, and egg yolks with "the ends of the fingers of the *right* hand," adding a lit-tle water when necessary until the paste is rather firm. He then advised working the dough until it becomes soft and glossy, making sure the paste is neither too stiff nor too soft.[13]

The next step involves rolling the paste into its characteristic paper-thin sheets—a process that requires a cool surface and chilled, hard butter. Today our refrigerators and freezers can easily keep butter cold and make all the ice we need, but in the nineteenth century, ice was an expensive commodity. As a result, making quality puff paste during the summer months was often difficult. To chill the butter, Carême suggested keeping it in a pail of cool spring water, then placing it in a cloth to squeeze out the excess water just prior to use.[14]

After the first sheet of paste is rolled out on a marble slab, pieces of the chilled butter are placed on top and then another sheet is rolled out over it to a length of three feet. It is then folded into three parts by doubling one part over the other, rolled out again, turned over and folded once more into three equal parts. Six and a half of these "turnings" are required for vol-au-vents, with periods of rest in between to prevent the pastry from getting too stiff. Since this paste needs to be thicker than for other types of pastry, the paste is folded in half on the last turn instead of in thirds—this was called a "half turn." Carême advised layering the pastry sheets between plates of pounded ice covered with paper to keep them cold between turnings.[15]

To make the vol-au-vent case, a pastry cutter is used to cut two circles out of two layers of puff pastry, each about 1/4 inch (5 mm) thick and 6 inches (15 cm) in diameter. A slightly smaller circle (4 1/2–5 inches or 12–13 cm) is then cut inside one of the circles and the center removed. The outer ring of this piece is attached to the rim of the larger circle to form a case with a base and sides—like a round box. The removed center serves as the lid and is either baked separately or placed on top and scored around the inside of the border to make it easier to remove after it is cooked.[16]

Baking vol-au-vents requires a well-heated and predictable oven—if the temperature is not high enough, the pastry will not rise; and if it is too hot, the surface will set before the heat penetrates through the pastry, making it gummy and tough. Carême advised removing the vol-au-vent case from the oven when it had "acquired a fine reddish colour," then carefully scooping out any soft crumbs. Even the slightest injury to the sides or bottom can allow the filling to ooze through the sides and spoil its appearance. *Cassell's Dictionary of Cookery* (1883) recommended reinforcing any thin spots with a small piece of pastry adhered with egg white. The case is then put back in the oven for a few minutes to dry out the inside and ensure the pastry is thick enough to hold the rich filling.[17]

The financière filling—also referred to as a ragoût in some recipe books—is made by sautéing sweetbreads, mushrooms, chicken or forcemeat, truffles, and cockscombs. This mixture is then gently simmered in a thick and rich brown sauce made from a game or chicken stock and a glassful of sherry or Madeira. Once heated through, the ragoût is added to vol-au-vent at the last minute to avoid saturating the pastry, although it can be briefly heated in the oven to keep warm. It is then garnished with crayfish, cockscombs, and mushrooms, or the cover is simply placed on top.[18]

By the late 1800s, ready-made vol-au-vent cases could be purchased in bakeries and pastry shops for home cooks. This rich indulgence is still served today, although it has been modified over the years to reflect modern trends. For example, individual portions are now popular, and bite-sized versions are often served with cocktails.[19]

ENTRÉE NO. 2

Pigeons' Braise, Sauce Madère
Lamb Chops, Milanaise
Arcade de Volaille • Turtle Steak
Fricassee de Poulets, à la Chevalier • Caliepash

"Entrées are small meats made up in various guises with sauces and
garnishing, as distinguished from the principal joints and roasts."
—Jessup Whitehead, *The Steward's Handbook and*
Guide to Party Catering, 1889

The entrées continued to flow into the seventh course at the
Thousand Dollar Dinner, bringing the total to eleven different dishes. This in itself was not unusual—as previously mentioned; it was typical for fancy dinners to feature up to ten entrées.
What Parkinson did differently was break them into two courses—five in the sixth course and six in the seventh. It is not clear
why he did this; usually the entrées were all served together,
whether the style of dining was French, Russian, or American (a
hybrid of the two adjusted to reflect American tastes and customs).

Perhaps he wanted to spread them out to place more emphasis on each individual dish; maybe it was a pacing tactic given the fact there were so many courses, or perhaps this is simply how he wanted to group the entrée dishes.

Although nineteenth-century cookbooks and menus don't mention the idea of two separate entrée courses, they do discuss the order in which entrée selections should be served, particularly for the Russian style of dining with its multiple courses. The most commonly accepted rule was to serve the entrées in the order of their delicacy, starting with the lighter dishes and ending with the richest. The idea was that they were all building up to the course featuring the main attraction—the roast. Parkinson followed this progressive concept, saving the choicest dishes for this second entrée course, including rich turtle (steak and caliepash) and tender pigeon—highly valued then and rarely served today.

As previously discussed in the chapter on soups, green sea turtle was hugely popular in the nineteenth century. Although turtle soup was the most famous, the sizable beast rendered many other dishes too, such as turtle steaks, cutlets, and fins (typically served in a brown sauce with port wine, button onions, and mushrooms), which Isabella Beeton referred to as "a luxurious side dish."[1] Many of these presentations originated in the Caribbean where sea turtles were plentiful. Turtle steaks and fins were apparently favorite breakfast dishes in the Antilles, and baked turtle, which involved mixing chopped turtle meat with port and other wines, then serving it in its own shell covered with pastry crust (like a meat pie), was the preferred style in the Bahamas.[2]

Like the filet mignon cut of beef, the fatty, gelatinous portion found along the turtle's upper shell (called the caliepash) was the most prized. Also known as the "monsieur," it was often added to green turtle soup to up the richness factor, as well as made into an indulgent dish.[3] Caliepash (also spelled calipash or callapash) had its roots in the West Indies and was often a byproduct of the tedious process of butchering or "dressing the turtle," featured alongside other turtle delicacies including calipee (the undershell or belly—also rich and gelatinous), the fins, and the lights (lungs), heart, and liver.

Hannah Glasse explains in detail how "To Dress a Turtle the West India Way" in her book *The Art of Cookery Made Plain and Easy*. After the undershell was removed, small cuts were made on the surface of the calipee meat in several places and pieces of butter seasoned with sweet herbs, salt, and cayenne pepper were inserted inside each slit. The meat was then dusted with flour and baked in a hot oven. The fins were stewed with veal gravy, Madeira wine, and seasoning. The lights, heart, and liver were stewed in a similar manner, but with more seasoning. Sometimes the lights and heart were stewed with the "callapash," then removed and served together in one dish, but the liver was always dressed by itself. At the end of her lengthy instructions, she says to display these various dishes on the table like so:

Calapee
Lights, heart & liver | Soup | Fins
Callapash[4]

Of these, it was the decadent caliepash that Parkinson chose to serve as part of his second course of entrées. Similar to the Bahamian baked turtle, caliepash involved stewing the rich meat with sherry and other seasonings, then baking the mixture in the turtle's own shell that had been lined with a pastry crust. Here is the version from *Mrs. Hill's New Cook Book: Housekeeping Made Easy* (1872) by Annabella P. Hill, a collection of post–Civil War Southern recipes:

> *Calipash.*—Scrape the meat from the "calipash;" immerse the shell in tepid water; rub and wash it until the shell is entirely clean. Wipe it dry and cover the inside completely with a light puff paste. Take enough of the nicest part of the turtle (saving the coarser pieces for soup) to fill the shape, put in a stew-pan with salt, pepper, mace or any other sweet herb used in cooking which may be preferred. Rub a dessert-spoonful of

flour into a quarter pound of fresh butter, drop into the stew pan and cover with cold water. Put the lid on the stew-pan, set it on the stove or on a trivet before the fire; stew gently, skimming off all the impurities until the meat is tender. Add a wineglass of mushroom "catsup" or any kind preferred, the same of Sherry wine. Stir together and pour into the shell. Put on an upper crust, making it large enough to fit exactly, notch it around tastily, and cut a slit in the center. Should there not be gravy enough, pour in sufficient boiling water to answer. Bake a light brown. Send to the table on a square dish to fit, as nearly as can be, the shell. When well arranged, this is a beautiful as well as savory dish.[5]

The other turtle dish Parkinson served in this second course of entrées was turtle steak. Considered by many to taste even better than beefsteak, turtle steak was often compared to veal and referred to as "Barbados beef" in the West Indies. In the nineteenth century it was as common there as beefsteak was in Britain. Raving about the virtues of turtle soup and steak, humorist Artemus Ward wrote: "As for me, give me turtle or give me death. What is life without turtle? Nothing! What is turtle without life? Nothinger still!"[6]

The steaks were taken from the thick part of the turtle's fins. One recipe from *The National Cookery Book* (1876) gives a very simple preparation with minimal seasonings, allowing the flavor of the turtle to shine. The steaks were sprinkled with salt, pepper, and mace, then floured and fried in a mix of butter and lard, and simmered in a little water for about fifteen minutes. Just before serving, a lemon was squeezed over the steaks.[7]

But it is more likely the turtle steak Parkinson served resembled the slightly more complex recipe Thomas Jefferson Murrey presents in *The Book of Entrées* (1886). He gives it a fancy name, "Green Turtle Steak, Epicurean," and says, "raw turtle steaks may be had from any first-class restaurant, and occasionally at fish-stands," warning, "It is not advantageous for small families to purchase whole turtles, or rather tortoises, for soup and steaks." To prepare his version, he instructs trimming away the turtle's thigh bone and flattening the meat into the thickness of a steak. He then says to melt two ounces of butter in a chafing dish, and when the dish is very hot, to add a teaspoonful of Worcestershire sauce, a tablespoonful of currant jelly, a gill of port wine, and a little salt. The steak was stewed in this sauce until tender, and served directly from the chafing dish.[8]

Americans enjoyed these and other turtle delicacies throughout the nineteenth century and into the twentieth. But their appetite for the rich-tasting meat caused demand to soon outpace the supply. These lavish dishes that were previously an integral part of fancy dinner parties and upscale restaurant dining are no longer legally available in the United States. The green sea turtles once nested in large numbers in Florida, but became severely threatened by overfishing and encroachment of their nesting habitat. In 1978 the United States passed a ban on the taking of green sea turtles from U.S. waters, as well as a ban on the import, export, or transshipment of turtles or products made from them. As a result, commercial aquaculture, which has helped some aquatic species such as oysters remain viable gastronomic choices, has never been developed with sea turtles in the U.S. and is not likely to occur in the future.[9]

L ike turtle, pigeon was another classic Philadelphia dish. Passenger pigeons were often the variety served on fine dining tables, as they were extremely plentiful. But as the enormous flocks migrated over vast portions of the U.S. every year, hunters relentlessly pursued them, causing the population to collapse by 1880. After the demise of this wild breed, chefs turned to domestic squab farms to provide plump and tasty birds for their recipes.[10]

Pigeon was served a number of different ways, including roasted, braised, or fricasseed or baked in jelly, pie, or dumplings.

Stewing was also a popular method, particularly served with peas, a presentation that came out of the culinary renaissance of seventeenth-century France. The recipe included by celebrated French chef La Varenne in his revolutionary cookbook *Le Cuisiner Francois*—potage de pigeons aux pois verts—calls for poaching the pigeons in stock and then garnishing them with lettuce, peas, and pieces of bacon.[11]

American cooks came up with their own versions for stewing pigeons. One common method was to place the birds between layers of cabbage, season them with salt and pepper, cover with a bit of broth, and stew until tender. Variations included adding a little butter, cream, and flour to thicken and enrich the liquid, as well as swapping pickled mushrooms and oysters for cabbage. Other recipes call for stewing the pigeons (which could be stuffed or not) in brown gravy with spices and mushrooms, or a little mushroom ketchup. But perhaps the most interesting is "Squabs in Olives." This cosmopolitan-sounding recipe calls for stewing the squabs in a mix of butter, onion, flour, mace, cloves, salt, and pepper and then adding the olives and stewing slowly for another hour.[12]

But braising was the method Parkinson chose to feature at the Thousand Dollar Dinner, borrowing his recipe from the French— Pigeons' Braise, Sauce Madère (pigeon braised in Madeira sauce). Braising uses moist heat to slowly simmer meat and/or vegetables in minimal amounts of liquid at a low temperature. This results in very little evaporation, allowing the food to retain its natural juices and flavor. In the days of open-hearth cooking, braising was done with a special pan called a braisière that featured a sunken lid to hold hot charcoal, effectively heating the food from above and below. The invention of the stove allowed braising to move from the fireplace to the stovetop or oven. Braising pans were also updated, trading the recessed lid, which was no longer necessary, for a deep, tight-fitting one.[13]

To make Pigeons' Braise, Sauce Madere, the pigeons are barded with bacon or salt pork,[14] placed in the braising pan and lightly browned in the oven before covering with a thin Madeira sauce—

a rich combination of Madeira wine, stock, gravy, butter, shallots, mushrooms, and concentrated Espagnole sauce (brown stock that is slowly simmered with brown roux, mirepoix, and tomato puree). The lid is then tightly placed on top of the pan to keep the moisture inside and the birds are slowly braised in the oven until tender.[15]

Like most other game, pigeon largely disappeared from American menus in the early part of the twentieth century, although they are still sometimes served at fancy restaurants and can be purchased through specialty markets. However, in France and other parts of Europe they continue to have a more significant culinary role, with squab among the most expensive meats available in French restaurants and through poultry farmers. These delicate, tender young birds are typically roasted, grilled, sautéed, or served en papillotes.[16] Because of their active existence and more diverse diet, wild pigeons are more flavorful, yet leaner and drier than those that are farm raised, requiring slow simmering to bring out their juiciness rather than roasting.[17]

WINES

Moet—Extra Sparkling Champagne
Vintage of 1846—Snider's special importation

By the time of the Thousand Dollar Dinner, Champagne had made its mark as a symbol of luxury, wealth, and decadence. Its refreshing bubbles were viewed as festive and complementary to all types of foods. As a result, this unique effervescent wine was a fixture at opulent dinner parties, paired with specific courses as well as offered throughout an entire meal.

Nineteenth-century cookbooks and menus suggest a number of different wine pairings with the entrée course, including Bordeaux, Oeil de Perdrix (a rosé wine) and Amantillado sherry, but Champagne is also often recommended. As previously mentioned, although the Champagne in 1851 would have been sweeter than today, it still would have been a pleasant accompaniment to the rich entrées, with their choice cuts of meat, buttery pastry, and creamy sauces. Not only would it have complemented the celebratory feel of these sumptuous dishes, but the acidity and bubbles would have also helped cut through the richness, allowing the diners to enjoy and experience the different flavors in each dish.[18]

The Champagne chosen by Parkinson for his entrée course was a "Snider's special importation." He is referring to Philadelphia wine merchant Jacob Snider, Jr. (1811–1866), an importer well known for his connections to the principal winemaking houses of Europe. An advertisement for Snider's shop, which was located at 76 Walnut Street, boasts of "wines and liquors of all countries, of direct importation from the growers and producers, to be had cheaper than at any other store. The only establishment where all wines are sold directly from the original package in which imported." The list includes sherries, Madeiras, ports, sparkling Champagne, sparkling Moselle, brandies of all sorts, Irish and Scotch whiskey, bourbon, Scotch ale, London porter, and stout, just to name a few.[19]

But apparently the wine business did not keep Snider busy enough. His fascination with mechanics and engineering led him to become an inventor too. For example, he designed, printed, and implemented the first book in the United States with raised letters for use by the blind—the Gospel of Mark from the New Testament. As the recording secretary of the Pennsylvania Institution for the Instruction of the Blind, he presented this copy to the Library Company in 1838, noting he had printed forty copies "in leisure moments from business in the Year 1833." To create the book, he put long-fibered paper through a small hydraulic press to print the pages and pasted two leaves together. The book utilized real letters, not braille, which had been invented in 1829, and while these raised-letter texts never caught on, the principle helped advance the technology.[20]

But Snider is probably best known for his work with artillery, most notably the invention of the "Snider rifle," a breech-loader that he marketed in England in 1859 after he apparently overextended his wine business and had to cut his losses. The British government accepted the rifle but Snider apparently never received compensation for his design, and ended up dying in poverty.[21]

ROAST

Spring Chicken on Toast, Capons, bardet • Spring Lamb, Mint Sauce

"Roasting should be done before a steady hot fire. Roasted meats
are greatly superior to those that are baked; the flavor is finer, and
they are more tender and juicy."

—*National Cookery Book*, 1876

We have now reached the pinnacle of the meal—the all-
important roast. Every one of the preceding courses in
Parkinson's dinner was leading up to this point. The roast is the
main attraction, the most anticipated of all the dishes. This has
been the case throughout the history of fine dining and continues
today—think of the iconic British Sunday roast or the roast turkey
that is the highlight of Thanksgiving dinner in the United States.

Typically the most expensive, extravagant item on the menu,
the roast was the ultimate way for a host to impress his or her
guests. Comparing a multicourse dinner to a house with many
rooms, nineteenth-century French food critic Grimod de la
Reynière likened the roast to a house's *salon* or principal apart-

ment. "The *salon* in a French house is the room on which a hospitable host spends all his spare money. It is furnished and decorated with the greatest care, because in this room the master receives his friends. Just a like process is pursued in respect to the roast that smokes upon his table. It is the dish that has cost him the most money, and on which he hopes to content and feast his guests."[1]

Unlike the entrée dishes, which could be prepared any number of different ways, the name of this course dictated the cooking method. Diners knew they would be getting succulent, mouthwatering cuts of meat, which, if they were lucky, had been roasted over an open fire for maximum flavor.

Roasting meat on a spit over or near an open fire is one of the oldest and most beloved cooking methods, imparting a rich, smoky flavor and a deliciously contrasting texture that is crispy on the outside, yet juicy inside. It is referred to as a dry-heat method of cooking, sealing in the food's flavorful juices, as opposed to a moist-heat method such as braising, which infuses moisture with liquids such as wine or stock. The best way to distinguish between the two is that a dry-heat technique such as roasting will give the meat a lovely brown color. But achieving this delectable caramelized exterior requires very high heat, which can prove challenging to the cook. The higher the heat and the longer the roasting time, the more significant the drying effects. Rotating the meat on a spit is the most effective way to retain the delicious juices.[2]

So even though the oven was a popular nineteenth-century invention, the roasting jack remained a fixture throughout the Victorian period, as many people considered meat cooked over an open fire to be far tastier.[3] The roasting jack was a rotating spit that sat in front of the fireplace. The meat was suspended from a bracket fixed to the top of the mantelpiece or a meat screen (a useful tool which served to reflect heat back toward the meat). A dish was positioned underneath to catch the succulent juices, which could be used for future cooking or to make gravy. Bottle jacks were roasting jacks with a wind-up mechanism that turned the meat automatically to cook it evenly.[4]

Escoffier argued that the oven did not provide a true dry-heat roasting experience since the steam that accumulated around the meat adversely affected its taste and texture. But "the spitted roast, on the contrary, cooks in the open in a dry atmosphere, and by this means retains its own superior flavor," he explained. He had a point—when we use an oven to "roast" foods, we are essentially "baking" them. Although the heat of the oven does surround the food with hot, dry air—it is an indirect method, not the direct contact with an open flame provided by roasting over a fire.[5]

Nevertheless, by the end of the nineteenth century the oven was fully entrenched in American kitchens, and cookbooks made sure to provide instructions for oven roasting. The main message was never to let the meat come in contact with any liquid, which would turn the roast into a stew. It was essential to place the meat on a wire rack in the roasting pan so that it was not sitting in its own fat and juices as it cooked. Any basting was done with a fatty substance such as butter or the meat's own drippings, but never any other liquid.

Some cooks circumvented the issue by using a tin kitchen, Rumford Roaster, or Reed's Roaster. The tin kitchen (also called a reflector oven) was a large, spherical tin box that was placed in front of the fireplace (or the cook stove once they came on the scene). It contained a roasting spit and a convenient door on one side for basting and tending the roast. The other side was open— the oven's metal surface reflected the heat of the fire back on the roast. This ingenious device made the process of roasting meat in front of a fireplace safer, easier, and less messy. Nineteenth-century cookbook author Maria Parloa recommended using a tin kitchen for roasting whenever possible, "as meat cooked before a bright fire has a flavor much nicer than when baked in an oven."[6]

The Rumford Roaster was another invention of innovative scientist Sir Benjamin Thompson (Count Rumford). Obsessed with the amount of heat and fuel that was wasted during the cooking process, Thompson devised an alternative roasting method—a custom-built closed range, which consumed much less fuel. His design incorporated several small fires instead of one large one, which allowed several different types of food to cook over one fire, which was more efficient and produced less smoke. Each cooking pot or pan had its own separate closed brick fireplace, complete with a private door and chamber to channel smoke up the chimney. When he invited some friends to sample a leg of mutton cooked in a Rumford Roaster versus one roasted on a spit, they all thought the one cooked in his roaster was tastier, and apparently enjoyed the "exquisitely sweet" meat with currant jelly. The Rumford Roaster was launched in Great Britain, and eventually imported into the United States, with many introduced in the best houses in Boston and nearby towns, although it never gained a wide audience.[7]

Yet another roasting device that came on the scene a bit later in the century was a Reed's Roaster, a closed box with a door at the end, allowing cooks to look at the meat without removing it from the oven. Even though Philadelphia Cooking School instructor Sarah Tyson Rorer called it "the best and most convenient pan that has come under my notice," she admitted that many families did not have the space for these contraptions and ended up using their ovens for roasting. Her method required "getting the oven very hot at first, in order to form a crust upon the outer side, then slightly cooled, to prevent the crust from burning, and finished at a moderate heat." She maintained that as long as the roast was properly basted, meat cooked using this technique would be nicely crisped on the outside, yet still juicy on the inside.[8]

The importance of the roast course lies in the fact that it showcased the most tender, flavorful meat—typically choice game, succulent butcher's cuts, and delicate poultry dishes, which were often barded, larded, or stuffed to ensure a juicy interior.[9] According to Grimod, in French cuisine, the roast was divided into great roast and little roast—*gros rot* and *petit rot*. Examples of the larger roast included venison, quarters of wild boar, beef, mutton, veal, lamb, and pork; the smaller roast were fowl, grouse, and small birds.[10] In America, game roasts were preferred and considered far superior, but poultry such as turkey, capon, pullet, duck, guinea fowl, and squabs were an acceptable substitute, as was roasted butcher's meat.[11]

S pring meats were from young animals, typically lamb and veal, as well as poultry. Since the Thousand Dollar Dinner took place in April, Parkinson would have had no difficulty obtaining the spring chickens and lamb for his menu. According to Boston Cooking School instructor Fannie Farmer, spring chickens began to appear in the market during January weighing about one and one-half pounds, and although poultry was available throughout the year, it was at its best from March until June.[12]

Although very tender, spring meats were sometimes less flavorful than those that had time to mature. Barding and larding were two methods used to enhance their flavor and prevent them from drying out during the roasting process. In his book *The Modern Housewife* (1851), nineteenth-century French chef Alexis Soyer observed that spring chickens were usually plain roasted like larger chickens, although he does mention the larding technique as a possibility. A roasting time of just twenty minutes was sufficient due to the chicken's diminutive size. To improve their appearance when roasted, he suggested "tying the legs upon paper to the spit, as directed for the turkey."[13]

But many cooks considered spring chickens too delicate to roast, preferring other cooking methods. For example, Sarah Tyson Rorer felt that full-grown poultry were the best for roasting, and insisted spring chickens should be broiled, fried, or smothered (with gravy). She also recommended that after being drawn (butchered), spring chickens should be placed in a cool, dry spot for at least twenty-four hours before cooking; if cooked as soon as they were killed, they could be hard and tough.[14]

Spring Chicken on Toast, the dish featured on Parkinson's menu, usually required broiling or boiling the chicken (not roasting) according to the recipes of the time. It seems like a simple preparation, perhaps not even fancy enough for dinner-party fare, but according to the *White House Cook Book* (1889), this recipe "was considered most excellent." To prepare using the broiling method, the chickens were split and flattened, then seasoned with salt and pepper and placed on a gridiron over a slow fire with a tin pan or plate on top to keep them flat. They were broiled for about ten minutes on each side and then removed to a tin pan and brushed with butter. They were put back in the oven for a few minutes, then taken out and set on slices of moistened buttered toast that had been laid out on a platter. A half cupful of cream was added to the drippings in the pan along with a little flour to make rich gravy, which was then poured over the chicken.[15]

Today we often think of toast as a breakfast food, or perhaps something to nibble on when we are sick, but serving foods over toast was very fashionable in late nineteenth-century America. Spring chicken was undoubtedly one of the most popular toppings, but mixtures featuring game birds such as partridge, snipes, woodcocks, and plovers were also served, as well as broiled sweetbreads, hashed meat, stewed oysters, and Welsh rabbit.[16]

This usage can be traced back to medieval times when toast was an important functional and edible tool. Referred to as sops or sippets, toast was used like a dipper to soak up soups and stews, as well as a receptacle for toppings. In sixteenth-century Britain, veal toasts (made with chopped veal kidney, egg yolks, sugar, rosewater, cinnamon, and ginger) were popular, as well as toasts topped with minced meat hashes. By the end of that century all kinds of foods were served on toast, such as egg, ham, bacon, anchovies, and melted cheese. In the Victorian period, "savoury toast" with toppings such as cheese, caviar, and potted birds[17] was a stylish way to end an English dinner.[18]

A delicacy that dates back to Roman times, capons are roosters that have been gelded and fattened, making them plump and tender, rendering more meat than any other fowl. They generally weigh between six and ten pounds and are considered the best age for eating when nine to ten months old. Philadelphia must have produced an ample amount of capons in the 1800s, since Fannie Farmer noted that the city furnished Boston with both chickens and capons until late in the century. She referred to them as "very large, plump, and superior eating."[19]

Capons were often stuffed with truffles, chestnuts, forcemeat, or oysters, roasted until a nice golden color, and then placed on a platter with an attractive border of watercress. But Parkinson served his barded, and a pan placed underneath would have caught any drippings, which could have been used to baste the capon and/or to make into a rich gravy to accompany the bird.

Lamb was the other spring meat Parkinson served for his roast course. Spring lamb (also called house lamb) was very expensive due to the extensive care it required.[20] Born during the winter months, these lambs were carefully housed, fed, and kept warm to ensure they were thriving and would yield flesh that was delicate and tender. To fatten them up, they were given special feed, such as white peas and bran, and a chalk-stone to lick. Their mothers were sent out to graze on fine grass, and then brought to nurse the lambs four times a day, who were encouraged to drink all the milk they wanted. They entered the market as early as March when two to three months old, typically weighing just five or six pounds.[21]

A welcome addition to the table during a season when game was scarce, lamb was "the choicest of spring meats" according to Thomas Jefferson Murrey—a dish with no rival for private dinner parties.[22] A spring lamb could be roasted whole or divided into halves or quarters, generally the fore quarter (shoulder, neck, and breast), hind quarter (loin and leg), or saddle (both hind quarters together). Each portion had its devotees. According to Eliza Leslie, the saddle of a delicate, plump lamb cooked whole was very fashionable for company dinners. However, both Sarah Tyson Rorer and French cooking school instructor Pierre Blot said the fore quarter (which was generally more costly) was considered the best part of the lamb.[23]

Parkinson does not specify which cut he presented his guests, but if he roasted a whole lamb it would have likely been on a spit in front of the fire, basted first with butter and then its drippings. If he roasted the quarters, he probably would have cooked them in the oven on a rack inside a tin pan. Like other young meats, lamb was preferred well done, with no noticeable redness when served. Mint sauce was considered the perfect accompaniment for spring lamb. As Eliza Leslie noted, "this is only used for roast lamb in the spring. When the lambs are grown into sheep, the mint is too old for sauce. But they harmonize very pleasantly when both are young." Making the sauce required stripping the leaves from a large bunch of fresh, well-washed mint and mincing them into small pieces. The mint was then mixed with just enough cider vinegar to create a thick sauce and sweetened with brown sugar.[24]

WINES

Extra Sparkling Moselle, Scharzberg
Vintage of 1846—Special importation from the cellars of
Dienhard & Jordan, Coblenz

The Moselle (or Mosel) wine region of Germany takes its name from the Moselle River, often called the "Bride of the Rhine" by German poets. Flowing into the Rhine at Coblenz, the Moselle meanders through some of the world's steepest and most beautiful vineyards. The vines are planted on tiny terraces that jut out of the sheer vertical slopes in order to bask in as much sunlight as possible during the brief, cool growing season. Because of the precipitous location of the vineyards, the grapes are cared for and harvested by agile, fearless workers who scurry up the steep cliffs, sometimes using ladders to get to the distant vines.[25]

Today considered one of the finest Riesling regions, the area has a reputation for light, crisp, "flowery" wines, particularly the southern portion. However, early in the nineteenth century, only the finest vineyards of the Moselle region produced Rieslings, since the Kleinberg (also known as Elbling) grape was the most commonly planted at the time. An ancient grape varietal lacking flavor and acidity, Kleinberg wines were considered bland, sweet, and not nearly in the same league as the region's Rieslings, which were "appreciated for their peculiar perfume," and deemed a delicious summer beverage.[26]

Even though Riesling thrives in Germany's cooler climate, the Moselle region was sometimes a bit too cool, making the grapes more difficult to grow. But a period of mild weather starting in 1819 graced the Moselle region with six excellent vintage years, creating a surge in the popularity of its wines. Between 1817 and 1840 the wine-growing population grew by 38 percent, also a result of the Zollverein (German customs union) allowing trade between the German states in 1834. Plantings of Rieslings increased, as did the quality of the wine. British tourists were drawn to the area for a chance to taste its delicate wines within their natural setting and catch a glimpse of the breathtaking scenery. Although the wine took a hit in the 1830s and 1840s when the weather conditions turned less favorable, the vineyards rebounded in the 1850s, producing three outstanding successive vintages.[27]

The Moselle wine served by Parkinson was a sparkling variety from the Scharzberg *grosslage* (a German geographical classification designating a collection of individual vineyard sites), located within the Saar district, considered the premier Moselle wine-producing area. When the French began perfecting the art of making Champagne in the nineteenth century, Germany sat up and took notice, quickly becoming the second biggest sparkling wine producing country. The success of Germany's bubbly (also called *sekt*), makes sense since its vineyards are located so far north. Just as in France, this makes the grapes more acidic but with a relatively lower sugar content, resulting in a crisp, refreshing, effervescent wine. Even in bad vintage years, Moselle Riesling was an excellent resource for this rapidly growing sparkling wine industry modeled on Champagne.[28]

Although the sparkling Moselle served by Parkinson was likely sweeter than today's versions, it would still have had enough acidity to cut through the richness of the roast meats, cleansing the palate and preparing his guests for the next course.

PIÈCES MONTÉES

Swiss Basket • Panier en Nougat • Cottage Basket
Vase Monté, with Fruit Glacé
Flora's Offering • Moorish Fountain • Indian Temple

VEGETABLES

White Potatoes • Corn • Tomatoes • Green Peas • Cauliflower
Asparagus
Sweet Potatoes • Hominy • Celery • Spinach • Dressed Lettuce

"Architecture is the first amongst the arts, and confectionery is the highest form of architecture."

—Marie-Antonin Carême

"No other country surpasses America in turnips, carrots, beets, cabbages, spinach, peas, beans, pumpkins, parsnips, lettuce, celery, radishes, onions, asparagus, melons, leek, cress, cucumbers, and tomatoes."

—James W. Parkinson, *American Dishes at the Centennial*, 1874

To our modern palates, elaborate sugar sculptures served alongside garden vegetables may seem like a very odd combination—perhaps the most unusual of the seventeen courses in the Thousand Dollar Dinner. But this was Parkinson's version of *entremets*, which means "between dishes" in French. In years past, all the dishes served after the roast, including vegetables and sweets, were called entremets, but now the term (if used at all) usually refers to just sweet dishes. The concept can be traced back to medieval times when the idea emerged to provide a form of entertainment between courses (*mets*) and also give the servants time to clear the table.[1]

Even though entremets were elaborate, outrageous, and sometimes even shocking, they were considered edible dishes. Called subtleties or sotelties in English, these extravagant creations were built to huge proportions, taking the shape of majestic castles and colorful gardens, as well as animals and other creatures, such as cooked peacocks served with their iridescent feathers and tethered live birds baked into pies.[2]

These captivating entertainments eventually evolved into impressive works of art known as *pièces montées*, which literally translated means "mounted parts." Admittedly this does not sound very appetizing, but the focus had shifted from taste and amusement to pure presentation. Although made from edible ingredients such as sugar, cake, and almond paste, these artistic pieces of confectionery were ornamental and not typically meant to be eaten.[3]

Although pièces montées didn't incorporate live entertainment, they were over the top in their own way—enormous, breathtakingly elaborate table centerpieces made out of patisserie. They reached the height of their popularity in the eighteenth and nineteenth centuries, with many designed to depict recognizable objects such as historic buildings or events, as well as tranquil scenes from nature.[4] As Charles Ranhofer noted in *The Epicurean* (1894), "The principal object is to flatter the eye of the guests by their regularity, their smoothness and their finish."

Culinary innovator Marie-Antonin Carême played a major role in the standardization of these elegant creations, the same French chef who helped popularize elaborate cold dishes set in jelly. His knowledge and appreciation of structural design was developed at an early age. When just sixteen, he began serving as an apprentice under one of the best pastry cooks in Paris, Bailly of the Rue Vivienne. Recognizing the young man's talents and enthusiasm, Bailly encouraged Carême to hone his craft in the print room of the Bibliothèque Nationale in Paris, where he spent hours studying architectural history books. He would then base his designs on these masterworks, which included elaborate structures such as temples, pyramids, and ancient ruins.[5]

In Carême's book, *The Royal Parisian Pastrycook and Confectioner* (1834), the section on pièces montées reads more like construction blueprints than a cookbook, going into great detail explaining how to build items such as: A Small Rustic House, A Grand Cascade of Sixteen Columns, A Turkish Cottage, A Grecian Fountain, A Venetian Pavilion on a Bridge, and Ruins of Athens. He stipulates that "the columns which best suit pièces montées are the Doric, the Ionic, and the Corinthian," giving precise measurements for the distances between them. He also specifies the ingredients that should be used for each type of building material— confectioner's paste for the *montans* (straight upright pieces), puff paste for small ornaments such as rings and half-moons, and a "softish" mixture of light and dark green almond and confectioner's paste for the moss used to decorate ruins and rocks.[6]

But the main component in pièces montées is sugar in one form or another. Items are fashioned out of sugar that is shaped, blown, drawn, spun, twisted, or woven, as well as layers of sponge cake, nougat, petits fours, candied fruit, dragées (colorful, bite-sized confectionery), and chocolate shavings. Classic *pièces montées à la française* are "built" on a metal framework with a central rotating piece that allows trays to be stacked in tiers one on top of another. The other construction option, *pièces montées à l'espagnole*, uses separate trays of confectionery arranged in layers, each supported by pillars.[7]

Sugar sculptures, also known as ornamental sugar work, were similar to pièces montées except that they were made solely of sugar. European confectioners brought this talent of turning sugar into works of art to America. They advertised their expertise through advertisements in newspapers and by featuring their completed works in shop windows, drawing customers to this unique craft.

Soon these designs were in high demand among America's upper class, with sugar sculptures gracing tables of the most exclusive dinners and social events. George Washington even employed his own private French confectioner to create sugar work for an inaugural celebration in 1789. Like pièces montées, sculptures could be modeled after known architectural designs—in fact, many often borrowed ideas directly from the works commissioned by European royalty. They could also be shaped into more fanciful objects such as flowers and celebratory items including wedding cake ornaments, Easter eggs, and Christmas decorations.[8]

In addition to his many architectural designs, Carême's instructions also include a wide array of other sculptures, including a harp, lyre, and globe; military objects such as a French helmet, a Grecian helmet, a French military cap and a naval trophy, and decorative objects such as a basket of spun sugar filled with meringues, a basket with apples d'api of almond paste, a vase with palm branches, a balloon of spun sugar, and a small tree of nougat with baskets. He also gives detailed directions for garden-like scenes such as an arbor of lattice work covered with vines, a grotto ornamented with moss, a Parisian hermitage, and a rustic rotunda. The intricacy of the items he describes is remarkable.[9]

Pièces montées were often designed to mirror the theme of the banquet, meal, or party where they were displayed. The items Parkinson chose to display were spring themed, a perfect tie-in for the April dinner—a vase and baskets filled with fruit, as well as a fountain, temple, and sculpture depicting Flora, the Roman goddess of flowers and spring. Parkinson was celebrating the season, its bounty, and everything that is new and fresh.

However, what was unusual was his placement of pièces montées among the seventeen courses—quite a few places before the desserts. By the nineteenth century the role of pièces montées had shifted a bit. As Charles Ranhofer specifies in *The Epicurean*, "table ornaments called pyramids are used for replacing the cold pieces in the third service for French dinners . . . and are placed on the table at the beginning and at the dessert for a Russian dinner." But Parkinson doesn't adhere to either protocol, instead serving them right after the roast and during the same course as the vegetables. Although it was common in the French style of dining to feature a mix of sweet and savory dishes during the entremets course that followed the roast, hot sweets, such as puddings, soufflés, croûtes of fruit, fritters (beignets), and savarins, were typically served with vegetables, not pièces montées. [10]

Other Parkinson menus from the same time feature pièces montées right before the desserts, as a lead-in to the sweet dishes, after the vegetables and other savory dishes. But this is not the case with the Thousand Dollar Dinner. The pièces montées and vegetables are followed by two more substantial savory courses before the pastry and other sweet courses. Perhaps once again the chef was simply trying to break up this very rich and lengthy dinner by providing an attractive, diverting interlude.

Another unknown is whether Parkinson constructed all the pièces montées himself, or if he had assistance from his skilled staff, freeing him up to manage the other aspects of the dinner. He would have had numerous chefs trained in various culinary specialties in order to pull off a dinner of this magnitude, but given his background, it's highly probable he had at least a hand in the design of the pièces montées.

Experience, precision, and attention to detail were required to make structures of this type. As Ranhofer stated, "Few workmen are capable of making these different styles of pieces, their talent being limited, for their use is confined to a very small number of

houses. Special care must be taken that they be faultlessly execut-
ed." Recommending that those skilled at making pièces montées
should concentrate solely on this ability, he surmised, "this art is
certain to become fashionable in the near future."[11]

Ranhofer's late nineteenth-century prediction unfortunately did
not ring true, and the popularity of pièces montées began to fade
in the twentieth century. They are still showcased at big banquets
and special events such as weddings and bridal and baby showers,
but for the most part have been replaced with floral arrangements
and other types of centerpieces.

A t the time of the Thousand Dollar Dinner, it had become very
fashionable for elaborate banqueting menus to feature special
preparations of rare, early season, or out-of-season vegetables as a
light course toward the end of dinner, which became known as
entremets de légumes.[12] Today's high-speed transportation methods
allow us to enjoy fresh produce year round. But for James
Parkinson, procuring these specialties would have hinged on how
quickly items could have been shipped to Philadelphia from
warmer locales without spoiling. Considering the Thousand
Dollar Dinner took place in April, it is quite a feat to offer eleven
different vegetables for this course, including out-of-season varieties such as corn and tomatoes.

A few of the items were probably purchased locally, such as celery (a late winter vegetable), spinach (in season all year long), and
hominy (dried corn that was sold in the Philadelphia markets in
great quantities). It is also possible Parkinson got his hands on
some hothouse vegetables. Many of Philadelphia's elite had expansive country homes in and around the city that functioned as rural
retreats. These large properties boasted lovely mansion homes surrounded by meticulously landscaped grounds, formal gardens, and
outbuildings including greenhouses and orangeries where rare,
tropical, and out-of-season plants bloomed year round.[13]

One of the most famous of these estates was Lemon Hill, the country residence of Henry Pratt, Esq., which was located on the Schuylkill River, not far from the Fairmount water works. The site included over two hundred square feet of greenhouse and hothouse growing space, said to be "unrivaled in the Union." In additional to rare and fragrant flowers and tropical plants, numerous fruit trees such as orange, lemon, banana, guava, cherimoya, and plantain flourished there in the warm, humid environment. There was also a "forcing ground" where vegetables such as asparagus, potatoes, cucumbers, and lettuce were planted for early harvesting.[14]

Merchant and banker Stephen Girard was another wealthy Philadelphian who was known to dabble in hothouse gardens. An 1829 Pennsylvania Horticultural Society report states that he is thought to be the first person to introduce artichokes among his circle of friends, having grown them in a small greenhouse on his country estate, which was also stocked with lemons, mandarin oranges, and many other kinds of fruit.[15]

But most of the vegetables on the Thousand Dollar Dinner menu were probably shipped from more temperate locations. Luckily for Parkinson, rapid expansions within the food and transportation industries were taking place during the nineteenth century. By the 1830s, better roads, canals, steamships, and trains were making it possible for food to travel longer distances more swiftly. Ice harvesting was also fully exploited, which allowed foods to stay cool, cold, or even frozen in transport. Although it was still the early days in the transformation to the vast network of interconnected shipping we now take for granted, Parkinson's influence surely helped him get what he needed to impress.

According to one guest's recounting of the sumptuous meal, Parkinson used both telegraph and express to obtain many of the vegetables. For example, the lettuce, green peas, and cauliflower were ordered from Georgia.[16] This "express delivery" was probably accomplished via a combination of rail, horse (wagon and/or stagecoach), and maybe even steamboat. All of these new transportation systems were beginning to interlock and even compete with each other at this time, but service and connections were still intermittent in the more remote regions.[17]

The earliest type of express service in the U.S. was the informal shuttling of letters, packages, and other goods by stagecoach drivers, who would stow particularly valuable items under their hat for safekeeping. Another method was simply handing off packages and money to friends, acquaintances, and even complete strangers traveling in the direction the items needed to go, having faith they would be delivered properly. It wasn't until the 1830s that a more formal, organized express delivery system was created, spurred on by the need for an inter-bank messenger service after the federal government dissolved the Second Bank of the United States in 1836 (the Federal Reserve of that era). These early companies were mainly concentrated in the Northeast, servicing major cities such as New York, Boston, Albany, Providence, and Philadelphia. Some are still in business today, such as American Express and Wells Fargo. They took advantage of the new rail links and steamship routes and expanded their services in tandem with these new transport methods. For destinations outside of these locations they fulfilled deliveries using stagecoach, horse-drawn wagons, and private couriers.[18]

At the time of the Thousand Dollar Dinner, express service offices were just beginning to open in southern states such as Georgia and South Carolina, springing up alongside the expanding rail lines in these regions. In 1840 the Georgia railroad was completed from Augusta to Greensboro, with many other links in various states of survey and progress. There was also a New York to Charleston steamship express service.[19]

But before the railroad boom, the Great Wagon Road was the principal highway for foot, horse, wagon, and eventually stagecoach traffic between Philadelphia and the southern states. Heading west from Philadelphia, this thoroughfare passed through Lancaster, York, and Gettysburg, Pennsylvania, before turning south and winding through Maryland, Virginia, North Carolina, and South Carolina, finishing up in Augusta, Georgia. By the end of the colonial era, it was the most heavily traveled road in America.[20]

This route was still in use in 1851, but with less and less traffic, as trains were operating pretty regularly in the northern states by then. However, the South's railways were less robust and focused more on moving cotton short distances to river and ocean ports.[21] It wasn't until 1860 that a continuous railway route linked the North and South. So the vegetables Parkinson ordered could have made their way north via a combination of stagecoach and train travel.

Stagecoach-steamboat combination routes were also common, so this was another possibility. For example, by 1819, one such itinerary left Baltimore in the morning and reached Philadelphia the same evening, and two other "red-eye" routes left in the evening and arrived in Philadelphia in the morning. Others traveled between Baltimore and Norfolk, Virginia.[22]

But, by the second half of the nineteenth century, the railroad would eventually win as the fastest, most direct shipping service. Railroads started out as short-distance, local carriers. Food was cargo from the very beginning, but before 1850 few railroads had more than one hundred miles of continuous track. Farming was much more localized, with farmers selling their crops within a limited radius of their farms. It wasn't economical or even really feasible to ship fruits and vegetables far away. In the early days of railroading, it was helpful for regional farmers to utilize this new transport method, but only for in-season foods, such as spring strawberries shipped from New Jersey to New York City via the Paterson & Ramapo line. It wasn't until mid-century that food was transported over greater distances. For example, in 1855 produce was sent from Rochester, New York, to New York City, and fresh peaches and apples were shipped to Chicago from southern Illinois in special cars attached to passenger trains for speedier delivery.[23]

The greatest difficulty was keeping vegetables cool and fresh. Ice was used during the mid-nineteenth century to ship perishables by boat and rail, but this was more common in the northern states where it was less prone to melting. Frederic Tudor of Boston devised insulated storage methods and containers after starting an ice shipping business in 1805. But it wasn't until 1842 that the concept was applied to railroad freight cars, when the *American Railroad Journal* announced that the Western Railroad of Massachusetts planned to introduce refrigerated railcars, using ice in the summer and powdered charcoal in the winter to keep foods from spoiling. Perishables including eggs, butter, lard, fish, oysters, vegetables, cheese, lemons, oranges, and berries were predicted as freight, although it appears fish and oysters were the only items ever included in the service.[24]

A number of other experiments with refrigerated cars occurred over the next few decades, including shipments of butter, cheese, meat, and poultry to New York City and Boston from western New York and Vermont, and meat and strawberries between Chicago and the eastern states. By the late 1860s, the refrigerated car was a viable business concept, even if it wasn't in widespread use quite yet.[25]

But the idea of "artificial seasons" quickly caught on. Rare vegetables and other items such as fruits, fish, and nuts were sent to northern markets by rail and steamboat from southern locales such as Charleston, Norfolk, and Savannah, and even Bermuda, starting in the early spring. By 1867, deliveries of tomatoes, potatoes, peas, cabbage, onions, strawberries, and cherries arrived in New York at least twice a week, some in shipments of hundreds of barrels.[26]

Refinements to the design of refrigerated cars continued throughout the rest of the century. In the 1870s, Georgia peach grower Samuel Rumph (often referred to as the father of the Georgia peach industry) was frustrated by the lack of a practical means to refrigerate peaches for transport and in 1875 invented a refrigerated railcar and crates that allowed him to ship peaches to larger markets in Boston, Philadelphia, and New York.[27] A couple of years later, the first long-distance train delivery of oranges was accomplished when fruit grower William Wolfskill shipped the juicy citrus from Los Angeles to East St. Louis.[28]

The full potential of long haul rail transport was becoming a reality. By the late 1880s, fast "specials" such as the Thunderbolt Express sped along the Illinois Central line from New Orleans to Chicago, bringing sweet Louisiana strawberries and tropical bananas from Central America to folks in the city. In 1884, railroads in Florida and Georgia were still sending watermelons in ventilated cars to seaports where they were loaded onto ships for passage to Philadelphia, Boston, and Baltimore. But just three years later, all-rail shipments were in place—seventeen cars of melons traveled the 1,300-mile journey from Valdosta, Georgia, to Boston via ten different railroads.[29] In the 1890s refrigeration became widely used for commercial transportation and the shipping of produce increased significantly.[30] No longer reserved solely for exclusive dinner menus such as Parkinson's, a variety of vegetables began to grace American dinner tables year round.

THE THOUSAND DOLLAR DINNER

BILL OF FARE*

EMPIRE AND KEYSTONE

[*Coat-of-Arms of the States of New York and Pennsylvania*]

APRIL 19TH, 1851.

———

Before Dinner.

Cognac of 1821.   *Wine bitters, with Madeira and Sherry.*

LA CARTE.

First Course.

OYSTERS.

Morris River Cove, on shell.

Wines.

Sauternes, vintage of 1846, especially selected from the stock of
WASHINGTON MORTON, *at Bordeaux.*

Second Course.

SOUPS.

Green Turtle.   Potage, à la reine.

Wines.

Snider's Imperial Cognac (in pint bottles).

---

*There are no known copies of the actual Empire and Keystone menu printed for what became known as the "Thousand Dollar Dinner." This is a transcription provided by R. B. Valentine from his own "well-worn" copy for a September 4, 1874 *Philadelphia Press* article, "Les Bon Vivants—An Old-Time Philadelphia Dinner."

Third Course.

Fresh Salmon, lobster sauce.   Baked Rock, à la Chambord.

Wines.

Extra Cabinet. Steinberg—Vintage of 1834.
Especially selected from the cellars of the DUKE OF NASSAU.

Fourth Course.

BOILED.

Turkey, celery and oyster sauce.   Chicken and egg sauce.   Beef Tongues.

Wines.

Champagne—Sparkling, of Peuvrel a Avize.
SPECIALLY ON TABLE.
Medoc—Haut Brion, 1841.   Burgundy—Cote Roti, 1839.

Fifth Course.

COLD DISHES.

Galantine de Dinde a la Gelee.   Jambon Decoree.
Salade a la Russe en bordure de Gelee.   Aspic aux huitres.
Boeuf a la mode.   Mayonnaise of lobster.
Salada de Volaille, a la Mode Anglaise.   Aspic de Volaille aux truffes.

Wines.

RARE OLD CASK.

Amontillado—Pale Sherry.
Specially selected from the private stock of THOMAS OSBORNE, *Esq.,*
of the house of Duff, Gordon & Co., Port Andalusia, Spain.

Sixth Course.

Entrée No. 1.
Filet de Boeuf, aux Champignons.   Vol au vent a la Financiere.

Riz de Veau, Sauce Tomate.   Cotelettes de Mouton.
Croquettes de Volaille.

Seventh Course

Entrée No. 2.

Pigeons' Braise, Sauce Madere.   Lamb Chops, Milanaise.
Arcade de Volaille.   Turtle Steak.
Fricassee de Poulets, a la Chevalier.   Caliepash.

Wines.

Moet—Extra Sparkling Champagne.
Vintage of 1846—Snider's special importation.

Eighth Course

ROAST.

Spring Chicken on Toast, Capons, bardet.   Spring Lamb, Mint Sauce.

Wines.

Extra Sparkling Moselle, Scharzberg.
Vintage of 1846—Special importation from the cellars of
DIENHARD & JORDAN, *Coblenz.*

Ninth Course.

PIECES MONTEES.

Swiss Basket.   Panier en Nougat.   Cottage Basket.
Vase Monte, with Fruit Glacé.
Flora's Offering.   Moorish Fountain.   Indian Temple.

VEGETABLES.

White Potatoes.   Corn.   Tomatoes.   Green Peas.
Cauliflower.   Asparagus.
Sweet Potatoes.   Hominy.   Celery.   Spinach.   Dressed Lettuce.

Tenth Course.

COUP DU MILIEU.

Sorbets au vin de Tokia.

Eleventh Course.

GAME.

Jack Snipe.   Teal Duck.   Woodcock.   Plover.   Rice Birds.
Celery hearts.   Saratoga Potatoes.

Wines.

Oeil de Perdrix.

Twelfth Course.

Diamond-back Terrapin.   Roast Potatoes.

Wines.

Rare old Amontillado Pale Sherry.
Specially selected and bottled in Europe. Imported October, 1850.

Thirteenth Course.

PASTRY.

Lemon Pudding.   Gateaux a la Parisienne.   Gelée au Madere.
Peach Pie.   Meringues de pomme.   Blanc Mange.
Cocoanut Pudding.   Gateaux a la Napolitaine.   Italian Cream.
Charlotte Russe.   Meringues a la Crème.   Gateaux Allemanda.
Wafers a la Francaise.

Wines

Sherry—Rare old mellow cask wine, pale, of Duff, Gordon & Co.
Madeira—Soft, old; vintage of 1811.
Port—Burmester, extra special importation.

Fourteenth Course.

CONFECTIONERY.

Mint Drops.   Raspberry Balls.   Chinese Almonds.   Nougat de provence.
Cream Candy.   Burnt Almonds.   Cream Drops.   Port Wine Drops.
Celery Seed.   Brandy Drops.

Fifteenth Course.

ICE CREAMS AND WATER ICES.

Biscuit glace.   Caramel.   Harlequin.   Lemon.
Cream au beurre.   Vanilla.   Strawberry.   Orange Water Ice.
Punche a la Romanine.   Champagne frappe a la glace.

Sixteenth Course.

FRUITS AND NUTS.

Apples.   Figs.   Walnuts.   Pecan Nuts.
Oranges.   Raisins.   Almonds.   Filberts.

Wines.

Rhenish—Soft, old, very rare extra Cabinet.
Marcobrunn of 1834, specially obtained from the cellar
of the DUKE OF NASSAU.

Médoc.
Montrose of 1840, very choice and delicate, bottled in 1844, and
especially selected from the stock of VALE & CO., *at Bordeaux.*

Seventeenth Course.

Cafe Noir.

LIQUERES.

Maraschino.   Curaçoa.

WINES and LIQUORS selected for this occasion from the stock of
JACOB SNIDER, JR., Philadelphia

JAMES W. PARKINSON, Caterer.

Parkinson's Ice Cream and Confectionery Saloon at 180 Chestnut Street in an 1839 watercolor. A thriving locale on Chestnut Street for over twenty years, this popular eatery was opened in 1830 by James W. Parkinson's parents, George and Eleanor. James took over the business in 1840 and managed it until 1851 when he closed this location. He opened his magnificent restaurant, confectionery, and garden café at 311 Chestnut Street in 1852. (*Historical Society of Pennsylvania*)

An 1876 watercolor depicting the southwest corner of Eighth and Chestnut Streets. Parkinson's former restaurant at 38 South Eighth Street, where the Thousand Dollar Dinner took place, was located in a three-story building at the far left of this image. Parkinson ran this location from 1846 until he moved his operations to 311 Chestnut Street. (*Historical Society of Pennsylvania*)

An 1862 "bank note" for fifteen cents credit toward a meal at Delmonico's on South William Street, New York City. It pictures the "Citadel" with its imposing Roman columns, the Delmonico's flagship restaurant, built in 1837. It was here where the friendly restaurant challenge between New York and Philadelphia began. (*New York Public Library*)

The young nephew of John and Peter Delmonico, Lorenzo Delmonico joined the family business in 1831 and by 1842 he had assumed management duties of the growing restaurant dynasty. A quick learner and savvy businessman, Lorenzo was the driving force behind Delmonico's successful reign. (*New York Public Library*)

The original "Citadel" was razed in 1890 and a new restaurant was built on the same location, opening in July 1891. Although undergoing numerous changes in ownership and management over the years, it still operates under the name Delmonico's. (*Museum of the City of New York*)

"Paris, New York & Philadelphia fashions for spring and summer 1854, published and sold by F. Mahan, no. 211 Chestnut Street, Philadelphia." At the time of the Thousand Dollar Dinner, Philadelphia was among the most influential cities in the world, and its elite kept up with the latest fashions. (*Library of Congress*)

A mid-nineteenth-century sketch of a magnificent formal table setting for more than thirty persons at the James Rush mansion on Chestnut Street, located near Parkinson's restaurant. This sketch gives a sense of how the Thousand Dollar Dinner may have been laid out. (*Library Company of Philadelphia*)

With its many stores, offices, theaters, museums, hotels, and public buildings, Chestnut Street was the lively "Broadway" of Philadelphia during the nineteenth century. The street and sidewalks bustled with strollers, shoppers, sightseers, carts, and omnibuses. James W. Parkinson cleverly placed his various restaurant locations in this area to capitalize on the bustling activity. This daguerreotype taken in the early 1840s of the north side of Chestnut Street between Second and Third streets shows a seed store, a flower shop, a "lard lamp" dealer, and a print shop. No doubt Parkinson was familiar with these establishments in his lifetime. (*Library of Congress*)

A December 1848 advertisement announcing the holiday arrival of Kris Kringle at Parkinson's Restaurant and Confectionery. Featuring a fantastic display of seasonal decorations, candy, and toys, Parkinson's was the first shop in America to offer visits with Santa Claus at Christmastime. (*Library Company of Philadelphia*)

"An Oyster Supper. We won't go home till morning." a circa 1852 lithograph, shows a group of men enjoying a meal of oysters, an enormously popular social event in the nineteenth century. An oyster supper party typically featured a wide variety of oyster preparations: fried, stewed, broiled, roasted, raw, and patties. Oysters were also served at formal dinners, often as a first course. (*Connecticut Historical Society*)

Salmon à la Chambord. This drawing from *The Modern Cook* by Charles Elme Francatelli (1845) shows the stylish à la Chambord method, which involved stuffing a fish with forcemeat, larding it with bacon, and braising it with white wine and seasonings. It was then garnished with decorative skewers of fish quenelles and cooked crawfish and a rich Chambord and Espagnole sauce. This method was actually created for carp at the Château de Chambord in France, but Parkinson chose to use rockfish (striped bass) as part of the third course for his Thousand Dollar Dinner.

Various wine and cordial glasses and decanters were used in the nineteenth century, considered the "golden age" of wine, when people began to enjoy high-quality wines in record numbers. It was the steward's duty to inform the butler which wines were to be served during each course, and to ensure that they were served at the proper temperature. (The Epicurean)

Galantines of Chickens, à la Reine. This fanciful dish, similar to what Parkinson served as part of his fifth course, is typical of the elegant, imaginative cold dishes that were so popular in the nineteenth century. Galantines are made from poultry, pork, game, veal or rabbit, stuffed with forcemeat and pressed into a symmetrical shape and then set in clear aspic (gelatin). (Confectioners' Journal, *April 1879*)

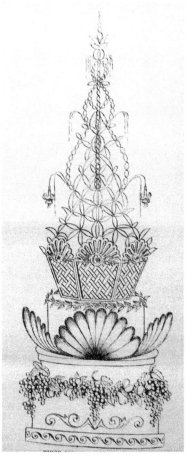

"Pièce Montée in Glacé Fruit." Pièces montées are impressive sculptures made entirely from edible ingredients such as sugar, cake, and almond paste. Designed to ornament and decorate fine dining tables, they are complex works of art that show off the skills of the confectioner who constructs them. Parkinson paired various pièces montées with vegetables for his ninth course as an *entremets*, "between dishes."(Confectioners' Journal, *February 1880*)

Vol-au-vent à la financière—literally translated as "a rich flight on the wind"—is a round case of puff pastry filled with a mix of sautéed sweetbreads, mushrooms, chicken or forcemeat, truffles, and cockscombs simmered in a rich brown sauce flavored with sherry or Madeira. Invented by French chef Marie-Antoine Carême in the early 1800s, vol-au-vent soon became a popular fixture on entrée courses throughout the nineteenth century, and was part of Parkinson's sixth course, the first entrée. (The Epicurean)

Reflecting the nineteenth-century trend of titling dishes after famous people and places, Gateaux à la Napolitaine is named for the city of Naples, Italy. A tall, delicate cake, it is constructed from thin round layers of pastry flavored with almonds, rose- or orange-flower water, and vanilla, sprinkled with sugar and then spread with fruit preserves. This exact confectionery was served as part of the Thousand Dollar Dinner's thirteenth course, pastries. (Confectioners' Journal, *February 1875*)

Mₐᵣₑₕ 1859

This 1859 photograph shows Parkinson's Restaurant and Confectionery on 311 Chestnut Street, complete with "Parkinson" carved in a stone frieze above one of the entrances. Philanthropist Frederick Kohn built this large "double house" in 1819 and resided there until his death in 1829. His widow continued to live in the mansion until James Parkinson purchased the building and opened his fashionable eatery in November 1852. (*Library Company of Philadelphia*)

This illustration shows the lush back garden area of Parkinson's Café and Restaurant on 311 Chestnut Street. A popular spot during hot Philadelphia summers, the large garden featured a fountain, walking paths, flowering trees, and shrubbery, and nightly illuminations and musical entertainments.
(*Historical Society of Pennsylvania*)

The only known portrait of James W. Parkinson, a caricature titled, "A Real Royal Personage," from the *Confectioners' Journal*, 1875. He would have been in his late fifties at the time. Parkinson had launched the *Confectioners' Journal* the year before and served as its highly successful and influential trade editor until his death in 1895. The informative, beautifully illustrated publication is now considered by culinary historians to be the most important resource for material about mid- to late- nineteenth-century American foods. (*Library Company of Philadelphia*)

COUP DU MILIEU

Sorbets au vin de Tokia

"The coup du milieu has a quasi-magical effect. Speaking only to its effects and not its causes, which we leave to the doctors to explain, we simply note that each gourmand then feels as he did when he first sat down, and is ready to do honor to a second dinner."
—Grimod de La Reynière, *Almanach des gourmands*, 1812

Parkinson's guests were now a little more than halfway through the seventeen courses on his extensive menu. No doubt the gentlemen diners were feeling pleasantly content and thoroughly impressed by all the rich dishes and fine wines they had enjoyed so far. Perfect timing for the *coup du milieu*, or midway pause—an opportunity to rest and refresh their palates.

A small glass of chilled or room-temperature spirits that was served after the roast, the coup du milieu emerged during the time of France's ancien régime, before the revolution. It was actually one drink in a three-part custom. The others were the *coup d'avant* (a glass of vermouth sipped in the drawing room before dinner) and the *coup d'après* (a glass of wine served after the soup).[1]

First popular in Bordeaux and other French seaside towns, it was introduced to Paris in the early 1800s. As nineteenth-century French food critic Grimod de La Reynière describes in his gastronomic masterpiece *Almanach des gourmands*, the type of drink served was usually a bitter liquor and/or spirit, such as an extract of Swiss absinthe,[2] Jamaican rum, or very old cognac. In addition to giving the diners a break from eating, the drink was thought to aid digestion. Grimod called the coup du milieu "a stroke of genius that makes a second dinner possible and has a way of redoubling the vigor of the weakest stomachs." He did warn, however, that it needed to be timed just right—too long of a delay could result in guests leaving with unfulfilled appetites.[3]

Even though Grimod maintained the coup du milieu must be "simple," the French had a very interesting way of presenting it. According to Grimod's description, the coup du milieu was typically served by "a young girl of 18 to 22 years, tall, blonde, shapely, engaging in all respects. Her sleeves are rolled up to her shoulders; in one hand, she carries a mahogany tray bearing as many glasses as there are guests, and in the other she holds a decanter of Jamaican rum, absinthe or vermouth." The girl would then walk around the table pouring a glass for each guest, starting with the most prominent, and then silently return to the kitchen. Guests were forbidden from taking any liberties with the girl, who was preferably a virgin. The custom became all the rage at Paris tables throughout the nineteenth century, particularly among lady guests, ironically.[4]

Between 1850 and 1900, the strong, bitter drink was often replaced by a sweeter choice, such as a rum sorbet or a glass of sherry or Roman punch.[5] It was still meant to break up the meal and cleanse the palate, but having it chilled or icy became customary. The other change was the placement of the drink or sorbet within the meal—it was now sometimes served before the roast instead of after.

Serving the sorbet before the roast gave the guests a chance to take time to pause before returning them to the significant part of the meal.[6] For example, in his descriptions of both French and American dinner menus, Delmonico chef Charles Ranhofer places the iced punch or sherbet between the entrée and roast courses.[7]

However, some menus still featured the roast before the sorbet, which is the case with Parkinson's Thousand Dollar Dinner. The sorbet was served as the tenth course, two courses after the roast. In any case, the "intermission" concept was the same. For Parkinson's guests, the sorbet would have been a welcome interlude in preparation for the rich game and terrapin courses that followed.

The term *sorbet* developed out of the Arabic word *sharbab*, traditionally a cold, sweetened nonalcoholic drink, which later became Anglicized as *sherbet* (and often used interchangeably with sorbet). *Sharabat* was a similar drink containing alcohol, which the Italians changed to *sorbetto* and the French adopted as sorbet. By the nineteenth century, a sorbet could signify either a chilled drink made from sugar and lemon pulp, or one that contained an alcoholic beverage and was very frothy and icy, like a modern-day frozen daiquiri. It was the second variety that became a standard offering during the midway pause, and eventually developed into the sorbets eaten with a spoon that are popular today.[8]

Sorbets were very fashionable during the Victorian era, a time when multicourse meals became more common and these icy refreshments served to cleanse the palate between courses. According to nineteenth-century British cooking instructor Mrs. Agnes Marshall (known as the "Queen of Ices"), "they should be of a light semifrozen nature, having only just sufficient consistency to hold together when piled up." She describes them as having lemon-water ice as a base, with the addition of some spirit, liqueur, or syrup for flavoring. The tangy-sweet lemon and cooling nature of the icy sorbet provided a refreshing contrast to the heat and rich flavors of the previous courses.[9]

These frozen drinks were also sometimes referred to as punches, with Roman punch the most popular—a mix of lemon peel, juice, sugar, and Jamaican rum.[10] The numerous other varieties included pineapple punch, imperial punch (made with pineapple, oranges, lemons, vanilla, cinnamon, rum, hock,[11] and champagne), marquise punch (made with Sauternes wine and brandy), and iced punch (like marquise punch but with the addition of orange, lemon, and rum and frozen like a granita).[12]

As was typical of that era, presentation was very important, and each punch or sorbet was served in pretty cups or glasses, or in some cases, unique molds made out of ice or other materials. Charles Ranhofer was well known for creating especially elegant punches and sorbets. His sunflower punch featured a mixture of pineapple water ice, Italian meringue, kirsch, and Champagne, which was poured into attractive sunflowers made from gum paste or pulled sugar. Another interesting concoction was Stanley punch, a colorful semifrozen combination of coffee, vanilla, lemons, kirsch, maraschino, and meringue. This punch was served inside a goblet adorned with a delicately poised heron. Formed out of gum paste, the realistic-looking bird stood on one leg surrounded by marshy reed grasses and cattails as if ready to take flight.[13] When Charles Dickens was honored at a Delmonico banquet in 1867, Ranhofer served a lemon and orange sorbet flavored with sparkling wine, kirsch, and prunelle (a sweet liqueur distilled from plums) inside cups made of ice (formed by freezing water between two cup-shaped molds).[14]

But Parkinson was the master at inventing delicious, eye-catching sorbets. For the Thousand Dollar Dinner, he pulled out every stop, creating a luxurious, rejuvenating sorbet using an extremely rare and expensive Hungarian Tokaji wine. According to guest R. B. Valentine, "This bold innovation could only have originated with an artist of genius." Valentine raved about not only the exquisite flavor, but also the "magical" result it produced. "It cooled our palates, whetted our appetites anew, and we went at it again with all the zest of a fresh start." This was exactly the effect Parkinson was striving for.[15]

Known as one of the world's greatest dessert wines, Tokaji wine (called Tokay in English) is named for the town of Tokaj in northeastern Hungary, nestled in the foothills of the volcanic Zemplen mountain range. Like French Sauternes, Tokaji is made from "botryized" grapes—those subjected to "noble rot." The discovery that the sinister-looking *Botrytis cinerea* mold plays a vital role in creating intensely sweet, highly flavorful wines occured independently of each other in Hungary, Germany, and France. But Tokaji is considered the first wine made this way—years before the similarly produced German Spätlese from the Rheingau region and Sauternes from France.[16]

As the legend goes, in the mid-1600s a Hungarian priest/winemaker was experimenting with local furmint grapes, curious about what would happen if he let them raisinate on the vine. Right before it was time for picking, a group of invading Turks raced through the region, forcing the priest to flee the area. By the time he returned, it was late fall and the grapes were a mess—shriveled, moldy, and seemingly unusable. But he decided to harvest the rotten grapes anyway. His frugality paid off: when the grapes were pressed, the small bit of wine that trickled out was like liquid gold. This lush honey was blended with table wine from the previous year to create the first "Tokay Aszu"—the archetype for one of the most indulgent, yet well-balanced sweet wines in the world.[17]

Botrytis cinerea requires fairly specific climatic conditions in order to provide its beneficial qualities. The proper balance of humidity and warmth is crucial—too much or too little can disrupt the process. But the Tokaj region happens to be the perfect setting for the mold to work its magic. Warm summer winds, protective mountains, and humid autumn mists from the nearby Bodrog and Tisza rivers provide the ideal conditions for botrytis to thrive. Tokaji is also aided by the fact that the region's grape varietals are well suited to this process, including the late-harvest, thin-skinned, acidic furmint grape, which is highly susceptible to botrytis. But even with all these positive factors in play, difficulties can arise. Botrytis often infects the grapes intermittently, forcing winemakers to pick them in stages. Some years it doesn't take hold at all, and no Tokaji is produced.[18]

Tokaji was also the first wine to be classified according to quality, predating the now-famous French classification system by over one hundred years. Hungarian Prince Rakoczi was the first to do this in 1700, and by 1737 Tokaji wines were categorized into first, second, third, and unclassed growths.[19] At the same time, the French were reluctant to acknowledge that rotten grapes were the secret behind their version of sweet wine (Sauternes). But Tokaji winegrowers openly disclosed their methods, and as a result, Tokaji was the only botrytis-infected wine ranked among the world's finest in the eighteenth century.[20]

Tokaji's popularity and status continued to flourish in the nineteenth century, gaining "an immense reputation for its great restorative and tonic qualities."[21] In his 1851 book, *A History and Description of Modern Wines*, Cyrus Redding refers to "Tokay" as the "King of Wines," made rich and syrupy in small quantities and considered "most precious." He describes it as having a powerful aroma, an earthy, astringent flavor, and a soft, oily taste. "The best wine of Tokay has so peculiar a flavor of the aromatic kind, and is so luscious, that the taste is not easily forgotten. In truth, it is more a *liqueur* than a wine."[22]

Toward the end of the nineteenth century, tragedy struck in the form of phylloxera, the tiny yellow aphid that spread throughout Europe, wreaking havoc on its vineyards, including those in the Tokaj region. Vineyards were slowly rebuilt but then ravaged once again by the First and Second World Wars. Then when Hungary fell under communist rule in 1949, Tokaji wine faced perhaps its greatest challenge. Wineries and vineyards were confiscated and nationalized, with wines from different regions pooled in the central cellar operations. The richly individualized Tokaji wines were blended with other lesser-quality wines, vineyards were neglected, and the centuries-old winemaking traditions were abandoned. As a result, the Tokaji wine produced in the 1980s would have been unrecognizable to the gentlemen at Parkinson's Thousand Dollar Dinner in 1851. Luckily there is a silver lining to this story. When the communists lost power in 1989, foreign investors swept into the Tokaj region and started working to restore the old vineyards to their pristine state. In less than five years, Tokaji wines were again available. Today winemakers are still recovering unkempt and deserted vineyards, but real Tokaji wine lives once again.[23]

ELEVENTH COURSE

GAME

Jack Snipe • *Teal Duck* • *Woodcock* • *Plover* • *Rice Birds*
Celery hearts • *Saratoga Potatoes*

"In former times small birds such as robins, thrush, snipe, and woodcock were roasted and greatly savored."
—James Beard, *American Cookery*, 1972

Now fully revitalized by Parkinson's unique, refreshing sorbet, his guests next tucked into a savory course of game birds. It might be difficult to imagine the tiny birds flitting about our backyards as food, but plump, delicate birds have long been a popular fixture on fancy banqueting tables. Europeans were very pleased to find an abundant supply of edible fowl when they started exploring and colonizing the New World. Many birds were similar to their European counterparts, including duck, partridge, quail, pigeon, and woodcock, allowing colonists to duplicate their favorite recipes.[1]

Unlike the bland, mass-produced fowl we are used to today, these small wild birds had a distinct, gamey taste. Parkinson referred to reedbirds as delicious, the plover as mouth-melting, and the woodcock as the "gamest game-bird of them all."[2] Estelle Woods Wilcox, author of *Buckeye Cookery*, also raved about the woodcock, claiming, "of game birds the woodcock outranks all in delicate tenderness and sweet flavor."[3] Not surprisingly, it was the most expensive bird in nineteenth-century public markets.[4]

However, game birds can be tricky to cook because of their small size and lean flesh, which has the tendency to dry out quickly. Parkinson does not specify the preparation method of the game birds on his menu, but it is likely they were roasted, as this was the preferred cooking technique. *The National Cookery Book* (1876) listed several birds that were always roasted, including canvasback, widgeon, mallard, teal, and black duck, as well as pheasants, grouse, and prairie hens. This cookbook recommended basting game birds in their own juices and dredging them with minimal flour. They could be presented to the table with or without their heads, according to preference. Snipe and woodcock were typically served with their heads on, as their long bills were a highly prized status symbol. Sometimes smaller birds were served with their claws still attached.[5]

To roast his game birds, Parkinson probably used a large stand-alone roaster equipped with a special rotating spit for roasting small game. In *The Epicurean*, Delmonico chef Charles Ranhofer describes a rotisserie-style roaster containing a five and a half foot long spit with six twenty-inch skewers designed to hold multiple wildfowl. For example, quails, partridges, and thrush could be roasted on one side, and snipe, woodcock, and plovers on the other, for a total of six rows of birds. "These spits are very useful for large dinners, for eight quails can be put on each skewer or forty-eight quails can be roasted at once without having them too crowded," said Ranhofer.[6]

Game birds were often barded or studded with lard to ensure juiciness, although this could mask the bird's natural flavor. Sometimes pigeons, quail, and woodcock were wrapped in grape leaves as well as barded.[7] Snipe and woodcock were often roasted without butchering them first, and while true epicures appreciated this method, the *National Cookery Book* called it "a disgusting practice, as articles of food offensive to man are often found in their stomachs."[8]

Another custom was roasting a small bird with the "trail" or intestines left inside and buttered toast placed underneath to catch the drippings. To serve, the toast was transferred to a hot dish with the birds positioned on top and gravy poured all around.[9] "Birds in a Grove" was another interesting dish, referred to as a "quaint old recipe" by James Beard. To make it, a large baking dish was generously lined with mashed potatoes and browned under a broiler. The game birds were then laid on top and sprigs of parsley placed among them to simulate the birds resting in a grassy field.[10]

Even though wild game was diminishing east of the Mississippi at the time of the Thousand Dollar Dinner, *The Market Assistant* by Thomas Farrington De Voe (1867) lists forty pages of "wildfowl and birds, called game" available in the markets of New York, Philadelphia, and Boston, with descriptions of numerous species of each type, including sandpipers, larks, quail, snipes, and plover. Reedbirds (also called rice buntings, rice birds, or bobolinks) were especially plentiful in the Philadelphia markets, as the region was very near to where they liked to feed. Plump and tiny, they were often brought to market strung on a twig or wrapped in vine leaves. And many cookbooks from the era devote whole chapters to game. Both *The Epicurean* and Eliza Leslie's *Directions for Cookery* have several pages of recipes featuring game birds cooked in various ways, including roasted, stuffed, stewed, baked in puddings and pies, as cold dishes, and with a mousseline sauce.[11]

But just as with the vegetables on his menu, obtaining these birds would have posed a challenge to Parkinson as they each were available in specific seasons. While some of the birds, such as the snipe and possibly the plover, were probably available in the Philadelphia markets in April, the woodcock, teal duck, and rice birds were probably not, as their seasons were summer and fall. According to guest R. B. Valentine's recounting of the Thousand

Dollar Dinner, the rice birds on the menu came from South Carolina, so perhaps the woodcock and teal duck also came from Southern locales. Sometimes small wild birds were captured and then caged and fattened up for eating later, so this is another possibility.[12]

Throughout the latter part of the nineteenth century, game birds began to slowly fall out of favor as a gastronomic choice in America, and were largely gone by the early twentieth century. Although some fancy restaurants still feature wildfowl on their menus, the number of recipes included in cookbooks has seriously dwindled. This is partly due to the introduction of more stringent hunting laws and the fact that some (such as the passenger pigeon) were hunted to extinction, but it could also be a reflection of the change in people's tastes. Most Americans are now used to mild-tasting domestic poultry and prefer basic white meat chicken to more "gamey" birds. While nineteenth-century cookbooks raved about the flavor of woodcock and snipe, a modern book on North American game birds refers to the eating quality of both as fair, with very dark, liver-like breast meat. [13]

Parkinson chose to pair his game birds with two vegetable side dishes that were very fashionable at the time: celery and Saratoga potatoes. Today celery is typically relegated to crudité platters or finely chopped to add crunch to chicken or tuna salad, but it was considered a high-status food in the nineteenth century, mainly because it was rather difficult to grow—it had to be blanched or protected by piles of soil in order to preserve the whiteness and sweetness of its stalks. The Victorians gave celery special treatment, creating distinctive stands or vases in which to serve them. Made of decorated glass or silver, the vessels could be tall and sturdy to hold the celery upright like a bouquet of flowers, or shaped like a low basket or oval "boat" to cradle the celery lying down.[14]

Celery was often prepared stewed, fried, or braised, but with Parkinson's stylish flair, it's likely he served raw celery in one of these elegant stands or vases. According to cooking school instructor and cookbook author Maria Parloa, "Celery should be scraped and washed and then put in ice water, to be made crisp, at least an hour before it goes on the table."[15]

Many people associate potatoes with Irish cooking and assume they must be an Old World food. But they actually originated in South America and were introduced to Europe by Spanish soldiers in the 1550s. Europeans then brought them back to the Americas when they started settling the New World. It wasn't until the 1700s that they began to gain wide acceptance in the United States.[16] Potatoes were stewed, boiled, baked, mashed, and made into croquettes and even small potato "marbles." But one preparation has perhaps become more popular than any other—the now-ubiquitous snack food known as potato chips.

Fried potatoes have been around in America since the early nineteenth century—Thomas Jefferson had a recipe for deep-frying raw sliced potatoes in his collection that dates to the early 1800s. And Mary Randolph, a distant cousin of Thomas Jefferson, featured directions on how "To Fry Sliced Potatoes" in her 1824 cookbook *The Virginia Housewife*. But it was a Saratoga Springs, New York, restaurant called Moon's Lake House that popularized this dish. The restaurant opened in 1853, and according to legend, in August of that year a fussy customer (some say it was railroad magnate Commodore Cornelius Vanderbilt) repeatedly sent his plate of "Moon's Fried Potatoes" back to the kitchen, complaining they were sliced too thick. In frustration, chef George Crum sliced up some potatoes razor-thin, fried them until crisp and seasoned them with extra salt. Other versions of the story credit Crum's sister Katie Wicks as the inventor, still others say it was the restaurant's owner Cary Moon or his wife. In any case, the style took hold, and by the 1870s, recipes for crispy Saratoga potatoes (sometimes called Saratoga chips) appeared frequently in American cookbooks.[17]

It is rather odd then that Parkinson's 1851 menu includes Saratoga potatoes—two years before Crum supposedly "invented" them. But it appears that fried potatoes were likely a specialty in the Saratoga Springs area prior to the 1853 Crum story. An entertaining 1849 *New York Herald* article discussing the "Comforts at Lake Saratoga" raves about the fried potatoes served at Loomis's Lake House, a resort predating Moon's. Just like Parkinson's pairing, these dinners also featured game birds such as woodcock and partridge, a detail affirmed by historian Dave Mitchell, who pointed out that all the lake houses in Saratoga Springs were famous for their fish and game dinners.[18] There is also a reference to Saratoga potatoes dated 1834 in the book *Reminiscences of Gideon Burton*, but it doesn't describe the preparation—just that the author ate it for breakfast while on a visit to Boston.[19]

So it seems highly probable that the Saratoga potatoes served by Parkinson were indeed the fried variety and had been known by that name even before 1853. Perhaps Parkinson had vacationed in the Saratoga Springs area and brought the recipe name and preparation home to Philadelphia, or maybe the dish had been making the culinary rounds earlier than previously believed.

WINES

Œil de Perdrix

A pale rosé wine made from the pinot noir grape, Œil de Perdrix is one of the prettiest shades a wine can be. Literally translated, Œil de Perdrix means "Eye of the Partridge," a reference to the wine's delicate salmon-pink color rather than the actual varietal. It is also used to describe very rare Champagne rosé.[20] A fresh, lively, fruity wine, Œil de Perdrix would have paired nicely with the rich game birds on Parkinson's menu.

There are conflicting reports as to how and where Œil de Perdrix originated, with both France and Switzerland vying for the honor. In the French version, it was created in the Champagne region of France in the Middle Ages, prior to the invention of the famous sparkling wine that is now its namesake. Most red wine grapes produce white juice; it is the skin of the grape that gives red wine its ruby hue. In an effort to compete with the rich, full red wines of Burgundy, winemakers in Champagne threw all their efforts into creating a fuller bodied white wine. But they couldn't figure out how to prevent the white juice from having brief contact with the red skins. As a result, all their attempts at making white wine from red grapes resulted in very pale wines ranging in color from vin gris (gray), to a slightly darkened white, to the most common shade—a light pink, referred to as Œil de Perdrix. Later, Benedictine monk Dom Pérignon perfected the method of creating white wine from red grapes that would end up being an important factor in the success of sparkling Champagne.[21]

Then there is Switzerland's story. Switzerland is not a huge wine-producing country due to the high altitude and colder weather—only 2 percent of its wine is exported. Most Swiss wine is from the western French-speaking cantons (provinces). It is the vineyards in one of these regions—Neuchâtel—that produce a fine rosé called Œil de Perdrix. Many Swiss sources claim this is the wine's birthplace, but it is more likely that the technique migrated there from France. It is now considered Neuchâtel's top wine, but because the name was never protected by the canton, rosé wine from any region in the world can be called Œil de Perdrix.[22]

DIAMOND-BACK TERRAPIN

Diamond-back Terrapin • *Roast Potatoes*

"Terrapins—This is a favorite dish for suppers and parties, and, when well cooked, they are certainly very delicious. Many persons in Philadelphia have made themselves famous from cooking this article alone."

—J. M. Sanderson, *The Complete Cook*, 1846

Like oysters, terrapins were a food equally common on the everyday supper tables of Quaker farmwives and the fine dining tables of the elite upper class. As previously mentioned, turtle dishes were extremely popular in nineteenth-century America, particularly in Philadelphia. When overfishing caused supplies of green sea turtle to dwindle, terrapin cookery developed as an alternative, and the terrapin was fondly referred to as "the bird." Also known as bay tortoises, they were found in brackish water along the eastern and southern coasts of the United States and soon became just as revered as their much larger ocean-dwelling relatives. James Parkinson was especially proud of this dish's American origins, stating, "What epicure does not know that all varieties of terrapin, and every style of serving it up, is entirely and exclusively American?"[1]

Slaves in Delaware, Maryland, and Virginia had included terrapins as part of their diet for years and were well aware of how tasty they were, but it wasn't until the early 1800s that the delicacy caught on, and they began showing up as an item for purchase in the Philadelphia markets. One publication from 1818 lists their price at $1 to $2 per dozen.[2]

Philadelphia cooks capitalized on this culinary discovery, and some even became famous for their turtle cuisine, such as Daniel and Elizabeth Rubicam, who ran the Washington Hotel at 20 South Sixth Street in Philadelphia. The Rubicams were the first caterers in Philadelphia to offer terrapin as a gourmet dish, and Mrs. Rubicam soon became known as the city's leading terrapin cook. In addition, a number of caterers including Peter Augustin, Robert Bogle, and James Prosser were highly respected for their terrapin soup. Many of these men were professional cooks of mixed-race heritage who had immigrated to Philadelphia from the West Indies or Haiti and were familiar with turtle cookery methods.[3]

Although there were numerous terrapin varieties, the diamond-back was the most sought after. Also called the saltwater terrapin, they were found in salt marshes from Massachusetts to Texas, but those from the Chesapeake Bay were considered the most delicious. Parkinson raved about these turtles, claiming they attained their "peculiarly high flavor" from feeding on Chesapeake wild celery.[4] The male terrapins (called "bulls") were usually small and tough, and sold by the hundred. The females were more desirable not only because their meat was more succulent, but also because of the possibility that they contained eggs, which "added greatly to the richness and appearance of this dainty dish." Egg Harbor terrapins from the Delaware Bay were also popular and fetched a high price.[5]

Not surprisingly, a friendly rivalry developed between these two regions (Baltimore and Philadelphia), each boasting that their style of terrapin dishes was the best. As Tillie May Forney stated in *Table Talk* magazine (1891), "If Philadelphia lays special claim to any one food luxury, it is certainly to terrapin. I once heard an epicure say that the Quaker City was the only place where the preparation of terrapin was properly understood. 'Baltimore,' he went on, 'delights in it, Washington eats it, New York knows it, but in Philadelphia it approaches a crime not to be passionately fond of it.'"[6] And in his memoir of New York high society, Ward McAllister compares Baltimore's terrapin stew (cooking the terrapin in a chafing dish with salt, pepper, and Madeira) to Philadelphia's Trenton stew (bathing the terrapin in a mixture of fresh butter and cream). Said McAllister: "I must say I agree with the Philadelphians."[7]

Baltimore's signature method used a base of brown sauce and wine, while the Philadelphia technique was creamy, like a white fricassee. Oddly enough, Maryland-style terrapin was also cream-based, just like the Philadelphia recipe. It was sometimes simply called terrapin stew. Preparing the terrapin was the same across the board—the live terrapins were placed in boiling water for a few minutes until the skin, shells, and nails could be removed easily. (Mrs. Rubicam actually goes one step further and stipulates the terrapins must remain in the pot until "quite dead.")[8]

For terrapin à la Baltimore, once the terrapin was cool, it was cleaned and the meat was cut into small pieces and sautéed in a saucepan with salt, pepper, a little nutmeg, and a glassful of Madeira wine. It was then added to a sauce made with half a pint of mirepoix (a mixture of chopped celery, onions, and carrots), a tablespoonful of flour, half a glassful of Madeira wine, a cupful of strong broth seasoned with salt and cayenne pepper, an ounce of fresh butter, and the juice of a lemon.[9] It was typically sent to the table in a chafing dish placed on a silver tray and served to each guest in a deep plate accompanied by pieces of toast.[10]

Elizabeth Rubicam's famous recipe for terrapins (Philadelphia-style) instructed saving the juices that drained out from the terrapins when cleaning them. This liquid was added to a saucepan along with the chopped terrapin meat and entrails (but no water), butter mixed with flour, and a seasoning blend of salt, cayenne, and black pepper. After stirring a short time, cream and Madeira wine were added and the terrapin served hot in a deep dish. Philadelphia's Franklin House Hotel tweaked the recipe a little by adding a dash of mace, a large tablespoonful of mustard, and ten drops of the gall (which was highly unusual since other recipes specifically instructed removing the gall-bladder as it imparted a bitter taste). Just before serving, the dish was embellished with the yolks of four hard-boiled eggs.[11]

In addition to these regional stews, there were numerous off-shoots with fancy names that were all cooked (and sometimes also served) in a chafing dish, such as terrapin à la McGovern (made with butter, salt, cayenne pepper, Madeira, lemon juice, and chopped parsley), terrapin à la Newburgh (stewed with raw eggs, truffles, and sherry), terrapin à la Bradley Martin (stewed with cream, sherry, oyster crabs, egg yolks, and truffles), and terrapin à la Robert Bonner (made with salt, pepper, madeira, egg yolks, butter, and cream). Other terrapin preparations included baked terrapin (baked in the shell and eaten with salt, pepper, and butter), terrapin pie (like chicken pie), and terrapin soup (either creamy or brown).

Because of its smaller size, the terrapin was much more manageable to cook than the colossal-sized sea turtle, and its reasonable cost allowed people from all economic levels to enjoy it. Many households would obtain a supply of live terrapins in the fall and store them through the winter during their hibernation phase in a barrel or cask located in the cellar. The *National Cookery Book* indicates that they did not need to be fed, but it does suggest throwing kitchen waste such as vegetable parings into the barrel to fatten them up. Prior to cooking they were placed in a tub of salt water overnight in order to remove any odor and ensure that they were still indeed alive. Those that appeared dead were discarded.[12]

By the late nineteenth century, terrapin was beginning to succumb to overfishing just like the green sea turtle. In *The Steward's Handbook and Guide to Party Catering* (1889), hotel cook Jessup Whitehead referred to the terrapin as "the subject of more speculative puffery and ingenious advertising to advance prices to the most absurd extremes than any other food-product of America." Although it appears Whitehead might not have been as impressed with the terrapin's culinary virtues as his contemporaries, his statement also reflects the fact that terrapin was becoming scarce and therefore expensive.[13]

In addition, it appears cooks had to be careful that they were getting the real deal. All types of turtles were substituted for the popular diamondback variety, and according to Whitehead, once seasoned and dressed with sherry it was impossible to tell them apart. "To pay $4 or $5 for a plateful, or $10 or $20 a quart for the prepared article is sheer infatuation, a fashionable craziness, a confession to being the dupe of cunning advertisers," he argued. He did admit, however, that tender, gelatinous terrapin or tortoise was "good eating as cooked in Maryland country-houses and susceptible of being highly flavored by skillful cookery."[14]

All these years of being in such high gastronomic demand caused the terrapin populations to fall to dangerously low levels by the twentieth century. In 1920, for example, only 823 pounds of Chesapeake Bay diamondback terrapins were harvested (at a cost of $125 per dozen turtles), compared to the nineteenth century's annual yield of 400,000 pounds.[15] Today diamondback terrapins are listed as a species of concern under the Endangered Species Act and are officially protected by several individual states.[16] Commercial harvest of terrapins ended in Maryland in 2007, but some states still allow terrapins to be hunted during specific seasons.[17]

WINES

Rare old Amontillado Pale Sherry
Specially selected and bottled in Europe, Imported October, 1850

During the first half of the nineteenth century, most sherries were sweet and heavy, reserved for sipping after dinner. But around the time of the Thousand Dollar Dinner the trend was leaning toward the consumption of lighter, drier wines, served as an aperitif or during the meal.[18] This is exactly the type of wine Parkinson chose to pair with the terrapin—a rare old Amontillado pale sherry.

Amontillado is an aged fino sherry—a full, sophisticated wine with nutlike undertones. Unlike other sherries, it gets minimal exposure to the protective flor yeast indigenous to Spain's Jerez region. If drunk when young, it would be nothing special, but the gradual aging process oxidizes and strengthens the wine, giving it a more intense, concentrated aroma, taste, and color as well as a higher alcohol content. However, not all finos become amontillados when they age—some just become old finos—retaining their lightness and freshness, and others actually lose their beneficial qualities and fizzle out. But when successful, the wine is soft, nutty, and delicious.[19]

As nineteenth-century wine expert Cyrus Redding stated, "The wine called Amontillado is not always the product of design. The quantity made is small. It is a drier wine than the common sherry, and is very often the result of accident." Winemakers have long puzzled over this mystery, attempting to influence the process by picking the grapes two to three weeks earlier than other varieties and then allowing them to ferment for two months or more. But even when grapes are taken from the same vineyard and treated in precisely the same way, only some casks will end up Amontillados, without the grower or the merchant being able to determine why.[20]

Amontillado sherry was a perfect match for the luscious terrapin. Turtle dishes almost always featured fortified Madeira or sherry as a flavor-enhancing ingredient. Serving the rich, creamy stew with a glass of Amontillado was a complementary pairing, adding layers of complexity to its taste.

PASTRY

Lemon Pudding • Gateaux à la Parisienne • Gelée au Madère
Peach Pie • Meringues de pomme • Blanc Mange
Cocoanut Pudding • Gateaux à la Napolitaine • Italian Cream
Charlotte Russe • Meringues à la Crème • Gateaux Allemanda
Wafers à la Française

"Pastry is an art that admits of no mediocrity—a good memory, taste, practice, and dexterity, being absolutely necessary in that branch of the business; for it is really from the manner of mixing the various ingredients of which it is composed that it acquires its good or bad quality."

—Eleanor Parkinson, *The Complete Confectioner,*
Pastry-cook and Baker, 1844

I t was now likely the wee hours of the morning. The savory courses were over, but the meal was not ready to wind down quite yet. It was time for Parkinson to show off his culinary prowess with confectionery.

By 1851 it was standard practice to save sweet dishes for the end of the meal, but it wasn't always that way. In prior centuries, sugar was used as a flavoring for all types of foods, and sweet dishes could be served at any point during a meal. It wasn't until the seventeenth century that a separate "sweets" category emerged, when it became customary for some foods to be seasoned only with salt, and others only with sugar.[1]

During the next two hundred years, sweet dishes slowly began to gravitate toward the last two dinner courses—the entremets and the dessert. The warm, sweet entremets were always served before the cold. For example, pies and tarts before crèmes and mousses, and fritters and pancakes before ice cream and sorbet. Fruits were left to the very end, with stewed fruits and compotes preceding fresh fruits and salads. The sequence of dishes was eventually rearranged to reflect the order we are now familiar with—savory before sweet.[2]

Parkinson was a master with all things sugary. He had trained with the best in the business, after all—his parents, George and Eleanor Parkinson, who ran a world-famous confectionery shop in nineteenth-century Philadelphia. As if he hadn't already amazed his patrons enough with the extravagant dishes served in the previous twelve courses, this was where he would really shine.

He began the first of four sweet courses with a "pastry" course featuring thirteen mouth-watering indulgences including pies, cakes, puddings, creams, meringues, and blancmange. In the nineteenth century, pastry was a rather broad term used to describe the sweet dishes that fell under the realm of the pastry cook, typically those that required an oven. Some menus had just one course of sweets, others had two or more—crèmes, glaces, and dessert in addition to pastry. Sometimes "pastry and dessert" were grouped together to conveniently include all types of sweets under one heading. The term *dessert* could designate all the sweets in a meal, or it could be a separate course used to categorize just fruits and confectionery. For especially extravagant occasions like the Thousand Dollar Dinner, the menu featured multiple divisions and headings.[3]

Today the sweets served in this course would fall under the "patisserie" umbrella in France, a term which includes confectionery and chocolates as well as creams, flans, puddings, fancy pastry, dough, and even ice cream.[4] In America, they are now simply grouped together as dessert, a term taken from the French word *desservir* (meaning to remove that which has been served). Dessert was the final course, signifying everything offered to guests after the previous dishes had been cleared away.[5]

Like pastry, pudding is another broad term within the world of desserts. Quintessentially British, pudding was originally a savory dish served at the beginning of a meal. Typically a mix of starch, eggs, milk, and a flavoring cooked in some kind of container, it was meant to whet the appetite before the more substantial meat course was brought out. Examples included carrot, pea, or potato pudding, cheese pudding, and batter pudding (a simple mix of butter, milk, flour, eggs, and salt). There was also suet pudding[6]—often served as an accompaniment to roast meat, it was boiled beforehand then cut into slices and laid in the dripping pan to brown a few minutes before serving.

Although savory puddings never went away completely, a preference for sweet puddings began to develop when sugar, molasses, chocolate, and vanilla became more available.[7] Blancmange is a good example of this transition. The version served by Parkinson was a smooth, almond-flavored, creamy-white pudding thickened with gelatin, but in the Middle Ages it was both a meat jelly made from pounded capon or veal and an almond-flavored dessert sweetened with honey. Blancmange was often considered difficult to make, as it had to be white and perfectly smooth.[8]

The resourceful Brits initially used an animal's stomach or intestines to boil puddings, and then eventually migrated to the pudding cloth when that was invented around the seventeenth century.[9] The pudding cloth was conveniently reusable, but keeping it clean and dry was very important. "The outside of a boiled pudding often tastes disagreeably; which arises from the cloth not being nicely washed, and kept in a dry place," warned cookbook author Maria Eliza Ketelby Rundell. "It should be dipped in boiling water, squeezed dry, and floured when to be used."[10] Later puddings were also steamed or baked in fancy molds or baking dishes, which is much easier and now the most common method. During this transitional stage, recipes would specify whether the pudding was baked or boiled.

Early English settlers brought their love of both puddings and pies (which could also be savory or sweet) to the New World, and by the nineteenth century they were among the most popular desserts in America. The line between them was often blurred, with the two terms used interchangeably. For example, many cream and custard pies such as almond, apple, coconut, lemon, and orange were listed in nineteenth-century cookbooks as puddings, but they were baked in a pie pan lined with a pastry crust or at least rimmed with a strip of pastry.

This would have been the case with the two puddings on Parkinson's menu—lemon and coconut. They are listed as puddings but would have been served with a bottom crust like a pie. Lemon and coconut were both popular dessert flavorings in Philadelphia—not only for puddings and pies, but also for cakes, candies, and frozen treats such as ice cream, sorbet, and water ice. This taste for the exotic developed from the fact that Philadelphia was a busy port city, receiving an abundance of tropical foods such as pineapples and coconuts from the Caribbean, and citrus fruits such as lemons and oranges from Portugal. As James Parkinson noted, American confectioners creatively used all these interesting flavors and ingredients to concoct a variety of delicious desserts.[11]

Decadent sweet-tart lemon pudding was a Philadelphia favorite. Mrs. Elizabeth Goodfellow, a talented pastry cook who operated a confectionery shop and supervised America's first organized cooking school during the first half of the nineteenth century, served the best-known version. Mrs. Goodfellow's lemon pudding was rich and custardy with ample amounts of butter, eggs, and sugar, and flavored with rosewater and wine or brandy in addition to lemons. It was so beloved that the recipe can be found in many manuscript cookbooks from the era and became the precursor of another popular dessert—lemon meringue pie.[12]

Coconut was the other pudding served by Parkinson. The product of swaying palm trees that line white-sand beaches in warm climates around the globe, perhaps no other food conjures up such vivid images of the tropics. They are unusual in look and taste—brown, hairy, and hard-shelled on the outside, with an inside kernel portion that is rich, white, and meaty. Coconuts are not easily classified, with much confusion about whether they are a fruit, nut, or seed. Technically, they are a drupe—a fruit with a hard stone, such as a peach or plum. Drupes have three layers, and when coconuts are brought to market, the fibrous outer layers have been stripped away, leaving just the hard, woody layer that surrounds the edible seed, or kernel.[13]

In the nineteenth century, Thomas Farrington De Voe categorized coconuts as nuts in his book *The Market Assistant*, calling them "the best flavored of all the foreign kinds. The white kernel, although hard, woody, and tough, in its fresh state, is said to be very nutritious, and, when grated, makes excellent puddings, pies, cakes, candy, etc."[14] Parkinson had a special affinity for New World coconuts, claiming those from the West Indies were "equal to the same nut in any other tropical country."[15] "Cocoanut" or "coconut" were common spellings through the early twentieth century, but eventually the "a" was dropped, possibly to avoid confusion with the word "cocoa."[16]

Just like puddings, pies started out as savory fare: beef, pigeon, veal and ham, fish and oyster, and potato pie, for example. Some, such as mince, combined sweet and savory components. But the bounty of fresh fruits in America allowed its citizens to quickly adopt fruit pies as a dessert favorite. In *Mrs. Hale's New Cook Book* (1857), Sarah Josepha Hale recommends gooseberries, currants, cherries, raspberries, plums, cranberries, and damsons for making large pies, with one pound of sugar to a quart of fruit as the proper proportion.[17]

Parkinson includes just one fruit pie on his menu—peach. Of course many of the fruits we associate with pie are available only in the late spring through the fall, which would have made it difficult for him to get access to them for his April dinner. Peaches are one of the earlier ripening fruits, so possibly he got his hands on some very early varieties from Georgia or even Bermuda. Or perhaps he used dried or preserved fruit to make the pie.

Peaches were first introduced to the southeastern United States more than three hundred years ago by Spanish explorers. It is thought that English and French settlers brought peach seeds with them to the northeastern United States. At first peaches in America were mostly grown in private orchards until commercial production took off in the nineteenth century.[18]

Parkinson must have had a particular fondness for the juicy fruit, as he featured peaches quite a bit on his menus—including peach tarts, peach ice cream, and peaches and ice cream. In *The Complete Confectioner* (1844), his mother Eleanor Parkinson listed recipes for peach ice, peach water ice, peach paste (made by mixing the fruit's pulp with sugar and heating it to marmalade consistency, then forming it into rings and knots so it could be candied or crystallized), and even peach water (described as a cooling drink for balls and routs).[19]

In the nineteenth century it was especially fashionable to name foods after famous people and places, and several of the desserts in this course reflect this trend. Naming a dish after a geographical location lent a mysterious element to a meal, summoning up images of distant horizons and alluring travel possibilities. Those dishes named for people were either a favorite of that famous person or created in their honor, as is the case with charlotte russe, which was technically named after two people.

"Charlotte" desserts originated in England at the end of the eighteenth century and are essentially puddings poured into a mold that has been lined with bread or sponge fingers. They can be served baked or unbaked. The most famous baked version is an apple charlotte, which incorporates buttered bread, stewed apples, and a breadcrumb topping. The name *charlotte* is thought to be in honor of Queen Charlotte, the wife of George III of England. Charlotte russe came a few years later. A luscious chilled dessert of vanilla Bavarian cream set in a mold lined with ladyfingers, it was created by French chef Carême at the beginning of the nineteenth century. Carême originally called the dish *charlotte à la parisienne*, but it is believed he changed it to charlotte russe in honor of Russian Tsar Alexander I.[20]

Variations of the popular dessert quickly emerged, including making the pudding as individual servings, and adding isinglass or gelatin to help "set" the pudding, which seemed to be a common American adaptation.[21] *The National Cookery Book* even has a recipe for "Florida Charlotte Russe" that specifies using "American" isinglass or gelatin (as opposed to the Russian isinglass listed in another recipe). However, it appears not everyone agreed with using gelatin. An 1898 *Table Talk* magazine article warns, "a genuine charlotte russe is not stiffened by gelatine but is made of whipped cream flavored and sweetened in various ways."[22]

Parkinson agreed. Even though he listed versions both with and without gelatin in the *Confectioners' Journal*, his favorite recipe involved lining a mold with thin sponge cake or ladyfingers, fastening the pieces together with icing, then filling it with double cream that had been whipped to a froth and then mixed with vanilla-flavored sugar. In his "humble opinion" this was "the most desirable and delicate of all the Charlotte tribe."[23]

The three cakes on Parkinson's menu followed the era's trend of geographically titled desserts—Gateaux à la Parisienne, Gateaux à la Napolitaine and Gateaux Allemanda—named after Paris, Naples, and Germany, respectively. The term *gateau* is yet another dessert classification that has had a variety of meanings, constituting "almost anything from a cream pie to an ornamented tall cake for a party," according to Jessup Whitehead. French for cake, it was derived from the old French word *guastral*, defined as fine flour and loaves and cakes made from it.[24]

Most often, the term *gateau* is used to describe fancy, lighter cakes, often freshly decorated with fruit or whipped cream. In broader terms, the French use the word to designate patisserie items based on puff pastry, short crust pastry (basic pie dough), sweet pastry, and Genoese and whisked sponges and meringues. Any number of ingredients can be added to these bases, including ground almonds, almond paste, chocolate, fruit (fresh, preserved, or dried), fondant or frosting, pastry and butter creams, liqueurs, and fresh cream.[25]

The three cakes on Parkinson's menu were indeed variations on this theme. The first, Gateau à la Parisienne, was a sumptuous cake that featured an almond- and pistachio-flavored pastry base topped with a rich sponge cake. As described by Carême in *The Royal Parisian Pastrycook and Confectioner*, making this cake was a time-consuming process that involved blanching the almonds, pounding them finely, and then soaking them in cream to create rich almond milk. The pistachios were also blanched and then washed and filleted before adding to the sponge, along with some preserved orange peel for additional flavor and texture. Versions of this cake eventually emerged with pureed fruit fillings, such as apple, peach, nectarine, plum, cherry, strawberry, currant, and gooseberry. Carême instructed cooks to frost these cakes with a meringue topping, but the Gateau à la Parisienne featured by American Nancy Lake in her cookbook *Menus Made Easy* was decorated with coffee icing, dried cherries, and whipped cream.[26]

Gateau à la Napolitaine was a delicate cake made from thin round layers of sweet pastry flavored with pounded almonds, rose or orange-flower water, and vanilla, sprinkled with coarse white sugar and then spread with fruit preserves. According to Parkinson, it was essential that this cake was "bold in form, and well proportioned." His recipe called for twenty of these pastry "flats," each one-third of an inch thick and eleven inches in diameter so that when the cake was fully mounted, it was thirteen inches high. It was typically frosted with meringue icing made with sugar, flour, cornstarch, and egg white. Once the meringue was dry, colored sugar or small bonbons were added. It could also be garnished with pistachios, more preserves, and an icing of glazed sugar. When served with cream, it was called *Gateau Napolitaine à la Chantilly*.[27]

The third cake, Gateau Allemanda, was a bit more substantial, similar to a soft, yeasty bread or coffee cake with a pâte brisée (short crust pastry) base and whole almonds for taste and garnish.[28]

In addition to being used as a frosting for gateaux, meringue was featured in many nineteenth-century desserts, including two on Parkinson's menu: Meringues de pomme and Meringues à la Crème. A sweet blend of stiffly beaten egg whites and sugar, meringue dates back to the sixteenth century, when European cooks first realized that whisking egg whites with birch twigs (for the lack of a better utensil) created a light, frothy mixture. It was eventually discovered that meringue hardens when baked at a low temperature (or simply left out in the air to dry), changing the texture to one that is pleasantly airy and crispy.[29]

Meringues de pomme was an interesting presentation in which peeled and cored apples were sprinkled with cinnamon and sugar and baked until tender. They were then arranged in a baked pie shell, and the cored centers were filled with orange marmalade mixed with crushed macaroons. The entire top of the pie was covered with meringue and baked until the meringue was browned. The cookbook *The Philadelphia Housewife* cleverly recommended swirling a peak of meringue over each apple to serve as a guide when serving the pie.[30] Meringues à la crème were tiny bite-sized baked meringues lightly flavored with vanilla and filled with cream or jelly.[31]

The other desserts featured in this course included Gelée au Madere (a molded gelatin dessert made from Madeira wine), Italian Cream (lemon-flavored custard often ornamented with crystallized or preserved fruits), and Wafers à la Française (light and crispy waffle-type cookies).

WINES

Sherry—Rare old mellow cask wine, pale, of Duff, Gordon & Co.
Madeira—Soft, old; vintage of 1811
Port—Burmester, extra special importation

SHERRY

All three wines served by Parkinson during this course of sweet pastry were fortified wines, what we now often refer to as dessert wines. Fortified wine is more robust than typical wines, made strong by the addition of a neutral spirit either during or after fermentation. The concept began in the early eighteenth century as a way to improve the taste of some types of wines that were otherwise tart or sour, and it also helped to keep them from spoiling when transported over great distances.[32]

Sherry was ubiquitous on nineteenth-century dinner tables. Extremely versatile, it ranged in style from bone dry to very sweet and could appear at just about any time during the meal—as an aperitif, paired with any number of the various courses throughout the meal, or with dessert at the end. It was also placed on the table in small decanters to add flavor and richness to soup.

In this course Parkinson chose a pale old mellow sherry. All sherry wine is naturally pale, a product of the chalky white soil of southern Spain's Andalucía region; darker shades are achieved during the aging and fermentation process. The solera blending system used to mature sherry in oak casks (where new wine gradually replaces the old) may contain wine that is decades old. According to an 1844 article, sherries that were mostly four or five years old, mixed with some of the choice reserve, were considered the highest quality.[33]

MADEIRA

Madeira is named after the island of the same name, situated four hundred miles off the coast of Portugal. Its prime location in the center of the Atlantic trade routes made it a busy stopping point for ships heading to and from Africa, Asia, and the Americas.

While there, sailors would load up on provisions, including wine. However, the intense heat of the ship's hold would cause the wines to go bad fairly quickly, so winemakers began to add clear brandy (neutral grape spirits) as a way to preserve them. But the fortifying spirit did more than that—it served to soften and deepen the flavor of the wine, as well as enhance the aging process.[34]

Ironically, the factors that had originally caused Madeira to spoil so rapidly—the heat and rocking motion of the ship—were found to be beneficial, creating wines that were rich and luscious. And the wine improved significantly with age, so the longer the voyage the better. Eventually the most sought-after Madeiras were those that had gone around the world, referred to as *vinhos da roda*. As Cyrus Redding noted in 1851, "Madeira wine is one of those which bears age remarkably well, and the wine has not yet been drunk too old. Its flavor and aroma perfect themselves by years."[35]

By the late seventeenth century, Madeira was trickling through Europe and its colonies. It soon became the most popular wine in colonial America, well known as a favorite of Thomas Jefferson and the other founding fathers. This was a direct result of the long-standing diplomatic alliance that had been forged between England and Portugal. The British were able to dominate the Madeira trade, and George III later enacted laws forbidding the importation of any other wine to the colonies. Since the colonists could purchase Madeira tax-free, it was consumed in great quantities and also used in a variety of sweet and savory dishes, including buns, cakes, and sauces.[36]

America's appreciation for the rich wine with caramel-flavored undertones continued through the 1800s. However, a fungus devastated Madeira's vineyards mid-century, causing shortages and high prices, making the wine too expensive for all but the wealthiest classes. Eventually the disease subsided, vineyards were replanted, and production returned to previous levels, bringing a corresponding reduction in cost. This outbreak would not have affected the Madeira served by Parkinson, as he wisely served a

well-aged vintage from 1811 (forty years old at the time of the dinner). In addition, Joshua Price, one of the dinner guests (who was
"as well known at that day as Independence Hall"), apparently
shared several bottles of one-hundred-and-fifty-year-old Madeira
that had been handed down to him by his great-great grandfather.
Reportedly "their great age was attested by the accumulations of
dust, cobwebs, and what not. These incrustations on the glass were
half an inch thick."[37]

PORT

Like Madeira, port also started out as an unfortified wine that ben-
efitted from the alliance between England and Portugal.
Unsophisticated and inexpensive, it was originally used to supply
British taverns when war and increased import duties made French
wine difficult to obtain. Eventually it was bottled (allowing it to be
stored in cellars and aged), and brandy was added during the fermentation process, which helped keep it fresh, preserved the flavor, and created a wholly different taste. Port became a powerful
wine that was also subtly sweet.[38]

The nineteenth century was particularly important for port. At
the beginning of the century, the amount of brandy added to port
was only about 3 percent, but an amazing vintage in 1820 that was
extremely lush, mature, and naturally sweet changed the way port
was made. Port shippers began adding greater amounts of brandy
earlier in the production process in order to stop fermentation and
retain sweetness. It was gaining recognition as a unique, interesting wine.[39]

Most port makers are called shippers because they initially
shipped their wine in casks from Portugal to British importers,
who would then bottle and label it with their own name or brand.
Although most port is now bottled in Portugal, the custom of
referring to port companies as shippers has persisted.[40] Parkinson
chose port imported by the Burmester family, who came to
Portugal from Germany in 1730 and began to specialize in port
about twenty years later. Today they are best known for their

mature tawny ports, traditionally known as "fine old tawnies." Faded to a tawny color by the aging process, these ports possess a smooth, silky mouthfeel and rich, nutty flavor with multilayered aromas that can include chocolate, coffee, caramel, raisins, nutmeg, and cinnamon.[41] These wines would have been a luxuriously fitting match for Parkinson's extravagant pastries.

CONFECTIONERY

Mint Drops • Raspberry Balls • Chinese Almonds • Nougat de provence
Cream Candy • Burnt Almonds • Cream Drops • Port Wine Drops
Celery Seed • Brandy Drops

"The confectioner's art is an accomplishment which may be ranked among the most desirable and graceful of all that pertains to domestic economy."

—The Art of Confectionery, 1866

Parkinson continued to showcase his skills with sweets by serving a course of confectionery, another somewhat blurry term in the realm of dessert foods. The *Larousse Gastronomique* provides perhaps the broadest, most basic definition: "food products based on sugar." Although sugar is the principal ingredient, it is combined with a variety of other components to create these confections, including milk, animal and vegetable fats, fruit, pectin, gelatin, flavored extracts, and colorings.[1]

Today we refer to confectionery as candy, but in the 1800s, it was usually lumped together as "sweetmeats." Wet sweetmeats were sipped or eaten with a spoon, such as jellies, preserved fruits in heavy syrups, marmalades, syrups, juices, cordials, ice creams, and ices. Dry varieties were finger foods—sugared comfits and flowers, nuts, candy creams, conserves, candied fruit, ratafias, and small cakes.[2] To add to the confusion, some confectioners were purely candy makers (they did not use flour in their shop), and others also made pastry.[3]

Just as today, vibrantly hued confections were considered more attractive than those that were transparent and colorless. But confectioners had to be careful—many of the substances used to color and brighten candies were actually poisonous, such as arsenic, lead, copper, and zinc. Safe alternatives were often found in nature, including the use of plants and spices such as saffron and marigold (to make yellow), spinach and raw coffee grains (to make green), and an insect called the cochineal (to make red).[4]

Cochineal is a bright crimson colorant made from the dried, pulverized bodies of the cochineal insect. Found in warmer locales, including Mexico, Central America, and the southwestern United States, they particularly enjoy feeding on cactus plants. Native Americans had recognized the cochineal's dye-making properties long before the Europeans arrived in the New World, forming plantations to harvest them in bulk. The Europeans soon caught on and were exporting cochineal overseas by the 1500s. (It is said that the coats of the highest-ranking British officials were dyed red with cochineal in the eighteenth century.) Chemists discovered that the carminic acid excreted by the insects could be mixed with aluminum or calcium salts to produce carmine, which was prized by confectioners as it produced an intense, brilliant scarlet color. Still used today as a food coloring, the use of cochineal has seen resurgence as the public eschews artificial colorings. It is also used in many cosmetics.[5]

Many of the flavorings used in the nineteenth century also came from natural sources, such as peppermint, anise, cinnamon, vanilla, orange, and lemon (which the *Confectioners' Journal* deemed the "most important"), but artificial flavors were already coming into play. For example, by the 1870s, an artificial version of wintergreen could be made by combining salicylic acid with methylic spirit.[6]

In some ways confectioners were more like chemists than cooks, as they had to make sure the precise amounts of these coloring and flavoring agents were combined, and they worked with substances such as tree gum and cream of tartar in order to make sure the candies set correctly and retained the proper texture. There were several stages of boiling sugar, involving precise temperatures and consistencies, requiring patience and attentiveness. In fact, the confectionery trade had its roots in the pharmacy—sugar was used in many medicines to act as a preservative and make them more palatable. Until about the end of the seventeenth century, only doctors and apothecaries made these confections. As demand and availability increased, nonmedicinal uses were quickly adapted, and confectionery became a separate business. Confectioners mimicked the physicians' formula (omitting the medicine), selling their version of candy lozenges.[7]

The mid-nineteenth century was a particularly exciting time for confectionery. Previously sugar had been considered a luxury item reserved for the wealthy, but by the 1830s, it had become cheaper to produce, refine, and distribute. As a result, there was a shift from rudimentary sweets like molasses and stick candies to more high-grade confectionery such as caramel creams and licorice. In addition, the introduction of steam power allowed manufacture on a much larger scale. This is evident by the surge in the number of confectioners operating in Philadelphia. In 1816 there were twenty known confectioners in the city, but by 1867 the number had risen to two hundred, and by 1874 the *Confectioners' Journal* estimated there were about four hundred.[8]

Parkinson's parents, George and Eleanor, were among the Philadelphians who took advantage of sugar's increased popularity. Their Chestnut Street store became the most famous and fashionable sweet shop in the city, serving specialties such as rich pies, cakes and creams, pretty jellies, flavorful cordials, and exquisite ice creams.[9]

James Parkinson had these very talented role models to teach him all the tricks of the trade. All his knowledge and training made him a fervent advocate for American foods, particularly confectionery, a skill dominated by the French for years. Parkinson was well aware of this fact—when he co-launched the *Confectioners' Journal* in 1874, the first issue admits the expertise of the French, stating, "the manufacture of confectionery, in its modern development . . . bears the distinctive artistic characteristics of French ingenuity and invention."[10]

However, this didn't stop him from voicing his disappointment and irritation that the world placed French culinary creations on such a high pedestal. "When we invent new devices in confectionery, we do not give them American names," he sadly confessed in *American Dishes at the Centennial.* "This would kill their sale. We give them French names; and yet the honest truth is that the best American confectionery is far superior to the best confectionery which is made in France."[11]

He backed this statement with the claim that almost all of the "French confectionery" sold in the United States at that time was really *American* confectionery. In addition, Americans who had traveled abroad had told him that they could not find confections equal to what they were accustomed to while visiting London, Vienna, Berlin, and even Paris. He felt his home city of Philadelphia outrivaled the entire world in the art of the confectionery.[12] Parkinson was well aware French confectioners were creative, innovative, and ambitious, but he wanted the world to know that by the 1870s America rivaled the French in this area.

So one can imagine that the confections he served even twenty years earlier at the Thousand Dollar Dinner were top-notch. There were four sophisticatedly flavored candy drops on the menu: mint, cream, port wine, and brandy. These would have been small, round, and slightly chewy, comparable to what we call pastilles today. To make drops, confectioners would add a flavored extract or essence to icing made from finely powdered refined sugar. The mixture was dropped from the end of a knife or a small drop pan[13] onto tin or copper plates or sheets of paper to form the flat, circular shapes. They were then placed in the stove for a few hours to dry. Drops of two colors were made by using a pan with two compartments to separate the different colored icings.[14]

Balls were round candies that were a little harder and slightly transparent, similar to hard candies. Parkinson's raspberry balls would have been made by melting gum arabic[15] in water, straining the mixture through a silk sieve, then boiling with sugar and a pinch of cream of tartar to the crack stage.[16] Some raspberry juice was added to the mixture and it was boiled again, then cooled and poured onto a warmed and lightly oiled marble slab. When it was somewhat hardened, the mass was cut into nut-sized pieces, each rolled into a ball and put on a sieve. The balls were then shaken about on the sieve until they were cold and round.[17]

According to *Confectioners' Journal*, creams were "soft, rich eating candies" with flavors such as almond, orange, and lemon. Apparently some confectioners considered their manufacture "a difficult and secret process," but Parkinson readily gives instructions on how to make them, stressing the importance of using "pure" flavorings from a "reliable maker." The process involved boiling refined sugar with water and cream of tartar until the mixture hardened when dropped into cold water. The mass was then placed on a marble slab to cool, and pulled vigorously (like taffy) until it turned white (Parkinson recommended using a hook to accomplish this). It was then placed back on the slab or a table dusted with sugar and braided into sticks or cut into pieces. Rose creams, a pretty pink color, were a popular variation, made by adding rose essence and a few drops of cochineal coloring to the mixture.[18]

Nougat was a nutty, chewy candy studded with blanched and dried almonds. There were many different varieties, including brown, white, pistachio, vanilla, and chocolate, with textures that could be either light and airy or firm and crunchy. "American nougat" included dried fruit and was stamped into shapes such as half-moons, rings, squares, and diamonds with a roller press. The *nougat de provence* served by Parkinson featured honey, sugar, almonds, egg whites, and orange oil as ingredients. Making this candy involved boiling the sugar and honey to the ball stage,[19] and then folding in stiffly beaten egg whites, giving it a snowy-white color and fluffy consistency. The almonds and orange oil were then added to the mixture. Once stirred into a thick paste, it was spread on a board, cooled, and cut into squares or other shapes.[20]

Comfits date back to the medieval period when the terms *confyt*, *comfect*, and *cumfitt* were used to describe sweetmeats made from fruits, roots, or flowers preserved with sugar. These terms eventually merged into the word *comfit*, and were limited to seeds or nuts coated in several layers of sugar. Producing comfits was one of the core skills of early confectioners, who were referred to as "comfitmakers" in sixteenth- and seventeenth-century England. Comfits were both eaten as confectionery and incorporated into other sweet dishes, such as the seed cake popular in the nineteenth century, made with caraway comfits rather than the plain seeds.[21]

Since regulating the heat was an important factor in making comfits, confectioners used a special copper comfit pan that was suspended from the ceiling or a beam over the stove or a charcoal fire. By swiveling it back and forth without touching the fire or stove, they could maintain a moderate heat. A pan containing clarified syrup[22] was placed nearby and kept hot, but not boiling. By modifying the proportions of sugar in the syrup, they could make comfits of varying textures, from smooth to crisp.[23]

Burnt almonds, also called prawlongs, prawlings, parched or crisp almonds, were made by boiling clarified sugar syrup and almonds to a high temperature, removing them from the heat, and stirring until the sugar dried to an almost powder form, thoroughly coating each almond. The almonds were then drained on a sieve and the loose sugar was vigorously shaken off. The process was usually repeated one or two more times to ensure a glossy coating.[24] Sometimes a few drops of essential oil such as rosewater, orange flower, jasmine, or bergamot were added to the syrup to impart a floral essence.[25]

These confections were apparently rather tricky to get just right, since readers of the *Confectioners' Journal* were constantly asking Parkinson the correct method for finishing or "polishing" burnt almonds. He recommended taking the fine sugar that had sifted through the sieve and boiling it with some water and gum arabic. This hot mixture was poured on top of the almonds, as they were turned over and over by another person. Once glazed, they were again shaken in the sieve, covered with a cloth, and allowed to dry. Another method was to rapidly mix the almonds with the sugar during the final glazing, then strew them on a marble slab and separate by hand.[26]

The last two comfits served by Parkinson were sugar-coated seeds—Chinese almonds and celery seed. Chinese almonds aren't actually almonds at all, but rather large, sweet, nontoxic seeds, or kernels, from special apricots grown solely for this purpose. With a taste and aroma similar to bitter almonds, sometimes they were soaked in a liqueur such as Maraschino or brandy for a couple weeks prior to coating them with sugar. They were often used in the nineteenth century as a substitute for bitter almonds in syrups, ices, and sweet almond paste, as only a small quantity was needed to impart a rich flavor.[27]

Sugar-coating celery seed was a similar process to making burnt almonds, but a little trickier and more time-consuming since the seeds were so tiny and required several coatings of sugar. The confectioner had to make sure to use a light hand with the syrup, using a "pearling cot" to produce a thin stream to evenly coat the seeds so that they didn't get too wet and clumpy.[28] They were then dried in the sun or an oven overnight and bathed in the sugar syrup several more times until the final product was about the size of "a large pin's head." According to Parkinson, they were "a beautiful little comfit or dragée."[29]

ICE CREAMS AND WATER ICES

*Biscuit glacé • Caramel • Harlequin • Lemon
Cream au beurre • Vanilla • Strawberry • Orange Water Ice
Punche à la Romanine • Champagne frappe à la glacé*

"There is no article of the dessert kind that deserves a more elevated position than well-made ices, as well for their intrinsic merit as for the agreeable goût which they impart to a well-ordered entertainment."

—James W. Parkinson, *Confectioners' Journal*, May 1879

Sweet, rich, and refreshing ices and ice creams—this was the course where Parkinson's guests were treated to the finest, most innovative culinary creations he could dish out—the *pièce de résistance* of the whole meal. James Parkinson was the unrivaled expert at crafting Philadelphia style ice cream, also called custard cream or Philadelphia cream, often considered the prototype of frozen desserts in America. During the second half of the nineteenth century, Parkinson's ice cream was renowned as the best of the best—

not only in Philadelphia, but throughout the United States. According to judge and writer Robert T. Conrad, Parkinson's creations were unforgettable, "like a wind from the 'Snowy Caucasus' sweeping over the traveler in the dusty plain . . . the *ne plus ultra* of art."[1]

Ice cream was not invented in America (forms of ice creams have been around since the thirteenth century), but both Philadelphia and the Parkinson family played significant roles promoting the icy indulgence. Often referred to as "Ice Cream City," Philadelphia was situated in a highly advantageous location, ideal for making excellent ice cream. The Schuylkill and Delaware rivers that sandwiched the city produced plentiful ice harvests each winter, and fresh, quality dairy ingredients were regularly delivered to its markets from local farms.[2]

As a staunch advocate for American foods, Parkinson boasted that the smooth and creamy ices made from rich Philadelphia cream were unique and original, a product of the region's fertile bounty. "This delicious dish smacked of the fat of the land," he said. He also claimed that his father's (George Parkinson) establishment was the first to *manufacture* ice cream, and the first to give Philadelphia ice cream "its celebrity throughout the country."[3]

And although he described the concept of edible frozen treats (such as iced-fruit waters, fruits molded in ice, iced custard, and sherbet) as dating back to the ancient Egyptians, he claimed that ice cream "as it is known by us" had its origins in America. He admitted that England, Italy, Germany, France, and Turkey made various water ices "of great delicacy," but their version of ice creams were "merely flavored *custards*, made of eggs, sugar and milk." They were "a nice dessert . . . but *not* ice cream," he said. In his opinion, no European city produced ice cream on par with what could be found in Philadelphia, Boston, New York, and Chicago in the late 1870s.[4]

According to Parkinson, in order to make ice creams of this caliber, it was crucial to use only premium ingredients—the best white sugar and finest flavors, and absolutely fresh, pure, rich, sweet cream. He stressed that the cream "cannot be too good," and "always kept on ice until wanted for use." Very closely monitoring the ice cream during the freezing process and exactly following the recipe directions was also critical. He assured readers of his *Confectioners' Journal* that these steps were well worth it, since "properly prepared and served they [ices] not only enrich and adorn the table of hospitality, but they largely contribute to the health and comfort of the customer."[5]

It's difficult to imagine that this famously decadent Philadelphia ice cream could be improved on, but Parkinson introduced and/or invented several of his own signature flavors, including pistachio ice cream, Parkinson's original ice cream punch, and Brahma's ice (a creamy frozen treat based on an authentic recipe from India, made with egg whites, curaçao, and orange-flower water). In fact, it was said that Parkinson could go into a confectionery store and "point out at least fifty different articles on the shelves" that were his own original inventions.[6]

It's no big surprise that he featured some of these delectable creations on the menu for the Thousand Dollar Dinner, including caramel ice cream, biscuit glacé (a rich custardy dessert made with sponge cake and vanilla liquor), and Champagne frappe à la glacé (a frothy ice made with the French sparkling wine). These elegant and complex flavors undoubtedly would have provided a unique experience.

Ice cream flavors in the nineteenth century were quite different from today, based on the ingredients that were fashionable and available at the time, with fruit flavors the most common. In the 1840s and 1850s the most popular flavors were vanilla, lemon, strawberry, and pineapple.[7] Keeping with what was in style, Parkinson includes three of these on his menu—vanilla, strawberry, and lemon, but what is probably most notable to our modern palates is the absence of chocolate.

The earliest printed reference to a frozen chocolate dessert is from a 1768 cookbook entitled *L'Art de Bien Faire les Glaces d'Office* by a Frenchman named Emy. His recipe—glace de crème au cacao—called for stiffly beating egg whites and sugar, mixing with cream until thickened, then adding roasted cacao beans and cooking the mixture in a warm water bath until the flavor of the chocolate permeated the cream. After an hour or two, he strained the mixture, then chilled it and froze it.[8]

But in the eighteenth century chocolate ice cream was still the exception, not the rule, mainly because the cacao beans used to make chocolate were expensive and difficult to process. Early recipes for edible chocolate required making a paste out of cacao beans, then adding sugar and other flavors (such as cloves and cinnamon). But through the mid-nineteenth century, chocolate was consumed mainly as a beverage, often served as an alternative to tea or coffee.[9]

In 1828 a Dutchman by the name of van Houten patented a way to simplify cacao processing by pressing out most of the fat and alkalizing the dry cocoa that remained. This changed the way hot chocolate was prepared and revolutionized the manufacturing of chocolate, allowing it to assume solid, liquid, and powdered form, paving the way for all kinds of chocolate dessert possibilities. In the decades that followed, recipes for chocolate blancmanges, mousses, creams, cream pies, custards, puddings, soufflés, and syrups began appearing more frequently in period cookbooks.[10]

Early chocolate ice cream recipes were more custardlike, with the addition of egg yolks, such as the recipe from *The Italian Confectioner* (1820), which called for a pint of cream, eight fresh egg yolks, half a pound of sugar, and four ounces of "good chocolate dissolved in a little warm water." Eleanor Parkinson's recipe for "chocolate ice" is very similar—fresh cream, eggs, sugar, and chocolate dissolved in water.[11]

Although Parkinson does include chocolate ice cream on later menus from the 1870s and 1880s, he probably didn't serve the flavor at the Thousand Dollar Dinner in 1851 simply because it was not that popular at the time. Or perhaps he preferred to serve flavors that were his signatures and he knew would be impeccable since there were still improvements to be made to chocolate ice cream.

In the mid-nineteenth century, ice cream and other frozen treats were getting more reasonably priced, but they were still a special treat mostly reserved for the wealthy due to the time and labor involved as well as the cost of the ingredients, particularly the ice delivery. They were most often served in special pleasure gardens or ice cream parlors, or as an elegant way to end a dinner party, and the flavors reflected this extravagance.

Parkinson divided icy desserts into six distinct classes, each featuring slightly different ingredients, textures, and serving specifications: creams, custards, water ices, frozen fruit, wine or liquor punches, and sorbets and graniti (semi-ices). "Philadelphia ice cream" was traditionally uncooked, made with just fresh cream, fruit juice, or pulp, sugar or sugared syrup, and flavoring such as vanilla beans, thoroughly blended for a smooth consistency and rich flavor. This was the style Parkinson's mother Eleanor featured in her book *The Complete Confectioner* (1844). However, James deviated from this version over time, incorporating eggs in some of his ice cream recipes.[12]

For example, in an 1876 *Confectioners' Journal* article, he includes recipes for vanilla, lemon, pineapple, and strawberry ice cream that list only cream, vanilla beans, sugar, and fruit as ingredients. But in another article in the same publication three years later, his definition of "cream ices" includes the addition of eggs. A specific example is his recipe for caramel ice cream, meant to conjure the essence of cream caramel candy. To make it, he instructs heating sugar, water, and lemon juice to make burnt caramel syrup, then folding it into a thickened cream and egg mixture. Other ingredients that enhance the flavor include lemon zest, cinnamon, and orange curaçao.[13] Perhaps experimenting with different flavors and ingredients led him to change things, adding eggs to thicken and enrich some of his ice creams.

Parkinson's description of custard was similar to ice cream, except egg yolks were used instead of whole eggs and the ingredients were heated over a fire until the mixture was thick and smooth, then rubbed through a sieve before freezing. His biscuit glacé (referred to as a "nectarous composition" by the *Philadelphia Inquirer*) was made in this manner. The "biscuit" was sponge cake that had been dried in the oven and pounded into a rich powder. It was then added to a heated and thickened mixture of cream, sugar, eggs, vanilla sugar, and vanilla liquor during the final freezing stage, before the ice cream was fully hardened. The concept took off and other versions emerged which featured biscuit, cake, shortbread, or even breadcrumbs (either toasted or plain).[14]

Biscuit ices were often frozen in special little boxes, or cases, made with sheets of very strong paper. Delmonico chef Charles Ranhofer frequently served these little packages with a pretty striped look. He would fill the cases halfway with biscuit ice cream, add a middle layer of fruits and macaroons, then another layer of the ice cream. After a brief freeze he would decorate the top with whipped cream tinted rose-pink.[15]

Harlequin ice cream was also a colorful rainbow of layers, formed by placing a small quantity of different types of ice creams in the same mold. The idea was similar to today's Neapolitan ice cream, but instead of the now-familiar vanilla-chocolate-strawberry combination, other flavors such as pistachio or pineapple were often included in order to provide an even greater contrast of hues. According to Eleanor Parkinson, it produced "a good effect for the table, but is not much admired on account of the jumble of flavours."[16]

In the nineteenth century, this concept of forming ices and ice cream into intricate shapes and molds was a popular way to present frozen desserts. Not only were the designs attractive and elegant, but the molds also made "turning the creams out and keeping them ready to dish up" easier. In order to create these designs, chefs would scoop ice cream into pre-chilled molds and place them in an icebox on a bed of salted ice. To remove the ice cream from the mold, they would carefully set it in warm water and then place the molded shapes back in the freezer until they were ready to decorate.[17]

Made out of pewter, copper, or tin, the molds for these designs ranged from simple fruits and flowers to elaborate replications of a scene or object, such as a wishing well or statue of Bacchus (the Roman god of wine) sitting atop a wine barrel. Other molds might seem odd and unappetizing to our modern tastes as they were meant to depict items such as cuts of meat, whole fish and fish heads, mushrooms, and pickles.[18]

Parkinson was a master at creating complicated frozen dessert creations. Examples of his artistry include an ice cream polar bear perched on an iceberg, an ice sculpture of intertwined dolphins balancing a frozen pudding, and an icy fruit bowl containing pears, apples, and peaches made out of ice cream, tinted and flavored "to imitate nature." But perhaps his most famous was a colorful nightingale suspended from a harp, created as homage to singer Jenny Lind, known as the "Swedish nightingale," a gesture that deeply impressed her.[19]

Today water ice is more of a casual thirst-quenching summer treat, a refreshing way to cool off while basking at the beach or watching a baseball game. But in the nineteenth century it was often served at elegant dinner parties. Parkinson described water ice as fruit pulp or juice mixed with syrup or sugar, lemon juice, and water sufficient to achieve a proper consistency when frozen. The *Confectioners' Journal* warned that the flavoring should be added in small increments to prevent overpowering the taste. Water ice was made from just about every kind of fruit, including peaches, apricots, redcurrants, lemons, grapes, cherries, pineapples, damsons (plums), raspberries, and even gooseberries. Orange was the flavor featured by Parkinson at the Thousand Dollar Dinner—his recipe called for a dozen Florida oranges and two lemons.[20]

Two types of frozen drinks were also included in this course—Punche à la Romanine (Roman punch) and Parkinson's own elegant invention, Champagne frappe à la glacé (literally translated as "Champagne hits the ice"). Served in ornate glasses with handles, frozen punches featured a base of rich lemonade mixed with a combination of liquor and fruit—slushy in consistency but still pourable. According to Parkinson, punches were usually served as "a half ice or semi-solid" alongside the soup course at dinners and banquets. They were "particularly adapted to be taken with turtle, gumbo, or any rich heavy soup," he said.[21]

As previously mentioned, punches were also a popular palate cleanser between courses. Delmonico chef Charles Ranhofer specified that punch or sherbet should be served between the last entrée and the roast. "The difference between sherbet and punch is that the former is a water ice into which some liquor is mixed, while punch is an ice either of water or cream mingled with a quarter as much Italian meringue and liquors."[22]

Punche à la Romanine (said to have been brought to Paris from Rome) had an interesting ingredient list: a quart of lemon water ice, flavored with a glass or two of rum, brandy, Champagne, and Maraschino. When frozen, it was combined with a meringue made from boiled sugar mixed with frothy whipped egg whites. It was then chilled and served in glasses with a small spoon.[23] Very decadent indeed.

Parkinson was once again showcasing his skills as an innovator by veering a little away from the norm by serving punch with a dessert course. In any case, these drinks would have provided an extra kick that was surely appreciated by the thirty gentlemen diners.

FRUITS AND NUTS

Apples • Figs • Walnuts • Pecan Nuts
Oranges • Raisins • Almonds • Filberts

"Fruit is man's luxury under all circumstances—his dessert."
—Thomas Farrington De Voe, *The Market Assistant*, 1867

Fruits are perhaps the oldest form of desserts. Naturally sweet and rich tasting, they were often featured at the end of a meal in ancient times, either fresh or dried, sometimes paired with honey, milk, or cheese dishes.[1]

In the eighteenth century, dessert (singular) was used to designate this final course of fruit and sweetmeats, which was either placed on the table after a meal or served at a separate table. Fruits could be served raw, cooked, stewed, or preserved as thick jams, in coulis, juices, and sorbets. During the colder months, an assortment of nuts, dried figs, and dates might also have been included.[2]

This idea and terminology came from the French word *desservi* (meaning the course after the table was cleared). In the French style of dining it was the first time in the meal the table was completely cleared. Up to this point, dishes were simply taken away and replaced by others. It was common to remove the tablecloth as well, revealing a second tablecloth underneath for the dessert.[3]

Since dessert was designed to impress, during the early to mid-eighteenth century, chefs would build fruit and sweetmeats into impressive pyramids decorated with flowers and candelabras. A century later, stately, elegant tazzas holding colorful displays of fresh fruits were placed down the middle of the table,[4] alternated with dried fruits, bonbons, and other preserved confections served on small round or oval glass plates. It was also fashionable to serve forced fruit growing in ornamental pots, arranged among the other dishes. "The garnishing needs especial attention, as the contrast of the brilliant-coloured fruits with nicely-arranged foliage is very charming," noted British cookbook author Isabella Beeton.[5]

By the second half of the nineteenth century dessert had evolved to signify a variety of sweet selections. This change had its roots in America, since dessert had developed a wider meaning there as early as the eighteenth century.[6] As Jessup Whitehead states in *The Steward's Handbook and Guide to Party Catering*, "It is the general custom to apply the term dessert to all the sweets that constitute the second service of the dinner . . . but 'dessert' alone means fruit, confectionery, very light sweets and ices."[7]

When fruit was served in its whole form, a whole set of etiquette rules developed around the most sophisticated way to eat it. As Eliza Leslie wrote in 1864, "It is very ungraceful to eat an orange at the table, unless having cut a bit off the top, you eat the inside with a teaspoon." Eventually specialized serving dishes and cutlery were introduced to make the experience easier and more elegant, such as orange cups designed to hold half an orange (similar to an egg cup or a grapefruit bowl), orange knives and peelers, and orange spoons with pointed tips. In her book *Practical Cooking, and Dinner Giving* (1878), Mary F. Henderson discusses "How they eat oranges in Havana." This innovative method involved piercing a fork through the center of the orange, holding it with the left hand like a handle, and then peeling the skin in strips from the top of the orange to the fork handle, leaving all the fibrous pulp on the fork.[8]

Even though all fruits and nuts were enjoyed, some were considered more appropriate for dessert than others, based on taste, appearance, and sweetness. Mrs. Beeton recommended pineapples, melons, grapes, peaches, nectarines, plums, strawberries, apples, pears, oranges, almonds, raisins, figs, walnuts, filberts, medlars, cherries, and all kinds of dried fruits, together with the "most costly and *recherché* wines." And among these types of fruits, there were preferred "dessert varieties," such as Williams apples and Houghton's seedling gooseberries. According to *The American Fruit Book* (1849), "A dessert apple should be of good size, handsome form, beautiful color, fair appearance, tender, crisp, juicy, and of a rich, fine flavor."[9]

Fruits were not only considered a delicious meal-ending treat, but also nutritious and even medicinal. According to Thomas Farrington De Voe, author of *The Market Assistant*, fruits produced "beneficial changes in the blood," and helped neutralize or remove "diseases lurking in the system." De Voe also noted the differences in the way fruits were consumed in the United States compared to Europe. The vast acres of open land in America available for growing fruit allowed a greater percentage of the population to partake of this bounty, he proclaimed. But in Europe, where space was often at a premium, it was another story. "Even to the wealthy, fruits are a luxury—a dessert," he said.[10]

According to James Parkinson, the quality of American fruits was also unparalleled. He felt the country's pears, peaches, cherries, plums, currants, raspberries, and strawberries equaled the best grown anywhere. Apparently this lusciousness was recognized overseas as well, since he claimed that American Greening and pippin apples were "among the most highly-prized dainties at the feasts of kings, queens, and emperors in Europe," and Tallman Sweets were shipped to England to supply the tables at Windsor Castle.[11]

But fruits had their seasons; so serving them fresh was not always possible depending on the time of year. Many fruits were also fragile and could spoil easily, so in the days before refrigeration, shipping and storing them was often difficult. However, there were some alternatives, such as placing citrus fruits stalk-end down in a vessel full of sand for cold storage.[12] Apples would also keep fairly well all winter in a root cellar.

Another way to enjoy fruits year-round was to preserve them in sugary syrup. In her cookbook *Seventy-five Receipts for Pastry, Cakes and Sweetmeats* (1828), Eliza Leslie described how to preserve fruits such as crab apples, cranberries, gooseberries, pineapple, peaches, plums, quinces, strawberries, and even pumpkin.[13]

Fruits were pared and cored or pitted, then cut in half, quartered, or sliced. Peaches could also be preserved whole, which involved peeling them first, then using a skewer to push out the pit. They were boiled until tender in a preserving kettle,[14] then carefully removed and set aside. The juice that remained was strained and combined with sugar (the general rule was a pound of sugar per pound of fruit). Sometimes flavorings such as lemon, cinnamon, or brandy (also a preservative) were added to the syrup. The fruit was put back in the kettle and boiled in the juicy syrup until thick. It was then transferred to large glass jars and the syrup poured over the top. When cool, a sheet of paper that had been dipped in brandy was laid on top to form a seal between the preserves and the lid. Sometimes the underside of the paper was also coated with egg white, which helped create a tighter seal, keeping out air and insects.[15]

Mrs. A. L. Webster, author of *The Improved Housewife* (1853), recommended checking on preserved fruit often "to see that it does not ferment." If this did happen, she advised pouring off the syrup, boiling it and then adding it back to the jar while still hot.[16]

So, even though sugar and brandy helped preserve the cooked fruit, it could still ferment over time, a longstanding predicament until the invention of a glass "fruit jar" by John L. Mason. Mason jars revolutionized fruit (and vegetable) preservation, making the task easier for home cooks and opening the door for a commercial industry. Patented in 1858, Mason's jar had a self-sealing screw-on zinc lid. A rubber gasket between the lid and glass zip ensured a tight seal. By the 1860s, these jars were being shipped throughout the United States.[17]

Since the rubber gasket prevented air from getting inside and spoiling the fruit, much less sugar was needed. As a result, cookbooks began differentiating between canning and preserving. In canning, fruit was kept fresh with or without sugar by sealing in airtight jars or cans, but preserves required a one-to-one ratio of sugar to fruit. As Marion Harland noted in 1871, "Within a few years canned fruits have, in a great measure superseded preserves. They are cheaper, more wholesome, and far less difficult to prepare."[18]

Crystallizing (extracting the juice and replacing it with sugar syrup) was another way to preserve fruits. The process was rather time consuming, involving boiling the fruit, making a sugar syrup, and then covering the fruit to allow it to absorb the sugar. When fully fermented, the fruit was removed from the syrup and rinsed with water. It could then be either glazed (dipped in thick sugar syrup and left to quickly harden) or crystallized (dipped in the same type of syrup but cooled and hardened slowly, thus causing the sugar covering the fruit to crystallize).[19]

Jessup Whitehead called crystallized fruits "a very acceptable dish for dessert; they ornament the table and please the palate." He recommended stacking them in an arrangement by color—using the darker hues such as greengages (a type of European plum) for the base, brighter tints such as apricots and oranges for the upper portion, and filling in any open spots with cherries and raspberries.[20]

Fruits were also made into marmalade, jams, and jellies. Marmalades and jams were made from fruit pulp that has been combined with sugar and boiled down to a chunky, yet somewhat firm, spreadable consistency. The sugar ratio was similar to making preserved fruit. However, Eleanor Parkinson advised against adding too much sugar, which would cause the mixture to crystallize. On the other hand, if not enough sugar was added or it wasn't sufficiently boiled, it would quickly ferment. Jellies were made using the juices of mucilaginous fruits (those that secrete a naturally gelatinous substance such as apples, quince, raspberries, and blackberries). The juice was clarified by filtering through a flannel bag, then an equal weight of sugar was added and the mixture was boiled until it was the consistency of jelly.[21]

Some fruits were served with a thin coating of sugary icing. Grapes made a particularly pretty presentation, typically on glass plates. Bunches of ripe, thin-skinned grapes were dipped into beaten egg white, then drained and rolled in a flat dish of superfine granulated sugar until they were completely coated. Individual fruits such as raspberries, strawberries, gooseberries, peaches, plums, and cherries were also prepared this way.[22]

Just as with fruits, a variety of nuts were consumed in the nineteenth century, but certain ones were more likely to be enjoyed with dessert, particularly almonds, brazil nuts, filberts, hickory nuts, pecans, and walnuts. Several different varieties of almonds were known, but the two most important were sweet almonds and bitter almonds. Sweet almonds were for eating—they were first blanched to remove the outer skin and then dried. Bitter almonds (which are actually poisonous in large amounts) were typically used only by confectioners who understood how to extract and safely utilize their strong, bitter taste.[23]

Walnuts also came in many varieties, with the English walnut (also called the Persian, Grenoble, or Madeira nut) the most popular. Native to the Iranian province of Gilan, it was grown in Europe and America by the nineteenth century. James Parkinson described it as large, fine flavored, and "highly valued as an article of dessert." Filberts were cultivated hazelnuts, generally imported from Europe. However, Parkinson preferred the American hazelnut due to its sweeter taste. "This nut is a most valuable adjunct to the dessert table, and when serious drinking is contemplated it is usually eaten with salt," he claimed.[24]

WINES

Rhenish—Soft, old, very rare extra Cabinet
Marcobrunn of 1834, specially obtained from the cellar of
the Duke of Nassau

Médoc
Montrose of 1840, very choice and delicate, bottled in 1844,
and especially selected from the stock of VALE & Co., at Bordeaux

MARCOBRUNN RHINE WINE

As early as the mid 1150s, Germany transported their wines up the Rhine River, supplying English kings and other nobility with dry wine. As a result, any wine shipped on the Rhine River was labeled "Rhenish," no matter where it originated.[25] By the nineteenth century, however, the definition of Rhenish wines had narrowed to designate wines produced in the valleys surrounding the Rhine, particularly the Rheingau, a small district in the vicinity of the Duchy of Nassau.[26]

During this timeframe, Germany's system of aristocratic wine estates equaled the quality of the great wine chateaux of France, with Rhenish wines as costly and celebrated as Bordeaux, well known for their ability to age better than any other wines. "In Germany the wine-culture may almost be said to assume the form of a passion, which pervades all classes from the prince to the peasant," wrote nineteenth-century German guidebook publisher Karl Baedeker. Wine cellars under the employ of the Duke of Nassau were particularly famous for their "Cabinet" wines.[27]

One of the most highly prized Rhenish wines was Markobrunner (also spelled Marcobrunner) from the village of Erbach, near the Markbrunnen (meaning boundary fountain). The Duke of Nassau spared no expense in maintaining and cultivating his vineyards. As a result, Marcobrunner were wines of exquisite flavor and bouquet.[28] This was the varietal chosen by Parkinson to pair with his ending course of fruit and nuts. In addition, the vintage he served was from 1834, considered one of the best years for Rheingau wines in the nineteenth century due to the decade's mild weather conditions. Once again Parkinson was treating his guests to the very best wine available at the time.

Château Montrose Médoc

Because the wines of the Médoc possess such a wide variety of qualities, the French have developed a growth system to classify them, the result of years of observation and study that can be traced back to the eighteenth century. As noted by wine expert Tom Stevenson, "The style of wine alters more radically over short distances in the Médoc than in any other French red wine district."[29]

For this final course, James Parkinson chose to serve Médoc from Château Montrose. The youngest of the cru (growth) classé vineyards, this wine would have been from fairly newly planted vines at the time of the Thousand Dollar Dinner in 1851. Construction on the chateau and the first grape plantings began around 1815, and the vineyard expanded quickly. By 1855 it boasted 237 acres of vines and second growth labeling of its wines, just one step below first growth, the top Bordeaux grading classification.[30]

Located within St. Estephe, the northernmost of the four communes that make up the Médoc district, the vineyard has soil that is rich in clay and slow to drain, enabling its vines to withstand hot, dry summers. The wines tend to be full-bodied and rich in tannins. An 1846 book on Bordeaux wines describes wines of the Upper Médoc as possessing the grand characteristics of superior delicacy, richness, and, especially, bouquet. This book also mentions the lack of terroir, or "that taste of the soil," typically found in the wines of the Lower Médoc.[31] Parkinson's choice probably was rich, full, and fruity, a suitable pairing for the fruit and nuts he served.

CAFÉ NOIR

Café Noir

LIQUERES

Maraschino • Curaçoa

"After a hearty dinner, especially if the food is rich in animal oil, a small cup of strong black coffee, drank without milk, but with a liberal allowance of sugar, is found to promote digestion and a lively flow of spirits."

—Joseph B. Lyman and Laura E. Lyman,
The Philosophy of Housekeeping, 1869

The evening had come and gone and it was now the early hours of the morning. The thirty gentlemen guests had been eating, drinking, and conversing for more than eleven hours. Things were finally winding down, but before they headed out into the soft glow of a new day, they were treated to a cup of dark, rich coffee accompanied by some sweet after-dinner liquors.

Today coffee is grown in warmer climates all over the world, but the tree is native to eastern Africa and Arabia—what is now

Ethiopia, Sudan, and Yemen. It is not known exactly when it was discovered that a robust stimulating drink could be made from the seeds (coffee beans) enclosed within the tree's small red berries. One legend tells the story of a goatherd who noticed his goats became agitated when they chewed the leaves of the coffee tree. Whatever the case, it was the Arabs who first enjoyed its virtues, establishing coffee houses as popular gathering places by the sixteenth century.[1]

Coffee was introduced into Western Europe in the 1600s where it became a fashionable drink among French nobility, and by the mid-nineteenth century it had infiltrated all social classes in France. In America, it was the Boston Tea Party in 1773 that led to the popularization of coffee in the colonies, a caffeinated alternative to the boycotted tea. American consumption of coffee slowly increased during the first half of the nineteenth century, aided by the War of 1812 when the tea supply was cut off. Coffee plantations had sprung up in Brazil and the Caribbean, making it easier for Americans to obtain. In addition, French styles were all the rage at this time, and Americans readily adopted the French coffee-drinking habit. By 1850, Americans drank almost four times as much coffee as they did tea.[2]

One reason the French style of coffee was so revered owed to its preparation method—a more sophisticated brewing technique that filtered the coffee. Americans tended to make coffee similar to today's instant coffee—adding ground coffee to boiling water. However this method required isinglass or egg white to clarify the muddy mixture, and a waiting period for the contents to settle. In *Directions for Cookery* (1844), Eliza Leslie gives detailed instructions:

> Allow half a pint of ground coffee to three pints of water. If the coffee is not freshly roasted, you should put in more. Put the water into the tin coffee-pot and set it on hot coals: when it boils, put in the coffee, a spoonful at a time, (stirring it between each spoonful,) and add two or three chips of isin-

glass, or lite white of an egg. Stir it frequently, till it has risen up to the top in boiling; then set it a little farther from the fire, and boil it gently for ten minutes, or a quarter of an hour; after which pour in a tea-cup of cold water, and put it in the corner to settle for ten minutes. Scald your silver or china pot, and transfer the coffee to it; carefully pouring it off from the grounds, so as not to disturb them.[3]

Not only was this technique time-consuming, it also resulted in a cup of coffee that was not nearly as fragrant, as much of the aroma was lost via evaporation. As Leslie warns, "If coffee is allowed to boil too long, it will lose much of its strength, and also become sour." In *The Dessert Book* (1872) by "A Boston Lady," the anonymous author so strongly opposes this method that she tells the reader, "Lay it down as a maxim, that no coffee can be good if it is boiled even for a minute. Water in a state of ebullition becomes more highly colored, indeed; but it fails to extract the delicate aroma and tonic properties of the powder; whilst the beverage into which it becomes converted is apt to produce flatulence, a sense of oppression, and many other physical discomforts, not to say positive injury."[4]

The method this author does recommend is the French style of filtering coffee with boiling water, or making use of one of the numerous types of *cafetières*, French coffee pots which brewed the coffee using an infusion of steam. Freshly ground coffee was placed in the upper portion of the pot and a strainer positioned over the top. Boiling water was slowly poured over it, and then the pot was covered and placed in a warm spot. When all the coffee had drained from the upper compartment to the lower one, it was ready.[5] Eliza Leslie advised using a cafetière called a biggin, fitted with a tin (not linen) strainer. She found those shaped in the form of an urn most practical, as they could be used to both make the coffee and bring it to the table.[6]

Many of us cannot fathom greeting the morning without a cup of hot, steaming, aromatic coffee. But the coffee served in this ending course was not a mild breakfast blend. The custom of serving coffee after a meal began among the French upper classes at the end of the seventeenth century. Known as *café noir*, this strong, black after-dinner coffee was also made in the French style. The difference was either less water or more coffee was used in order to make it more robust. In addition, after the coffee was brewed, it was filtered through the coffee pot two or three times before serving, which increased the strength.[7]

The stimulating effects of café noir were thought to speed digestion and relieve "the sense of plentitude in the stomach," especially advantageous after a large dinner.[8] The strong coffee was served in petite, elegant "half" cups called demitasses and could be sweetened with sugar, but no accompanying milk or cream. It was often paired with some sort of after-dinner liqueur, which was sometimes added to the coffee. Jules Arthur Harder (chef de cuisine of San Francisco's Palace Hotel) recommended the addition of brandy, kirschwasser, or rum. These spirits could be burnt with sugar before adding to the coffee by pouring a small quantity over a lump of sugar in a teaspoon resting on the cup. Called *brulo*, it helped facilitate digestion and excited the faculties of the mind, Harder commented.[9]

During the seventeenth century, coffeehouses popped up all over Europe, first in Italy, England, and France. These coffeehouses were meeting places where a wide variety of subjects could be discussed. The caffeinated beverage was an intellectual stimulant, encouraging energetic conversation. In addition to coffee, other beverages including liquor, tea, and hot chocolate were typically served, as well as some food items. By 1700 there were more than two thousand London coffeehouses, occupying more space and contributing more rent than any other trade.[10]

The custom was brought over to America, where coffeehouses could be found in the financial districts and marketplaces of Boston, New York, and Philadelphia starting in the late 1600s. Just as in Europe, these places offered spirits as well as coffee, serving as a sort of businessman's tavern. However, unlike the European coffeehouses, those in colonial America sometimes functioned as a courthouse for trials, particularly in New York. General assembly and council meetings were also sometimes held there.[11]

American coffeehouses became very important for merchants and sea captains transporting goods around the world. One of the most famous was Philadelphia's London Coffee House, established in 1754 by newspaper publisher William Bradford. Named after the famous London institution, it was frequented by many ship captains and travelers, who used it as a place to exchange messages and post and hold auctions. Merchants gathered at noon to read newspapers, discuss prices, and schedule the shipping of goods. New York City's unofficial auction house and commodity exchange was the Exchange Coffee House, opened in the 1730s. About twenty years later the Merchants Coffee House took over this role and became known as the most celebrated coffeehouse in New York.[12]

LIQUEURS

The liqueurs Parkinson chose to follow the dark café noir were Maraschino and curaçoa (also known as curaçao), both extremely popular in the nineteenth century. As one author noted, they were "more extensively used than any other liqueurs. So much is this the case that it is a matter of custom to speak of the one as the king and the other as the queen of liqueurs." Toward the end of the century, however, these liqueurs were more often used as a flavoring for foods, particularly desserts, such as ice cream, soufflés, puddings, custards, and fruit compotes. They were also incorporated into many cocktails and punches.[13]

MARASCHINO
Today Maraschino cherries are most often known as the super-sweet garnish added to an ice cream sundae, as in the phrase "with

a cherry on top." But the Marasca, or black cherry, is also mashed and fermented to produce a bittersweet colorless liqueur, called Maraschino di Zara, named after Zadar, the picturesque historical town in Croatia where it originated. These cherries grow wild along the coast of the country's Dalmatia region.[14]

To make the liqueur, the small black cherry (also called a gean) is combined with crushed cherry pits, giving it a subtle bitter almond flavor. The mixture is put through a distillation process similar to brandy and then sweetened with sugar or cane syrup before it is aged and filtered. It is one of the few liqueurs in the world produced by distillation.[15]

In the mid-nineteenth century it was very fashionable in Europe to end a dinner with a glass of Maraschino or other liqueur after coffee. The practice soon spread to England and America.[16] Apparently women had a particular affinity for Maraschino. According to Scottish journalist E. S. Dallas, "The liqueur is made so sweet that women take to it as flies to honey and as moths to candles. It is a curious fact in natural history that the fair sex prefer a sweet liqueur to the finest wine; and they have such a tendency to Maraschino."[17]

Curaçoa

Also called curaçao, this liqueur was originally made using the dried peels of the laraha citrus fruit from the island of Curaçao, located off the coast of Venezuela. A descendant of the Valencia orange, the laraha evolved after efforts to grow the orange in the hot, dry climate failed. Although the bitter fruit was determined inedible, the peels were found to be fragrant and well suited to make a pleasant liqueur. The process involved macerating the peels with a little cinnamon and a few cloves in sweetened brandy, producing two different types of curaçao—one white and the other red.[18]

Eventually the manufacture of the liqueur moved to Amsterdam, and Seville oranges were used as a substitute. It was also often made at home—recipes for replicating curaçao abound in nineteenth-century cookbooks, encyclopedias, and liquor guides. *Goodholme's Domestic Cyclopaedia of Practical Information* (1889) gives the following instructions for making curaçao:

> A fair quality can be made at home by taking the rind of six oranges, peeling off as thin as possible, without retaining any of the white skin. Put it into a glass jar with a cover closing tight; pour over it a quart each of best brandy and rectified spirits of wine. Let it steep in a warm place for a fortnight; then strain the liquor carefully away from the orange peel. Melt two pounds of loaf sugar into a wineglassful of water, and when nearly cold, pour it into the liquor, stirring well. Then bottle it off, and use as required.[19]

Today there is still one company that makes curaçao liqueur using the island's laraha fruit, but many different liquor houses also make versions of the orange liqueur. These are often sold as "triple sec," and can be colorless, yellow, orange, or a "Caribbean" blue.[20]

AN OVATION

"On Saturday evening, the 19th instant, thirty gentlemen sat down to a dinner at J. W. Parkinson's, South Eighth St. below Chestnut, which for magnificence outvied anything ever seen in the United States."

—*Philadelphia Evening Bulletin*, April 1851

Perhaps the richest, most elegant, elaborate and poetical entertainment ever gotten up in this country, was achieved in this city last week by the accomplished confectioner and caterer, James W. Parkinson.

—*American Courier*, April 1851

SUNDAY, APRIL 20, 1851, 6 A.M.

The slender, tapered candles had burned down to their wicks, the ice in the buckets was melted, and the buffet was lined with empty wine bottles. Only bits and crumbs remained on the cake stands that had proudly displayed the elaborately decorated gateaux and other confections. Parkinson's thirty guests were still seated around the table, lingering over their coffee and liquors, discussing politics, the economy, and other affairs of the day. Some puffed on cigars. They were relaxed, satiated, and getting drowsy.

The eventful evening was finally at an end. As if on cue, master chef James Parkinson strode into the banquet room from the kitchen, his beaming face flushed from the heat of the ovens, the exertion from being on his feet for so many hours, and the thrill of his success. Upon seeing the creator of the sumptuous feast they had just experienced, the men were on their feet, clapping and nodding their resounding approval. Parkinson humbly took a bow, once again thanking them all for coming and giving him the chance to show them the exceptional food and preparations available in the city of Philadelphia.

The men rose from their chairs and stretched their arms and legs. The waiters assisted them in gathering their belongings. The guests all made sure that they took their menu as evidence of their privileged attendance at this extravagant feast. As they said their good-byes to Parkinson, both the New Yorkers and Philadelphians thanked him once again and took a last look around, etching every vivid detail in their minds. They slowly descended the stairs, retrieved their coats and bags, and stepped out into the muted light of the morning. A cluster of shiny carriages was waiting to take the New York gentlemen to their hotel, and the Philadelphians back to their residences. Their bags were loaded as they said their good-byes and stepped into the carriages, sighing as they sat down, resting their heads back against the cushioned seats. They all welcomed the thought of a good, long sleep but their minds still swirled around the past twelve hours. The Thousand Dollar Dinner was over.

Unfortunately James W. Parkinson is no longer a household name in America or even his home city of Philadelphia. But his achievements and impact are significant. Both he and the Delmonico family had used their confectionery skills as a springboard—first making a splash through their popular sweet shops and then expanding into the restaurant business. However, while Delmonico's concentrated on setting the tone for fine dining, James Parkinson strived to make his eateries an engaging experience on many levels. Parents could bring their children for ice cream, courting couples could enjoy a stroll in the gardens, ladies could enjoy lunch in the ladies' salon, and those seeking an elegant dinner had their choice of seating—the main public dining area, a private parlor, or outside in the garden during warmer months. Parkinson's even served breakfast.[1]

And although Parkinson was successful for many years, he may have had a somewhat more difficult road than the Delmonico family. After his parents died, he was essentially running the show alone, unlike the Delmonicos, who kept bringing new family members into the fold. Parkinson had a sister, Eliza, who married a confectioner named Samuel Hutchison, but they divorced in 1842 and there is no record that he and James ever went into business together. Parkinson was also briefly married and had a daughter, Ida, but again, it doesn't appear she ever joined the restaurant business. Although James did have financial support from General Cadwalader and a full staff of cooks and waiters, unlike Delmonico's, he never had the endless rotation of relatives to assist him with managing the restaurant.[2]

Perhaps because of this, he suffered from overextending himself and his operations, making his restaurant empire a shorter lived venture than Delmonico's. He was undoubtedly an energetic and driven culinary genius, which is how he managed to pull off such a venture as the Thousand Dollar Dinner and maintain his reputation as a first-class caterer and restaurateur. Ultimately, however, he was not able to sustain the enormous financial cost of Parkinson's Gardens on Tenth and Chestnut. After sinking a small fortune into trying to make it profitable, he was forced to abandon the establishment in the 1860s. As noted by author Harold Kynett, "Parkinson's suffered from the modern vice of over-reaching its capacities. Too much entertaining yielded too small dining checks." But he was by no means a failure. The opulent restaurant and entertainment venue was just one of his many ventures that secured him a spot in culinary history. Plus, he was able to continue sharing his vast gastronomic knowledge through other avenues.[3]

Parkinson continued to dabble in the restaurant business, open-ing an ice cream and confectionery shop on New York's Broadway in 1863, known as the Parkinson Caramel Depot. Announcing its grand opening, the *New York Times* referred to it as "the largest, coolest and most unique Ice Cream Saloon in the Metropolis, where the New York public can procure Parkinson's celebrated Philadelphia Ice Cream, Sherbets, Ices, etc.—world renowned for a half century past."[4] Just as his other locations, it was clean and beautifully decorated, with lush and elegant furnishings. N. P. Willis in the *Home Journal* added that in a very short time Parkinson "established a reputation for ice creams, summer bever-ages, and all things, in fact, that are taken 'for the stomach's sake,' that might well be envied by any caterer in the city or country. Philadelphia's loss is certainly our gain."[5]

By 1875 he had returned to his Philadelphia roots, opening a restaurant and café in his large private home on Walnut Street. He continued to specialize in ice creams, ices, confectionery, caramels, and dessert bonbons. In addition, he took advantage of his spa-cious residence by offering rooms for rent—either furnished or unfurnished, as well as providing catering services in his amply supplied dining rooms.[6]

Parkinson also had a journalistic side. In 1874 he wrote a lengthy testimonial in response to the Grand Duke Alexis of Russia, who visited the United States in the early 1870s and later claimed that American cookery was nonexistent and the best American cooks "were all French." Parkinson's essay, published as an editorial in the *Philadelphia Press* newspaper and also as a pam-phlet printed later entitled *American Dishes at the Centennial*, extensively sang the praises of the numerous "exclusively and dis-tinctively" American foods and dishes, meticulously pointing out the duke's inaccuracies. It was two years before Philadelphia's Centennial Exhibition (America's first official world's fair), and Parkinson declared that the rest of the world would see and taste the true excellence of American cuisine at this celebration. "American dishes at home, at the great fair in 1876, will lead to

American dishes abroad," he predicted. "America, therefore, should become, and may become, the fashion."[7]

Just a few months later, Parkinson launched the *Confectioners' Journal* with Edward Heinz (no relation to the Pittsburgh food family), serving as its highly successful and influential trade editor until his death in 1895. The informative, beautifully illustrated publication is now considered among culinary historians to be the most important resource for material about mid- to late nineteenth-century American foods. Columns written by professional confectioners shared detailed trade secrets, an "Answers to Correspondents" section (often written by Parkinson himself) provided thorough explanations to all kinds of food questions, advertisements for culinary goods and services reflected the most current techniques and technology of the day, and historical and industry news kept readers up-to-date and knowledgeable.[8] From 1882 to 1884, Parkinson was also editor of *Caterer and Household* magazine, a publication that fused light literature with gastronomy.[9]

Parkinson was a busy and productive force right up until the time he died. The fact that he kept reinventing himself and finding new ways to share his immense culinary skills shows his capacity for creativity and innovation. His culinary creations and innovative marketing techniques have infiltrated our modern culture, such as deliciously flavored ice creams and ices and "visits with Santa" at Christmas. He made sure customers paying a visit to one of his restaurants or confectionery shops had an entertaining, unforgettable experience. His written endeavors were thoughtful and informative.

Parkinson was a tireless advocate for American foods, continuously voicing the idea that an "American style" of cooking truly exists. If he were alive today, he would probably be disappointed to see the rise of American "fast food." But hopefully he would be pleased to see the range and caliber of foods available throughout the country, the trend toward shopping at farmer's markets and buying local. He would also be able to realize that his wish has indeed come true—America's culinary influence has proliferated throughout the world, sometimes fusing with the foods from other nations to provide a unique, global eating experience.

Delmonico's, which lost the friendly wager to Parkinson, remained a beacon of fine dining long after Parkinson's death. It was a restaurant dynasty that ended up ruling New York's appetite for expertly prepared food and service for nearly a century, from the 1830s through the 1920s. But Prohibition effectively ended the carefully cultivated family business.[10] The Delmonico name does continue to live on, with specialties such as Delmonico steak (developed by Chef Alexander Filippini in the 1880s). And the Delmonico name once again graces the name of a number of restaurants in New York City (owned by Delmonico's Restaurant Group), New Orleans, and Las Vegas (both owned by chef Emeril Lagasse). However, these restaurants have no connection to the Delmonico family or the original business.[11]

At this point you may be wondering the obvious question: "What would the Thousand Dollar Dinner cost today?" The purchasing power of $1,000 in 1851 would now be about $32,000, and the original dinner may have cost more; it is unclear whether the amount was just for the meal.[12] Some of the foods Parkinson featured are now difficult or impossible to procure, such as terrapin, green sea turtle, wild Atlantic salmon, and perhaps some of the game birds.

But, as we learned with mock-turtle soup, creative cooks can always come up with alternatives, which would be necessary to find modern price comparisons for a sampling of items served to the thirty guests at the 1851 dinner. For instance, East Point oysters (from Cape May, New Jersey) are the closest modern match to the Morris River Cove variety served by Parkinson. To make turtle soup, "fresh wild-caught boneless snapping turtle" could be substituted for sea turtle and farmed Atlantic salmon could be substituted for the wild. For the various fowl, wild turkeys, squab (pigeon), poussin (spring chickens), and quail (as a substitute for the game birds) can all still be procured. Likewise, some of the other meats, such as boneless beef chuck roast for the boeuf a la mode and veal sweetbreads for the Riz de Veau, Sauce Tomate are available. For the meats alone, the price would be more than $2,000.

Fruits and vegetables are in greater supply than in 1851, with some no longer the exotic or out of season delicacy of more than a century and a half ago—such as cauliflower, celery, navel oranges, and Medjool dates. Although Parkinson made all his desserts, it is safe to assume that many of them would have to be baked elsewhere today, and once again, alternatives would be necessary. For the pièces montées, a macaroon tower or a croquembouche (choux pastry balls stacked into a cone shape and laced with threads of caramel) could be substituted. Lemon tarts and marjolaines (gateaux with layers of hazelnut-almond meringue) remain favorites and can still be purchased, as can various types of confectionery. All of this is not inexpensive, however, and the desserts would cost several hundred dollars. We could re-create Parkinson's famous caramel ice cream using premium ingredients such as cream, organic eggs, superfine sugar, and curaçao (which could be used later in the dinner to serve with the coffee). The ingredients would be about $100, and adding the Tokaji for the sorbets au vin de Tokia and French roast coffee would push the cost to $200.[13]

The ingredients, such as the meats, vegetables, and eggs, and prepared foods would be many times the cost of the entire 1851 dinner. Then one must think of the labor required. To prepare and cook all of this food for thirty people, one would not only require a large specialized kitchen, but also sous chefs, a head chef, and other kitchen workers. Waitstaff and kitchen help such as dishwashers in order to replicate the dinner would be necessary, and if all of these support personnel were required to work for more than twelve hours, the costs would far exceed that of the ingredients.

And how would these dishes taste if we tried to prepare this dinner today? It is likely that many of the meats would not be as flavorful unless they were from small, local farms. Modern poultry is often plumped up with a saline solution and would taste less gamey than what Parkinson served. The Atlantic salmon would be farmed, not wild-caught. The oysters might be smaller. Many of the fowl would have to be purchased frozen, not fresh. And several of the presentations might seem odd or even unappetizing, such as the various cold dishes set in gelatin or the eating of very tiny songbirds. On the plus side, with today's modern transportation methods, obtaining the various out-of-season fruits and vegetables would not be a problem.

For the wines served, it is difficult to convert prices, because several of the bottles were shared from private collections, although one source does mention that the cognac cost $6 a pint at wholesale, which would run about $190 in today's money.[14] In 1851, all the wines of this caliber were produced in Europe, so they had to be shipped great distances in order to reach America. Restaurateurs and wine suppliers had to wait for the ships carrying the wines they wanted to buy, so Parkinson may have had a limited supply of his own to draw from. However, for this extravagant meal, he would have obtained the best wines he could, which would have included those from the city's private cellars.[15]

The wines would have also looked and tasted different. In the nineteenth century, red wines were lighter in color and more tannic than they are today. White wines (including Champagne) were much sweeter and darker hued than many modern vintages. Wine experts refer to this era as wine's "first golden age." As explained by Paul Lukacs, author of *Inventing Wine*, during this time record numbers of people began to appreciate and acquire high quality wines. Wine production increased significantly and the public progressively sought fine, quality wines. By 1851 a wine-drinking culture was emerging in upper-class America. The men at the Thousand Dollar Dinner were from the East Coast and likely well educated—they would have known something about wine.[16]

It is also important to note that these gentlemen would have been drinking pre-phylloxera wines. About a decade after Parkinson's 1851 dinner, a plant louse called *Phylloxera vastarix* was accidently imported into Europe from America and began attacking the roots of grapevines, devastating thousands of acres. The only way the vineyards were saved was though grafting the rootstocks with those from American varieties, which were resistant to phylloxera.[17]

Many wine experts believe that "French wine lost something when it was forced to graft all of its vines over to American rootstock"—a certain flavor, texture, and even purity. Those lucky enough to have tasted one of these very old, highly prized bottles claim the wine is silkier, more concentrated and intense, with an incredible scent and a long, lingering finish. However, this may be due to a variety of factors. As noted by wine expert Hugh Johnson, the phylloxera invasion "was not one event." As their vines were dying, vineyard owners tried almost anything to save them, including the use of manure and sulfur to fertilize and strengthen the roots, which increased yields dramatically. They also started adding sugar to the must before fermentation, experimented with temperature control, and started bottling earlier.[18]

If Parkinson were planning this meal today, he wouldn't be limited to European wines. As Lukacs explains, a great revolution in the world of wine has taken place over the past forty years—there has been an expansion of wine and wine making at the highest levels. Today, we would be able to enjoy quality wines from all over the globe to pair with the various foods.[19]

Nonetheless, the cost of comparable wines is incalculable, but serving rare and vintage wines today for thirty persons over multiple courses could easily exceed $10,000.[20]

While it would be difficult to create a modern version of the Thousand Dollar Dinner, the legacy of that meal is what matters most. It showcased regional specialties and laid the groundwork for a distinctive American cuisine that could rival those of Europe. It promoted the use of local ingredients, an idea increasingly valued today. But perhaps the best way to celebrate James Parkinson's remarkable feat is to toast him the next time you are proud of a dish or drink you prepared for others to enjoy.

NOTES

An Invitation

1. Built in 1849, the Jayne Building was officially ten stories (including its two-story tower); at 130 feet in height it was America's tallest building at the time. Funded by Dr. David Jayne with money he earned from his patent medicine business, the imposing Venetian Gothic style structure was located on Chestnut Street below Third. Korom, *The American Skyscraper, 1850–1940*, 31–33; Wolf, *Philadelphia: Portrait of an American City*, 191. How and when the gentlemen arrived and the specifics of the dinner were reconstructed from extensive research in period newspaper articles, advertisements, and other historical documents.

2. The Camden and Philadelphia Steamboat Company began operations in May 1838, having its termini at Bridge Avenue, Camden, and just below Chestnut Street, Philadelphia. About two years later, through a special act of the Pennsylvania Legislature (April 11, 1840), the company was authorized to hold real estate in Philadelphia not exceeding an assessed valuation of $200,000 (increased to $300,000 in 1843), and immediately purchased the Lafayette Block at the foot of Walnut Street. Reserving enough land for a ferry building and hotel, the ferry company transferred the balance of the land to the Camden and Amboy for a freight station. The hotel was long known as Bloodgood's, and until 1862, its parlor was used as the waiting room for the railroad passengers. In the latter year a waiting room was erected on the Walnut Street wharf. Charles S. Boyer, "An Address Delivered Before the Camden County Historical Society," Oct. 11, 1911, *Annals of Camden*, No. 3 Old Ferries, Camden, New Jersey, privately printed.

3. Klopfer, *Travel, Reminiscences and Experiences*, 81.

4. Freedley, *Philadelphia and Its Manufactures*; Weigley, *Philadelphia: A 300-Year History*; Littell, *Littell's Living Age*, vol. 31; "Strawberries and Cream," *Sunbury American*, April 12, 1851. Root and de Rochemont, *Eating in America—A History*, 324, 327. Thomas, *Delmonico's: A Century of Splendor*, 70-71.

5. New types of silverware proliferated in nineteenth-century America when it became stylish to serve consecutive individual dinner courses. Three- and four-tined dinner forks were rare in America until the mid-nineteenth century, but by

1860 they were considered essential. During this period, numerous forks for other uses emerged, intended for pastry, salad, fruit, strawberries, sandwiches, bread, and ice cream. Spoons were developed for sorbet, bouillon, chowder, cream soup, preserves, jam, jelly, eggs, lemonade (later iced tea), and grapefruit, as well as ladles for ice cream, mayonnaise, and oyster stew. Blunt-bladed knives for fish, butter, and salad were also introduced (Smith, *The Oxford Companion to American Food and Drink*, 537–38). However, not all of these would have been placed on the table at the same time. For a dinner party of this size, plates and silverware were changed after each course, washed immediately, and used again for the following courses. Dessert spoons and forks were brought out with these courses (Ranhofer, *The Epicurean*, 9–10).

6. Pillsbury, *From Boarding House to Bistro*, 23.

7. Pillsbury, *From Boarding House to Bistro*, 31; Lobel, *Urban Appetites*, 109.

8. Wolf, *Philadelphia: Portrait of an American City*, 179.

9. Lobel, *Urban Appetites*, 108.

10. Williams, *Food in the United States*, 153.

11. Parkinson, *American Dishes at the Centennial*, 26; Lobel, *Urban Appetites*, 106; "A Grand Dinner," *Andrew County Republican* (Savannah, Missouri), Oct. 2, 1874.

12. Parkinson, *American Dishes at the Centennial*, 26.

13. The cost of the dinner varies according to the source—some say $1,000, but the *Evening Bulletin* listed a price of $900, and guest R. B. Valentine said the "Philadelphia entertainers" paid the caterer (Parkinson) $1,500 for the banquet—$50 a plate. In any case, it was an exorbitant amount of money for that time period. However, it is important to note that while Parkinson kept track of the cost, he apparently did not accept any profit for himself. According to Valentine, "all that he asked was the pleasure of showing to our friends from New York what the culinary and confectionery art could do in his native city of Philadelphia." Parkinson, *American Dishes at the Centennial*, 22, 32; "City Bulletin," *Evening Bulletin*, April 26, 1851.

14. Parkinson, *American Dishes at the Centennial*, 22, 26.

15. The new service style was called *à la russe* because it was said to have been introduced by the Russian ambassador in France in 1810. Belden, *The Festive Tradition*, 34.

16. Williams, *Food in the United States*, 153; Visser, *The Rituals of Dinner*, 198–203.

17. Parkinson, *American Dishes at the Centennial*, 26–28.

18. Visser, *The Rituals of Dinner*, 197–98, 203.

19. Gaskell, *Gaskell's Compendium of Forms*, 777.

20. Parkinson, *American Dishes at the Centennial*, 32.

21. Parkinson, *American Dishes at the Centennial*, 32.

22. The Italian version of the family surname was actually Del-Monico, but when the brothers first set up shop at 23 William Street the sign read Delmonico's. According to one family legend, they decided it was less expensive to change their

names than have the sign repainted. Andrews, "Delmonico's," *American Heritage,* August–September 1980, 3.

23. Smith, *The Oxford Companion to American Food and Drink,* 185–86; Andrews, "Delmonico's," *American Heritage,* August–September 1980, 3.

24. The current Delmonico's Restaurant at this 56 Beaver Street location has no connection to the Delmonico family or original business. It has been renovated to duplicate the elegance of the original building. The Pompeian pillars are still used to support the portico, private rooms are available for discreet dining, the bursting wine cellar offers a variety of choices, and the menu offers Delmonico-style cuisine. Lagasse, *Emeril's Delmonico: A Restaurant with a Past,* xiii.

25. Lobel, *Urban Appetites,* 122; Brown, *Delmonico's: A Story of Old New York,* 16.

26. Andrews, "Delmonico's," *American Heritage,* August–September 1980, 4; Smith, *The Oxford Companion to American Food and Drink,* 186.

27. Schwartz, *Arthur Schwartz's New York City Food,* 56.

28. Schwartz, *Arthur Schwartz's New York City Food,* 56, 62, 64; Choate and Canora, *Dining at Delmonico's,* 27.

29. Scharf and Westcott, *History of Philadelphia,* 988–89.

30. Ice cream saloons had bare floors, whereas ice cream parlors were carpeted. Funderburg, *Chocolate, Strawberry and Vanilla: A History of American Ice Cream,* 76.

31. Hines, Marshall, and Weaver, *The Larder Invaded,* 28–29; Woloson, *Refined Tastes,* 81; "Hot House Grapes," *Philadelphia Inquirer,* Nov. 11, 1847, 4.

32. During the 1840s, Parkinson also partnered with a confectioner named R. B. Jones, with the business advertised and listed in city directories as "Parkinson, R.B. & J.W., confectioners" and "Jones & Parkinson, confectioners." Their partnership dissolved in 1851. It is not clear if this is the same Col. Richard B. Jones who owned the Exchange Hotel on Dock Street in Philadelphia and later a fine dining restaurant for "ladies and gentlemen" on Arch Street; Megargee, "Seen and Heard in Many Places," *Philadelphia Times,* June 10, 1897, 4.

33. A member of Philadelphia's influential Cadwalader family, General George Cadwalader (1806–1879) served during the Mexican-American War and the Civil War. Besides his military accomplishments, he was a successful real estate investor and lawyer. Cadwalader Family Papers, Historical Society of Pennsylvania, http://hsp.org/sites/default/files/legacy_files/migrated/findingaid1454cadwalader-part1.pdf.

34. "City and Business Notices," *Philadelphia Inquirer,* Jan. 1, 1849, 1; "Famous Old Caterer Dead," *Philadelphia Times,* May 16, 1895, 2.

35. "Parkinson, Provider for Epicures," *Public Ledger,* Dec. 1, 1907.

36. Megargee, "Seen and Heard in Many Places," *Philadelphia Times,* June 10, 1897, 4.

37. Hines, Marshall, and Weaver, *The Larder Invaded,* 29.

38. "Parkinson, Provider for Epicures," *Public Ledger,* Dec. 1, 1907.

39. "Old Kriss Kringle's Head-quarters," *North American,* Dec. 30, 1846, 3; Katz, Solomon, and Weaver, *Encyclopedia of Food and Culture,* 40; "Famous Old Caterer Dead," *Philadelphia Times,* May 16, 1895, 2.

40. "Parkinson's Restaurant," *Gleason's Pictorial Drawing-Room Companion*, May 28, 1853, 44; "Touches of Old Philadelphia," *Philadelphia Record*, Oct. 5, 1909.

41. "Parkinson's Restaurant," *Gleason's Pictorial Drawing-Room Companion*, May 28, 1853, 44.

42. "Parkinson's Restaurant," *Gleason's Pictorial Drawing-Room Companion*, May 28, 1853, 44; Watson and Hazard, *Annals of Philadelphia and Pennsylvania in the Olden Time*, 155.

43. Foster, "Philadelphia in Slices," *New York Tribune*, Dec. 28, 1848.

44. Wolf, *Philadelphia: Portrait of an American City*, 188.

45. Megargee, "Seen and Heard in Many Places," *Philadelphia Times*, May 28, 1897.

First Course: Oysters

1. Schwartz, *Arthur Schwartz's New York City Food*, 30.

2. Kurlansky, *The Big Oyster*, 23; Schwartz, *Arthur Schwartz's New York City Food*, 29.

3. Cannato, *American Passage*, 25.

4. Published in Stockholm in 1702, Holm's book was based on Peter Lindestrom's manuscript journal and the notes of his grandfather, Johan Campanius, who had been a Lutheran pastor in New Sweden from 1643 to 1648. An engraver by trade, Holm ironically never visited America. Carol E. Hoffecker, *New Sweden in America*, 354. New Sweden was a Swedish colony along the Delaware River on the mid-Atlantic coast of North America from 1638 to 1655 and included parts of the present-day American states of Delaware, New Jersey, and Pennsylvania.

5. Ingersoll, *The Oyster Industry*, 144.

6. "History of the Eastern Oyster" Fact Sheet—Partnership for the Delaware Estuary, Feb. 2002.

7. O'Neill, *American Food Writing*, 1–2.

8. Schwartz, *Arthur Schwartz's New York City Food*, 29; Perkins, *The Story of an Oyster*, 5.

9. "History of the Eastern Oyster" Fact Sheet—Partnership for the Delaware Estuary.

10. Schwartz, *Arthur Schwartz's New York City Food*, 29–30.

11. Parkinson's Restaurant A La Carte. Menu from the International Electrical Exhibition of the Franklin Institute.

12. Weygandt, *Philadelphia Folks: Ways and Institutions in and About the Quaker City*, 140, 145.

13. Leslie, *Miss Leslie's Lady's House-book*, 287–88.

14. Williams, *Savory Suppers and Fashionable Feasts*, 191, 193; Leslie, *Miss Leslie's Lady's House-book*, 287–88.

15. Weygandt, *Philadelphia Folks: Ways and Institutions in and About the Quaker City*, 143–44.

16. A precursor to today's thick tomato ketchup, catchups were concentrated and flavorful liquids similar to soy or tamari sauce. They had their roots in Asian cuisines, from the Chinese word *ketsiap* or *ke-tsiap*. Nineteenth-century versions were made from a number of foods, including walnuts, mushrooms, oysters, fish, and lobster, as well as grapes and tomatoes, and were much thinner than today's ketchup. *Dictionary of Gastronomy*, 234; Diamond, *Mrs. Goodfellow: The Story of America's First Cooking School*, 144.

17. *The Oyster Epicure*, 13.

18. *Caterer and Household* was published in Philadelphia from 1882 to 1887. James W. Parkinson served as its editor from 1882 to 1884. Mott, *A History of American Magazines: 1865–1885*, 100.

19. *The Oyster Epicure*, 12; Parkinson, *American Dishes at the Centennial*, 28.

20. A Frenchman who immigrated to the U.S. in 1855, Pierre Blot helped enlighten New Yorkers to the wonders of French food through giving lectures in the culinary arts, publishing a series of cookbooks and magazine articles, and eventually launching a cooking school in 1865 that he dubbed the New York Cooking Academy.

21. *The Oyster Epicure*, 9.

22. *The Oyster Epicure*, 11, 13.

23. Williams, *Savory Suppers and Fashionable Feasts*, 234–35.

24. *Philadelphia Inquirer*, Sept. 19, 1906, 6.

25. Huneker, *New Cosmopolis*, 89–90.

26. Parkinson, *American Dishes at the Centennial*, 10.

27. Kurlansky, *The Big Oyster*, 47–48.

28. Fisher, *Consider the Oyster*, 45.

29. *The Oyster Epicure*, 25.

30. Originally referred to oysters harvested from Great South Bay near the town of Blue Point, Long Island. Now a collective term for a medium-sized, mild East Coast oyster. Reardon, *Oysters: A Culinary Celebration*, 237.

31. Claiming to be the oldest social organization speaking the English language, "The Colony in Schuylkill" or "Schuylkill Fishing Company" was founded as a men's fishing club in 1732 by a few of the original Philadelphia settlers, many of whom immigrated with William Penn to the New World. Their first meetinghouse, which they called "the castle," was built on the west side of the Schuylkill River when the area was still a wilderness. In 1781 the group was renamed "The State in Schuylkill" and for generations they fished in the city's streams, then cooked and ate what they caught themselves, each one serving the other. Diamond, *Mrs. Goodfellow: The Story of America's First Cooking School*, 69–70.

32. Weygandt, *Philadelphia Folks: Ways and Institutions in and About the Quaker City*, 140.

33. Interview with Dave Bushek, Haskin Shellfish Research Lab, May 2013.

34. Mints, *The Great Wilderness*, 128.

35. Delaware estuary: Oyster Industry. Franklin Institute website. http://www.fi.edu/fellows/fellow7/dec98/history/oyster_history.html.

36. Oysters of the Delaware Bay. http://www.cumauriceriver.org.

37. "Oysters! The Bivalves in Philadelphia Where They Come From," *Philadelphia Inquirer*, February 21, 1870, 8.

38. Mints, *The Great Wilderness*, 132; Oysters of the Delaware Bay. http://www.cumauriceriver.org.

39. Edelmann, *U.S. 1 Newspaper*, August 24, 2005.

40. "History of the Eastern Oyster" Fact Sheet—Partnership for the Delaware Estuary, Feb. 2002.

41. "History of the Eastern Oyster" Fact Sheet—Partnership for the Delaware Estuary, Feb. 2002.

42. Interview with Dave Bushek, Haskin Shellfish Research Lab, May 2013; "History of the Eastern Oyster" Fact Sheet—Partnership for the Delaware Estuary, Feb. 2002: Mints, *The Great Wilderness*, 125.

43. For example, pollution from sewage and chemical plants located in the Delaware Bay can contaminate the oyster beds, so the state of New Jersey monitors water quality, determining what areas can be open. In addition, large storms can wreak havoc on the bay's delicate saltwater balance. For instance, in 2011 Hurricane Irene and Tropical Storm Lee pushed fresh water into the bay, lowering salinity and diluting the water, causing oyster mortalities. When Hurricane Sandy was bearing down on the area the following year, New Jersey temporarily closed state waters to shellfish harvesting as a precaution given the expected heavy rainfall. Rising ocean levels due to climate change pose the same potential problem. Interview with Dave Bushek, Haskin Shellfish Research Lab, May 2013.

44. Kiesel, "The Surprise of Sauternes," *Food & Wine*, October 1998. www.foodandwine.com/articles/the-surprise-of-sauternes; Page and Dorenburg, *The Food Lover's Guide to Wine*, 2011. The wine's origin determines the spelling. Sauternes is the French wine. An American wine made in the style of Sauternes is called a sauterne.

45. Tarmy, "To Every Wine (Sauternes, Sauternes, Sauternes) There Is a Reason," Bloomberg, May 1, 2013.

46. Prial, "In Defense of the Sweet," *New York Times*, Nov. 1, 1987.

47. MacNeil, *The Wine Bible*, 137; Sauternes Wine Information—Wine Types Wiki website—http://www.winetypeswiki.com/wine/sauternes.

48. MacNeil, *The Wine Bible*, 137; Sauternes Wine Information—Wine Types Wiki website—http://www.winetypeswiki.com/wine/sauternes; Joseph and Rand, *KISS Guide to Wine*, 87.

49. MacNeil, *The Wine Bible*, 138–39.

50. *The Oyster Epicure*, 14.

51. Marshall, *What's a Wine Lover to Do?*, 216.

52. *The Oyster Epicure*, 14–15.

53. Reardon, *Oysters: A Culinary Celebration*, 4.

SECOND COURSE: SOUPS

1. Gaskell, *Gaskell's Compendium of Forms*, 421–23.
2. *Party-giving on Every Scale*, 178–80.
3. Wright, *The Best Soups in the World*, 7.
4. Gode Cookery (http://www.godecookery.com/); Flandrin, *Arranging the Meal*, 58, 68; Rumble, *Soup Through the Ages*, 3.
5. Flandrin, *Arranging the Meal*, 58.
6. Williams, *Food in the United States*, 25.
7. Flandrin, *Arranging the Meal*, 6.
8. Smith, *Souper Tomatoes*, 10.
9. Lincoln, *Mrs. Lincoln's Boston Cook Book*, 119.
10. Beeton, *Mrs. Beeton's Cookery Book and Household Guide*, 48.
11. Owen, *Choice Cookery*, 191–92.
12. Williams, *Savory Suppers and Fashionable Feasts*, 224.
13. Schweitzer, "The Turtles of Philadelphia's Culinary Past," *Expedition*, 41; Williams, *Food in the United States*, 26.
14. Whitehead, *The Steward's Handbook and Guide to Party Catering*, 462; De Voe, *The Market Assistant*, 311.
15. Rumble, *Soup Through the Ages*, 112; *The Edinburgh Encyclopedia* (1832), 381.
16. Leslie, *New Receipts for Cooking*, 34.
17. Ude, *The French Cook*, 54.
18. Leslie, *New Receipts for Cooking*, 34–35.
19. De Voe, *The Market Assistant*, 311; Schweitzer, "The Turtles of Philadelphia's Culinary Past," *Expedition*, 38.
20. Schweitzer, "The Turtles of Philadelphia's Culinary Past," *Expedition Magazine*, 38; Hines, Marshall, and Weaver, *The Larder Invaded*, 21.
21. Kimball, *Fannie's Last Supper*, 43–44; Schweitzer, "The Turtles of Philadelphia's Culinary Past," *Expedition*, 42.
22. Williams, *Food in the United States*, 27.
23. Arlene Burnett, "Slow Food: Turtle Soup Is a Throwback to an Earlier Elegant Time," *Pittsburgh Post-Gazette*, June 26, 2008; "Snapper Soup," Eat Your World—http://eatyourworld.com/destinations/united_states/pennsylvania/philadelphia/what_to_eat/snapper_soup; George Ingram, "Into the Soup: A Rich Snapper Soup Starts with Plenty of Turtle Meat—and Patience," *Philadelphia Inquirer*, April 24, 2002.
24. Pepin, "Soup, Beautiful Soup," *New York Times*, March 31, 1991; Blot, *Handbook of Practical Cookery*, 61.
25. "Home & Garden: Q&A," *New York Times*, August 14, 1985; Dallas and Kettner, *Kettner's Book of the Table*, 118.
26. Marquise de Créquy, *The French Noblesse of the XVIII Century*, 158; Rumble, *Soup Through the Ages*, 72, 222; Sala, *The Thorough Good Cook*, 114–15.
27. "Potage à la Reine: The French origins of a Dutch soup," Coquinaria—http://www.coquinaria.nl/english/recipes/07.2histrecept.htm.

28. Rumble, *Soup Through the Ages*, 35.

29. Ferrières, *Sacred Cow, Mad Cow: A History of Food Fears*, 114; "Potage à la Reine: The French origins of a Dutch soup," Coquinaria—http://www.coquinaria.nl/english/recipes/07.2histrecept.htm.

30. Hale, *Mrs. Hale's New Cook Book*, 55.

31. Pepin, "Soup, Beautiful Soup," *New York Times*, March 31, 1991. Translated as "velvety" in French, the term *velouté* is used to designate a basic white sauce made with veal, chicken, or fish stock; it may also be used to signify soup. Davidson, *The Oxford Companion to Food*, 827.

32. Rothert, *The Soups of France*, 11.

33. "Experience Cognac," Beverage Alcohol Resource—http://www.experiencecognac.com/cognacfood.php.

34. MacNeil, *The Wine Bible*, 157–60; Lukacs, *Inventing Wine*, 89; Johnson, *Vintage: The Story of Wine*, 189.

THIRD COURSE: FISH

1. Schwartz, *Arthur Schwartz's New York City Food*, 29.

2. O'Neill, *American Food Writing*, 1.

3. Parkinson, *American Dishes at the Centennial*, 9–10.

4. Blot, *Hand-book of Practical Cookery*, 460.

5. Leslie, *Directions for Cookery*, 42.

6. Whitehead, *The Steward's Handbook and Guide to Party Catering*, 63. The Spanish, or espagnole sauce, is a combination of a dark roux and meat stock, and one of the five important "mother sauces" in classical French cuisine from which many other brown sauces are derived.

7. Hines, Marshall, and Weaver, *The Larder Invaded*, 51; Smith, *The Oxford Companion to American Food and Drink*, 534; Parkinson, *American Dishes at the Centennial*, 9.

8. Smith, *The Oxford Companion to American Food and Drink*, 515–16; *Stoddart's Encyclopaedia Americana*, 422–23; *The New American Cyclopaedia*, 569.

9. Parkinson, *American Dishes at the Centennial*, 27.

10. De Voe, *The Market Assistant*, 191–92.

11. Filippini, *One Hundred Ways of Cooking Fish*, 51. The coral can also be used to make colorful, deep-red "lobster butter," by mixing it thoroughly with fresh butter and a little cayenne, then pressing it through a sieve.

12. Jackson, *Seafood*, 329.

13. Parkinson, *American Dishes at the Centennial*, 9.

14. Leslie, *Miss Leslie's New Cookery Book*, 82.

15. Beard, *James Beard's New Fish Cookery*, 313.

16. David, *Italian Food*, 167–68; Dallas and Kettner, *Kettner's Book of the Table*, 104.

17. Hooker, *The Book of Chowder*, 87.

18. Filippini, *One Hundred Ways of Cooking Fish*, 51.

19. Ranhofer, *The Epicurean*, 333.

20. Simon and Howe, *The Dictionary of Gastronomy*, 339.

21. Ude, *The French Cook*, 241.

22. Stevenson, *The Sotheby's Wine Encyclopedia*, 343.

23. *Cozzens' Wine Press*, 114.

24. Lukacs, *Inventing Wine*, 77; MacNeil, *The Wine Bible*, 541; Johnson, *Vintage: The Story of Wine*, 288.

25. Reynolds, *Teetotaler*, 181–82.

26. Johnson, *Vintage: The Story of Wine*, 290; Kloster Eberbach: The Wine Estate of the former Cistercian abbey (Fact Sheet)—http://kloster-eberbach.de/fileadmin/media/Weingut/pdf-Dateien_Weingut/Image _brochure_2011.pdf.

27. Kloster Eberbach: The Wine Estate of the former Cistercian abbey (Fact Sheet)—http://kloster-eberbach.de/fileadmin/media/Weingut/pdf-Dateien_Weingut/Image_brochure_2011.pdf.

28. *Ridley & Co.'s Monthly Wine and Spirit Trade Circular*, issue 444, part 55, 372.

29. *Cozzens' Wine Press*, 114.

Fourth Course: Boiled

1. Zanger, *The American History Cookbook*, 70.

2. Flandrin, *Arranging the Meal*, 146–47.

3. Dolby, *The Cook's Dictionary and House-keeper's Directory*, 71–72; Leslie, *Miss Leslie's Lady's House-book*, 235.

4. Leslie, *Miss Leslie's Lady's House-book*, 235.

5. Mackenzie, *Mackenzie's Five Thousand Receipts*, 163.

6. Dolby, *The Cook's Dictionary and House-keeper's Directory*, 71–72.

7. Mackenzie, *Mackenzie's Five Thousand Receipts*, 163.

8. Lee and Leslie, *The Cook's Own Book, and Housekeeper's Register*, xiv–xv.

9. Von Rumford, *The Complete Works of Count Rumford*, 177; Dolby, *The Cook's Dictionary and House-keeper's Directory*, 71–72.

10. Smith, *The Oxford Companion to American Food and Drink*, 164; Dolby, *The Cook's Dictionary and House-keeper's Directory*, 71–72.

11. Von Rumford, *The Complete Works of Count Rumford*, 177. Scientist and inventor Benjamin Thompson was born on March 26, 1753, in North Woburn, Massachusetts. Largely self-taught, his inquisitive mind led him to pose scientific questions at an early age. He studied heat and friction and is probably best known as inventor of the Rumford fireplace. In the 1770s he joined the Loyalists in Boston to serve as a spy and informant for the British army. He later worked for the Bavarian government and was given the title of Count Rumford of the Holy Roman Empire for his years of service.

12. Dolby, *The Cook's Dictionary and House-keeper's Directory*, 72; Lee and Leslie, *The Cook's Own Book, and Housekeeper's Register*, xiv–xv.

13. Sanderson, *The Complete Cook*, 21; Smith, *The Oxford Companion to American Food and Drink*, 477.

14. Smith, *The Oxford Companion to American Food and Drink*, 477; "History of the Pressure Cooker," *Miss Vickie's Pressure Cooker Recipes*—http://missvickie.com/

15. "Low Energy Cooking Bygones"—http://comestepbackintime.wordpress.com /tag/digester-cookers/.

16. Ronald, "Garnishing and Dishing Hot Meats," *Table Talk*, 1897, 120.

17. Henderson, *Practical Cooking and Dinner Giving*, 168.

18. Chambers, *Chambers's Information for the People*, 1875.

19. Alexis Soyer trained at the Grignon restaurant in Paris and immigrated to England in 1830, becoming *chef de cuisine* at the Reform Club in London in 1837. He popularized many kitchen innovations, including gas stoves, refrigerators cooled by cold water, and ovens with adjustable temperature controls. He also authored several cookbooks and was extremely charitable, opening soup kitchens in Ireland during the famine and later assisting the British army.

20. Soyer, *The Modern Housewife*, 208.

21. Soyer, *The Modern Housewife*, 208.

22. Soyer, *The Modern Housewife*, 208.

23. Smith, *The Turkey: An American Story*, 4–5.

24. Smith, *The Turkey: An American Story*, 13; Smith, *The Oxford Companion to American Food and Drink*, 598.

25. Smith, *The Oxford Companion to American Food and Drink*, 598; Beard, *American Cookery*, 223; Brillat-Savarin, *A Handbook of Gastronomy*, 103, 115. Jean Anthelme Brillat-Savarin was a French lawyer, politician, and author of a celebrated work on gastronomy, *Physiologie du goût* (The Physiology of Taste), a clever, insightful series of anecdotes and observations on food published in 1825. He was forced to leave France during the French Revolution and went to Switzerland and the United States, where he lived from 1794 to 1796. He returned to France in 1796 and became a judge of the court of cassation during Napoleon's consulate.

26. Smith, *The Turkey: An American Story*, 43.

27. *National Cookery Book*, 87; Smith, *The Turkey: An American Story*, 28.

28. "Partakers of Our Plenty," Plimoth Plantation website—http://www.plimoth .org/learn/thanksgiving-history/partakers-our-plenty; Anderson, "Talking Turkey About the REAL 1st Thanksgiving," *Chicago Tribune*, November 19, 2006.

29. Smith, *The Turkey: An American Story*, 67–68; Siskind, "The Invention of Thanksgiving: A Ritual of American Nationality," 43.

30. Smith, *The Turkey: An American Story*, 68–69.

31. "Thanksgiving History," Plimouth Plantation website—http://www.plimoth .org/learn/MRL/read/thanksgiving-history; Smith, *The Turkey: An American Story*, 72–73; Anderson, "Talking Turkey About the REAL 1st Thanksgiving," *Chicago Tribune*, November 19, 2006.

32. "Thanksgiving History," Plimoth Plantation website—http://www.plimoth .org/learn/MRL/read/thanksgiving-history; Anderson, Talking Turkey About the

REAL 1st Thanksgiving," *Chicago Tribune*, November 19, 2006; Williams, *Savory Suppers and Fashionable Feasts*, 196.

33. MacNeil, *The Wine Bible*, 162–65.

34. Lukacs, *Inventing Wine*, 115; MacNeil, *The Wine Bible*, 164.

35. Johnson, *Vintage: The Story of Wine*, 217; Stevenson, *The Sotheby's Wine Encyclopedia*, 171; Johnson and Robinson, *The Concise World Atlas of Wine*, 44.

36. Lukacs, *Inventing Wine*, 156–57; Marshall, *What's a Wine Lover to Do?*, 215–16; MacNeil, *The Wine Bible*, 171–73.

37. Lukacs, *Inventing Wine*, 79; Johnson, *Vintage: The Story of Wine*, 201. *Terroir* is the French term for a vineyard's entire growing environment, including altitude, climate, soil, slope, and any other significant factors that may affect the life of a vine and the quality of grapes produced. Each vineyard is said to have its own terroir.

38. Lukacs, *Inventing Wine*, 79; Johnson, *Vintage: The Story of Wine*, 201.

39. Lukacs, *Inventing Wine*, 78–79; Johnson, *Vintage: The Story of Wine*, 201.

40. Lukacs, *Inventing Wine*, 80.

41. Cocks and Feret, *Bordeaux and Its Wines*, 75.

42. MacNeil, *The Wine Bible*, 237–38.

43. Johnson, *Vintage: The Story of Wine*, 299; Gilbey, *Treatise on Wines and Spirits of the Principal Producing Countries*, 22; Parker, *The Wines of the Rhône Valley*, 34.

FIFTH COURSE: COLD DISHES

1. Bode, *European Gastronomy*, 150.

2. Aron, *The Art of Eating in France*, 123.

3. Ibid.

4. Ranhofer, *The Epicurean*, 722.

5. Whitehead, *The Steward's Handbook and Guide to Party Catering*, 55.

6. Ranhofer, *The Epicurean*, 7.

7. Flandrin, *Arranging the Meal*, 3, 21.

8. Flandrin, *Arranging the Meal*, 101.

9. Whitehead, *The Steward's Handbook and Guide to Party Catering*, 55.

10. Bode, *European Gastronomy*, 110–12.

11. These are meats, poultry, fish, or game coated with a brown or white sauce, glazed with aspic, and served cold. *Larousse Gastronomique*, 257.

12. Ranhofer, *The Epicurean*, 722.

13. Fussell, *Masters of American Cookery*, 170–71; *Larousse Gastronomique*, 50–51; Gouffé, *The Royal Cookery Book*, 276.

14. Carême, *The Royal Parisian Pastrycook and Confectioner*, 252.

15. Gouffé, *The Royal Cookery Book*, 471.

16. *National Cookery Book*, 86; Leslie, *Miss Leslie's New Cookery Book*, 273.

17. Started in Louisiana and made famous by chef Paul Prudhomme, a turducken is a boned chicken stuffed inside a boned duck stuffed inside a turkey; with dressing layered between each. Smith, *The Turkey: An American Story*, 36.

18. Williams, *Savory Suppers and Fashionable Feasts*, 241; Smith, *The Turkey: An American Story*, 36.

19. The fleshy red outgrowth on the top of a cock's head, traditionally used as a garnish in many French dishes. *Larousse Gastronomique*, 312.

20. *Larousse Gastronomique*, 51; Ranhofer, *The Epicurean*, 766.

21. Cracknell and Kaufmann, *Practical Professional Cookery*, 544.

22. Gouffé, *The Royal Cookery Book*, 471. Montpellier was a flavored butter seasoned with herbs such as parsley, chervil, and tarragon, and sometimes other ingredients including nutmeg, shallot, garlic, hard-boiled eggs, and anchovies. *Larousse Gastronomique*, 187; Carême, *The Royal Parisian Pastrycook and Confectioner*, 227–28.

23. Gouffé, *The Royal Cookery Book*, 466.

24. Kimball, *Fannie's Last Supper*, 184, 189.

25. Williams, *Savory Suppers and Fashionable Feasts*, 122, 280.

26. Dodgshun, Peters, and O'Dea, *Cookery for the Hospitality Industry*, 49; Bode, *European Gastronomy*, 148–51.

27. Stevenson, *The Sotheby's Wine Encyclopedia*, 321–22.

28. Stevenson, *The Sotheby's Wine Encyclopedia*, 321–22.

29. Walker and Walker, *To the Heart of Spain*, 38–39.

30. Marshall, *What's a Wine Lover to Do?*, 176; Stevenson, *The Sotheby's Wine Encyclopedia*, 324.

31. Marshall, *What's a Wine Lover to Do?*, 176; Stevenson, *The Sotheby's Wine Encyclopedia*, 322; MacNeil, *The Wine Bible*, 439.

32. MacNeil, *The Wine Bible*, 444.

33. Brooke, *Sketches in Spain and Morocco*, 86.

34. Whitehead, *The Steward's Handbook and Guide to Party Catering*, 233.

SIXTH COURSE: ENTRÉE NO. 1

1. Ude, *The French Cook*, vi.

2. Senn, *The Menu Book?*, 144.

3. Flandrin, *Arranging the Meal*, 66–67.

4. Flandrin, *Arranging the Meal*, 73.

5. The culinary term for the thymus gland (in the throat) and the pancreas (near the stomach) in calves, lamb, and pigs. *Larouusse Gastronomique*, 1170.

6. Flandrin, *Arranging the Meal*, 5–7; Visser, *The Rituals of Dinner*, 198; Jurafsky, "Entrée," *The Language of Food* blog.

7. Hill, *The Book of Entrées*, 3; Aron, *The Art of Eating in France*, 112–13.

8. Bode, *European Gastronomy*, 145.

9. Bode, European Gastronomy, 146; Aron, *The Art of Eating in France*, 118; Hill, *The Book of Entrées*, 8.

10. Jurafsky, "Entrée," *The Language of Food* blog; Hill, *The Book of Entrées*, 7.

11. *Larousse Gastronomique*, 1282.

12. Simon and Howe, *Dictionary of Gastronomy*, 178; *Larousse Gastronomique*, 1282.
13. Carême, *The Royal Parisian Pastrycook and Confectioner*, 2.
14. Carême, *The Royal Parisian Pastrycook and Confectioner*, 4.
15. Carême, *The Royal Parisian Pastrycook and Confectioner*, 4; *Cassell's Dictionary of Cookery*, 666.
16. Davidson, *The Oxford Companion to Food*, 832–33; *Larousse Gastronomique*, 1282.
17. Carême, *The Royal Parisian Pastrycook and Confectioner*, 4; *Cassell's Dictionary of Cookery*, 1096.
18. *Cassell's Dictionary of Cookery*, 1096; *Larousse Gastronomique*, 1282–83.
19. *Larousse Gastronomique*, 1282.

Seventh Course: Entrée No. 2

1. Beeton, *The Book of Household Management*, 100–104.
2. Whitehead, *The Steward's Handbook and Guide to Party Catering*, 463.
3. Davidson, *The Oxford Companion to Food*, 710; Schweitzer, "The Turtles of Philadelphia's Culinary Past," *Expedition*, 41.
4. Glasse, *The Art of Cookery, Made Plain and Easy*, 257–58.
5. Hill, *Mrs. Hill's New Cook Book*, 144.
6. Brewster, *The Edinburgh Encyclopaedia*, 381; Whitehead, *The Steward's Handbook and Guide to Party Catering*, 463–64.
7. *National Cookery Book*, 52.
8. Murrey, *The Book of Entrées*, 15.
9. Stickney, *Aquaculture of the United States*, 286–87.
10. Hines, Marshall, and Weaver, *The Larder Invaded*, 60; Smith, *The Oxford Companion to American Food and Drink*, 436. Squabs are young pigeons, just old enough where they are about to leave the nest. They are typically never more than four weeks old and do not weigh more than fourteen ounces. Simon and Howe, *The Dictionary of Gastronomy*, 360.
11. La Varenne, *Le vrai cuisinier François*, 12.
12. *National Cookery Book*, 109; Hale, *Modern Household Cookery*, 188–89.
13. *Larousse Gastronomique*, 153; Simon and Howe, *The Dictionary of Gastronomy*, 82.
14. Technique for cooking meats where the meat is wrapped in a layer of pork or bacon fat before roasting or braising to help maintain the moisture of the meat while it cooks and prevents it from drying out. Also called larding.
15. *Larousse Gastronomique*, 466; Simon and Howe, *The Dictionary of Gastronomy*, 341; Fellows, *A Selection of Dishes and the Chef's Reminder*, 159.
16. *Larousse Gastronomique*, 887; Smith, *The Oxford Companion to American Food and Drink*, 252; Davidson, *The Oxford Companion to Food*, 605.
17. Fisher, *The Cooking of Provincial France*, 121.

18. "The Art of Dining," *Harper's*, 136; Menu: "Salons De Parkinson, Le Quatre Fevrier, 1853," Menu Collection, Library Company of Philadelphia.

19. Church, *Bizarre, For Fireside and Wayside*, April–October 1852, 187.

20. Wolf and Korey, *Quarter of a Millennium: The Library Company of Philadelphia, 1731–1981*, 155.

21. Jacob Snider Papers, The New York Public Library Rare Books and Manuscripts Division, Accession # *85M21; "Jacob Snider, Inventor," *Belgravia*, vol. 11, no. 1432, June 11, 1867, 3. Breech-loading rifles ultimately revolutionized warfare. The bullets were loaded into a chamber at the back of the gun, resulting in a shorter reloading time and the ability to load multiple bullets at once.

EIGHTH COURSE: ROASTS

1. Kirwan, *Host and Guest: A Book About Dinners*, 164–65.

2. Trubek, *Haute Cuisine*, 22–23; Stevens, *All About Roasting*, 8–9.

3. Flanders, *Inside the Victorian Home*, 105; Escoffier, *A Guide to Modern Cookery*, 116.

4. Flanders, *Inside the Victorian Home*, 103–5.

5. Stevens, *All About Roasting*, 8–9.

6. Williams, *Food in the United States*, 69, 220.

7. Wilson, *Consider the Fork*, 89–90; von Rumford, *The Complete Works of Count Rumford*, 237.

8. Rorer, *Mrs. Rorer's Philadelphia Cook Book*, 80–81.

9. Aron, *The Art of Eating in France*, 113; Bode, *European Gastronomy*, 152.

10. Kirwan, *Host and Guest: A Book About Dinners*, 164–65.

11. Ranhofer, *The Epicurean*, 2.

12. Farmer, *The Boston Cooking-school Cook Book*, 240.

13. Soyer, *The Modern Housewife*, 290.

14. Rorer, *Mrs. Rorer's Philadelphia Cook Book*, 167.

15. Gillette, *The White House Cook Book*, 80.

16. Leslie, *Miss Leslie's Directions for Cookery*, 59, 84, 387, 432.

17. "Potting" was an economical way to use up bits of cold meats and preserve them for long periods of time. Potted birds were usually made from pigeon meat that was seasoned with mace, allspice, pepper, and salt, slathered with butter and then covered with a thick flour paste. The birds were baked and cut into small pieces when cold. These pieces were then pounded to a paste and packed very tightly together in small jars. Butter or meat drippings were poured over the top and then the mixture was covered with paper to form a tight seal. If potted properly, these meats would keep for months. Henderson, *Practical Cooking and Dinner Giving*, 208.

18. Smith, *The Oxford Companion to American Food and Drink*, 589; Davidson, *The Oxford Companion to Food*, 799–800.

19. Farmer, *The Boston Cooking-school Cook Book*, 240.

20. Daniell, "Spring Meats and Vegetables. How To Buy and Use Them," *American Kitchen*, March 3, 1899, 17.

21. DeVoe, *The Market Assistant*, 73.

22. Murrey, *Practical Carving*, 18.

23. Leslie, *Miss Leslie's New Cookery Book*, 182; Rorer, *Mrs. Rorer's New Cook Book*, 235; Blot, *What to Eat, and How to Cook It*, 126.

24. Leslie, *Miss Leslie's New Cookery Book*, 315.

25. Redding, *A History and Description of Modern Wines*, 231–35; Johnson, *Wine*, 118–19; Marshall, *What's a Wine Lover to Do?*, 158.

26. Redding, *A History and Description of Modern Wines*, 231–35; Banfield, *Industry of the Rhine*, 182–86.

27. Johnson, *Vintage: The Story of Wine*, 388–89, 395; Lukacs, *Inventing Wine*, 158.

28. Johnson, *Vintage: The Story of Wine*, 395; Lukacs, *Inventing Wine*, 157–58.

NINTH COURSE: PIÈCES MONTÉES • VEGETABLES

1. Aron, *The Art of Eating in France*, 114; *Larousse Gastronomique*, 462.

2. *Larousse Gastronomique*, 885; Woloson, *Refined Tastes*, 156–57.

3. *Larousse Gastronomique*, 885; Davidson, *The Oxford Companion to Food*, 762–63.

4. *Larousse Gastronomique*, 885.

5. *Larousse Gastronomique*, 220.

6. Carême, *The Royal Parisian Pastrycook and Confectioner*, 197–210.

7. *Larousse Gastronomique*, 885.

8. Woloson, *Refined Tastes*, 156–65.

9. Carême, *The Royal Parisian Pastrycook and Confectioner*, 197–210.

10. Ranhofer, *The Epicurean*, 1029; Bode, *European Gastronomy*, 111.

11. Ranhofer, *The Epicurean*, 1029.

12. Bode, *European Gastronomy*, 159.

13. Chesney, "The Root of the Matter: Searching for William Hamilton's Greenhouse at The Woodlands Estate, Philadelphia, Pennsylvania," *Historical Archaeology of the Delaware Valley, 1600–1850*, 273.

14. Hovey, "Notices of some of the Gardens and Nurseries in the neighborhood of New York and Philadelphia taken from Memoranda made in the Month of March last," *American Gardener's*, May 1835, 160–63.

15. "Report of the committee appointed by the Horticultural Society of Pennsylvania for visiting the nurseries and gardens in the vicinity of Philadelphia," July 13, 1830, *The Register of Pennsylvania: devoted to the preservation of facts and documents and every other kind of useful information respecting the state of Pennsylvania*, January to July 1831, 114.

16. Parkinson, *American Dishes at the Centennial*, 27.

17. Davidson and Sweeney, *On the Move: Transportation and the American Story*, 29.

18. Grossman, *American Express: The Unofficial History of the People who Built the Great Financial Empire*, 38–47; Warner, "Forefathers of the Express," *Express Gazette*, 1921, 54–55.

19. Warner, "Forefathers of the Express"; Stimson, *History of the Express Companies: And the Origin of American Railroads*, 156–60.

20. Rouse, *The Great Wagon Road*, ix.

21. U.S. Census Bureau, *Report on the Agencies of Transportation in the United States at Tenth Census 1880*, 308–9.

22. Holmes and Rohrbach, *Stagecoach East: Stagecoach Days in the East from the Colonial Period to the Civil War*, 168.

23. White, *The American Railroad Freight Car*, 28–29.

24. Ibid., 272.

25. Ibid., 272–73.

26. De Voe, *The Market Assistant*, 322–23.

27. Henry, "Ga. Blueberry Knocks Peach Off Top of Fruit Pile," Associated Press, July 22, 2013; "Peaches," GeorgiaInfo—An Online Georgia Almanac.

28. Davidson and Sweeney, *On the Move*, 78.

29. White, *The American Railroad Freight Car*, 28–29.

30. Cook, "Food and the Fast Track," *Countryside & Small Stock Journal*.

Tenth Course: Coup du Milieu

1. *Larousse Gastronomique*, 347.

2. A potent, high-alcohol elixir and spirit made from the wormwood plant, invented in Switzerland in the 1700s by Frenchman Dr. Ordinaire. Simon and Howe, *Dictionary of Gastronomy*, 9.

3. *Larousse Gastronomique*, 347–48.

4. *Larousse Gastronomique*, 347–48; Flandrin, *Arranging the Meal*, 96–97.

5. *Larousse Gastronomique*, 347; Flandrin, *Arranging the Meal*, 97.

6. Bode, *European Gastronomy*, 152; Aron, *The Art of Eating in France*, 118.

7. Ranhofer, *The Epicurean*, 2, 9.

8. Davidson, *The Oxford Companion to Food*, 717.

9. Marshall, *Mrs. A. B. Marshall's Cookery Book*, 487.

10. Marshall, *The Book of Ices*, 32.

11. British term for German white wine, originating from Hochheim on Main. *Dictionary of Gastronomy*, 220.

12. Flandrin, *Arranging the Meal*, 97.

13. Ranhofer, *The Epicurean*, 1003.

14. Davidson, *The Oxford Companion to Food*, 717.

15. Parkinson, *American Dishes at the Centennial*, 31.

16. Johnson and Robinson, *The Concise World Atlas of Wine*, 218; MacNeil, *The Wine Bible*, 540.

17. MacNeil, *The Wine Bible*, 593–94.

18. Johnson and Robinson, *The Concise World Atlas of Wine*, 218; MacNeil, *The Wine Bible*, 594–95.

19. Johnson and Robinson, *The Concise World Atlas of Wine*, 218.

20. Lukacs, *Inventing Wine*, 122–23.

21. *Library of Universal Knowledge*, 450.

22. Redding, *A History and Description of Modern Wines*, 282–85.

23. Johnson and Robinson, *The Concise World Atlas of Wine*, 218; MacNeil, *The Wine Bible*, 24, 591–93.

Eleventh Course: Game

1. Smith, *The Oxford Companion to American Food and Drink*, 251; Davidson, *The Oxford Companion to Food*, 330.

2. Parkinson, *American Dishes at the Centennial*, 11–12.

3. Williams, *Food in the United States*, 129.

4. De Voe, *The Market Assistant*, 180.

5. *National Cookery Book*, 103–4.

6. Ranhofer, *The Epicurean*, 223–24.

7. Flandrin, *Arranging the Meal*, 14.

8. *National Cookery Book*, 104.

9. Beard, *American Cookery*, 244–45.

10. Beard, *American Cookery*, 245.

11. De Voe, *The Market Assistant*, 146–80; Beard, *American Cookery*, 245.

12. De Voe, *The Market Assistant*, 146–80; Smith, *The Oxford Companion to American Food and Drink*, 251; Parkinson, *American Dishes at the Centennial*, 27.

13. *National Cookery Book*, ix; Hehner, Dorsey, and Breining, *North American Game Birds*, 106–8.

14. Williams, *Savory Suppers and Fashionable Feasts*, 110–11.

15. Parloa, "Everything About the House," *Ladies Home Journal*, November 1891, 29.

16. Davidson, *The Oxford Companion to Food*, 627.

17. Smith, *The Oxford Companion to American Food and Drink*, 236–37; Smith, *Fast Food and Junk Food*, 571; Burhans, *Crunch! A History of the Great American Potato Chip*, 18–21.

18. "Notes from the Watering Places," *New York Herald*, Aug. 2, 1849, 1; e-mail correspondence with Dave Mitchell, Oct. 8, 2014.

19. Burton, *Reminiscences of Gideon Burton*, 35.

20. Gillespie-Peck, *Winewoman@Bergerac. France*, 231.

21. Johnson, *Vintage: The Story of Wine*, 212 and 270; "Swiss Wine: Oeil de Perdrix," *Rhi's Foodie Life Blog*, June 29, 2014.

22. Johnson and Robinson, *Concise World Atlas of Wine*, 205; MacNeil, *The Wine Bible*, 584; "Oeil-de-Perdrix," Fine Swiss Wine website.

TWELFTH COURSE: DIAMOND-BACK TERRAPIN

1. Parkinson, *American Dishes at the Centennial*, 10.
2. Willcox, *A History of the Philadelphia Savings Fund Society*, 57–58.
3. Hines, Marshall, and Weaver, *The Larder Invaded*, 21, 50.
4. Parkinson, *American Dishes at the Centennial*, 10.
5. Schweitzer, "The Turtles of Philadelphia's Culinary Past," *Expedition*, Winter 2009, 42; Forney, "Terrapin and Canvas-Back Ducks," *Table Talk*, 1891, 93.
6. Forney, "Terrapin and Canvas-Back Ducks," *Table Talk*, 1891, 93. Tillie May Forney was an author and journalist born in Washington, D.C., in 1861. She was the youngest child of journalist and politician John W. Forney, the "epicure" she refers to in the article. Willard and Livermore, *A Woman of the Century: Fourteen Hundred-seventy Biographical Sketches Accompanied by Portraits of Leading American Women in All Walks of Life*, 296.
7. O'Neill, *American Food Writing*, 101.
8. Filippini, *One Hundred Ways of Cooking Fish*, 96; Weaver, *35 Receipts From the Larder Invaded*, 37.
9. Filippini, *One Hundred Ways of Cooking Fish*, 96.
10. Heppe, *Explanations of All Terms Used in Coockery* [sic], 321.
11. Sanderson, *The Complete Cook*, 72.
12. *National Cookery Book*, 52.
13. Whitehead, *The Steward's Handbook and Guide to Party Catering*, 459.
14. Whitehead, *The Steward's Handbook and Guide to Party Catering*, 459.
15. U.S. Fish & Wildlife Service—http://www.fws.gov/international/cites/cop16/diamondback-terrapin.html.
16. Defenders of Wildlife website—http://www.defenders.org/diamondback-terrapin/what-you-can-do.
17. National Aquarium website—http://www.aqua.org/explore/animals/diamond-back-terrapin.
18. Simpson, *Creating Wine: The Emergence of a World Industry 1840–1914*, 178.
19. Johnson and Robinson, *The Concise World Atlas of Wine*, 164; Johnson, *Vintage: The Story of Wine*, 321; Johnson, *Wine*, 54.
20. Timbs, *The Mirror of Literature, Amusement, and Instruction*, 233–37; Redding, *A History and Description of Modern Wines*, 203–8.

THIRTEENTH COURSE: PASTRY

1. Flandrin, *Arranging the Meal*, 80.
2. Flandrin, *Arranging the Meal*, 80; Bode, *European Gastronomy*, 161.
3. Whitehead, *The Steward's Handbook and Guide to Party Catering*, 49.
4. Aron, *The Art of Eating in France*, 123. In nineteenth-century France both sweet and savory pastry were called *pâtisserie*, but today savory pastries are usually made by the chef or cook (*cuisinier*) and sweets are the domain of the *pâtissier*. (*Larousse Gastronomique*, 855).

5. *Larousse Gastronomique*, 414; Flandrin, *Arranging the Meal*, 104.

6. Suet is the protective fat around the kidneys of beef or mutton.

7. Williams, *Savory Suppers and Fashionable Feasts*, 170; Smith, *The Oxford Companion to American Food and Drink*, 481.

8. *Larousse Gastronomique*, 124.

9. Smith, *The Oxford Companion to American Food and Drink*, 481. The concept of savory puddings cooked inside an animal's stomach is still in use, as with haggis, considered the national dish of Scotland.

10. Rundell, *A New System of Domestic Cookery*, 136.

11. Parkinson, *American Dishes at the Centennial*, 15.

12. Diamond, *Mrs. Goodfellow: The Story of America's First Cooking School*, 158, 225.

13. Davidson, *The Oxford Companion to Food*, 198–99.

14. De Voe, *The Market Assistant*, 396.

15. Parkinson, *American Dishes at the Centennial*, 15.

16. Smith, *The Oxford Encyclopedia to American Food and Drink*, 135.

17. Hale, *Mrs. Hale's New Cook Book*, 332.

18. Smith, *The Oxford Encyclopedia to American Food and Drink*, 439.

19. Parkinson, *The Complete Confectioner*, 52, 69, 73.

20. Davidson, *The Oxford Companion to Food*, 159; *Larousse Gastronomique*, 248–49.

21. Isinglass is obtained from the swimming bladder of certain fish, especially the sturgeon (which yields Russian isinglass). It contains collagen, which when heated with water produces a pure gelatin. Davidson, *The Oxford Companion to Food*, 409.

22. *National Cookery Book*, 242–43; "Créole Recipes," *Table Talk*, February 1898, 71.

23. Parkinson, "Answers to Correspondents," *Confectioners' Journal*, June 1879, 16.

24. Davidson, *The Oxford Companion to Food*, 333; Whitehead, *The Steward's Handbook and Guide to Party Catering*, 325; *Larousse Gastronomique*, 199.

25. *Larousse Gastronomique*, 198–99.

26. Carême, *The Royal Parisian Pastrycook and Confectioner*, 19–20; Carême, *Le Pâtissier royal parisien ou Traité élémentaire et pratique de la pâtisserie ancienne et moderne*, 212–16; Lake, *Menus Made Easy*, 169–71.

27. Lake, *Menus Made Easy*, 170; Crawford, *French Confectionary Adapted for English Families*, 39; Kenney-Herbert, *Sweet Dishes: A Little Treatise on Confectionery and Entremets Sucrés*, 84; "Napolitain Cake, Historie," *Confectioners' Journal*, February 1875, 8.

28. Crawford, *French Confectionary Adapted for English Families*, 42, Carême, *The Royal Parisian Pastrycook and Confectioner*, 19.

29. Diamond, *Mrs. Goodfellow*, 160.

30. Aresty, *The Delectable Past*, 194.

31. Hérisse, *The Art of Pastry Making*, 97.

32. Lukacs, *Inventing Wine*, 118–19.

33. *The Penny Magazine of the Society for the Diffusion of Useful Knowledge*, 435.

34. Lukacs, *Inventing Wine*, 119.

35. MacNeil, *The Wine Bible*, 500; Redding, *A History and Description of Modern Wines*, 266–67.

36. Staib, *The City Tavern Cookbook*, 146, 352.

37. Kellogg, *The Encyclopaedia Britannica*, vol. 24, 1899, 609. Joshua Price was a member of the Society of Friends and belonged to one of the first families of Philadelphia. *The Living Age*, Volume 31, 274.

38. Lukacs, *Inventing Wine*, 116–17.

39. MacNeil, *The Wine Bible*, 484–85.

40. MacNeil, *The Wine Bible*, 484.

41. Mayson, *Port and the Douro*, 207–8; Stevenson, *The Sotheby's Wine Encyclopedia*, 337–38.

FOURTEENTH COURSE: CONFECTIONERY

1. *Larousse Gastronomique*, 326.

2. Sugared comfits were seeds or nuts coated in sugar. Conserves were a thick, sticky mass made by pounding fresh herbs, flowers, or fruits with sugar. Ratafias were small macaroons, typically made with bitter almonds or apricot kernels.

3. Diamond, *Mrs. Goodfellow*, 57–59; *The Art of Confectionery*, 14; *Larousse Gastronomique*, 326.

4. *The Art of Confectionery*, 15–20.

5. Davidson, *The Oxford Companion to Food*, 196; "Cochineal and Carmine," *Confectioners' Journal*, April 1875, vol. 1, no. 5, 17.

6. "Flavors," *Confectioners' Journal*, June 1875, vol. 1, no. 7, 11.

7. Smith, *The Oxford Companion to Food and Drink*, 89; "The Word Confectionery," *Confectioners' Journal*, December 1874, vol. 1, no. 1, 1.

8. Smith, *The Oxford Companion to Food and Drink*, 89; Chapman, *The Candy-Making Industry in Philadelphia*, 4; Freedley, *Philadelphia and Its Manufacturers*, 231; "The Word Confectionery," *Confectioners' Journal*, December 1874, vol. 1, no. 1, 1.

9. Scharf and Westcott, *History of Philadelphia, 1609–1884*, vol. 2, 988–89.

10. "The Word Confectionery," *Confectioners' Journal*, December 1874, vol. 1, no. 1, 1.

11. Parkinson, *American Dishes at the Centennial*, 5.

12. Parkinson, *American Dishes at the Centennial*, 5.

13. A pan with a narrow lip on the right side, so that when it is held in the left hand, the drops can be detached with the right.

14. Day, "The Art of Confectionery," *The Pleasures of the Table*, 22–23; Parkinson, *The Complete Confectioner*, 43.

15. A tasteless and odorless gum secreted by the acacia tree found in North Africa, Egypt, and northwest India. Useful in many types of confectionery, it helps prevent

sugar from crystalizing, is used as a glaze, and is a basic ingredient in gum, licorice, and marshmallows.

16. Sugar boiled to a very high temperature (295–310°F). The resulting syrup forms threads that are stiff (brittle) and break easily. Used for brittles, toffees, glazed fruit, hard candy, pulled and spun sugar. "Cooked Sugar Stages," www.joyofbaking.com/StagesOfCookedSugar.html.

17. Gouffé, *The Book of Preserves*, 265.

18. Parkinson, "Answers to Correspondents," *Confectioners' Journal*, April 1880, vol. 7, 22; "On Creams," *Confectioners' Journal*, April 1875, vol. 1, no. 5, 17; Rorer, *Home Candy Making*, 59.

19. Sugar boiled to 242–248°F. The resulting syrup forms a firm but pliable, sticky ball that holds its shape briefly. Used for caramels, butter creams, nougat, marshmallows, Italian meringues, gummies, and toffees. "Cooked Sugar Stages," www.joyofbaking.com/StagesOfCookedSugar.html.

20. Parkinson, "Nougat, and Its Various Preparations," *Confectioners' Journal*, December 1875, vol. 2, no. 13, 20.

21. Day, "The Art of Confectionery," *The Pleasures of the Table*, 6; Davidson, *The Oxford Companion to Food*, 207.

22. Because sugar in the nineteenth century was often discolored and/or dirty, it had to be clarified before it could be used in confectionery. This was done by boiling the sugar in clear water with an egg white and straining it through a clean napkin, resulting in clear syrup. Day, "The Art of Confectionery," *The Pleasures of the Table*, 8.

23. Davidson, *The Oxford Companion to Food*, 207; Parkinson, *The Complete Confectioner*, 44.

24. *The Art of Confectionery*, 72; Parkinson, *The Complete Confectioner*, 28.

25. Day, "The Art of Confectionery," *The Pleasures of the Table*, 7.

26. Parkinson, "Answers to Correspondents," *Confectioners' Journal*, February 1879, vol. 5, no. 49, 18; Parkinson, "Answers to Correspondents," *Confectioners' Journal*, February 1880, vol. 6, no. 61, 20.

27. Anderson, *Food of China*, 168; Parkinson, "A Brief Account of the Principal Herbs, Roots, Barks, Woods, Seeds, Gums, Fruits, Nuts, Flowers, Blossoms, etc. used in Confectionery, Cookery and Pharmaceutical Confects," *Confectioners' Journal*, April 1875, vol. 1, no. 5, 17; Day, "The Art of Confectionery," *The Pleasures of the Table*, 7.

28. A pearling cot resembled a funnel with a small hole in the center fitted with a spigot in order to pour out the syrup in a thin stream. Parkinson, *The Complete Confectioner*, 44.

29. Parkinson, *The Complete Confectioner*, 44–46; Parkinson, "A Brief Account of the Principal Herbs, Roots, Barks, Woods, Seeds, Gums, Fruits, Nuts, Flowers, Blossoms, etc. used in Confectionery, Cookery and Pharmaceutical Confects," 21. *Dragées* (the French word for comfit) are a great specialty within French confectionery. Davidson, *The Oxford Companion to Food*, 256.

FIFTEENTH COURSE: ICE CREAMS AND WATER ICES

1. Parkinson, *American Dishes at the Centennial*, 19.
2. Hines, Marshall, and Weaver, *The Larder Invaded*, 57; Woloson, *Refined Tastes*, 78.
3. Parkinson, "Ice Cream," *Confectioners' Journal*, August 1879, vol. 5, no. 55, 22; Parkinson, "Ice Cream and Ice Cream Machinery, Ancient and Modern," *Confectioners' Journal*, March 1876, vol. 2, no. 15, 12.
4. Parkinson, "Ice Cream and Ice Cream Machinery, Ancient and Modern," *Confectioners' Journal*, March 1876, vol. 2, no. 15, 12.
5. Parkinson, "Food in Ices," *Confectioners' Journal*, May 1879, vol. 5, no. 52, 14.
6. "Parkinson," *Confectioners' Journal*, June 1875, vol. 1, no. 7, 12.
7. Weaver, *35 Receipts From the Larder Invaded*, 43.
8. Quizno, *Of Sugar and Snow: A History of Ice Cream Making*, 41–42.
9. "Ice Cream," Food Timeline, http://www.foodtimeline.org/foodicecream.html# firstchocolate; Woloson, *Refined Tastes*, 99.
10. Williams, *Food in the United States*, 47; Smith, *The Oxford Companion to American Food and Drink*, 122.
11. Jarrin, *The Italian Confectioner*, 125; Parkinson, *The Complete Confectioner*, 76.
12. Parkinson, "Food in Ices," *Confectioners' Journal*, May 1879, vol. 5, no. 52, 14; Parkinson, *The Complete Confectioner*, 72.
13. Parkinson, "Food in Ices," *Confectioners' Journal*, May 1879, vol. 5, no. 52, 14; "On the Method of Proceeding for the Composition of Ice Creams," *Confectioners' Journal*, June 1876, vol. 2, no. 18, 22; Weaver, *35 Receipts from the Larder Invaded*, 23.
14. Parkinson, *American Dishes at the Centennial*, 19; "On the Method of Proceeding for the Composition of Ice Creams," *Confectioners' Journal*, June 1876, vol. 2, no. 18, 22; Weir and Weir, *Ice Creams, Sorbets and Gelati*, 100–101.
15. Ranhofer, *The Epicurean*, 982–83.
16. Parkinson, *The Complete Confectioner*, 74; Oliver, *Lee's Priceless Recipes: A Valuable Collection of Tried Formulas and Simple Methods*, 145.
17. Smith, *The Oxford Companion to American Food and Drink*, 314; Cooke, *Cookery and Confectionary*, 187–91.
18. Smith, *The Oxford Companion to American Food and Drink*, 314; Ranhofer, *The Epicurean*, 1019–24.
19. Weaver, *35 Receipts from The Larder Invaded*, 43; "How to Make Ice Dishes," *Confectioners' Journal*, May 1880, vol. 8, 25.
20. Parkinson, *The Complete Confectioner*, 77–78; Parkinson, "Food in Ices," *Confectioners' Journal*, May 1879, vol. 5, no. 52, 14; "On the Method of Proceeding for the Composition of Ice Creams," *Confectioners' Journal*, June 1876, vol. 2, no. 18, 22.
21. Parkinson, "Food in Ices," *Confectioners' Journal*, May 1879, vol. 5, no. 52, 14.
22. Ranhofer, *The Epicurean*, 1001.

23. Parkinson, "Food in Ices," *Confectioners' Journal*, May 1879, vol. 5, no. 52, 14; Parkinson, *The Complete Confectioner*, 78; Weir and Weir, *Ice Creams, Sorbets and Gelati*, 213.

SIXTEENTH COURSE: FRUITS AND NUTS

1. *Larousse Gastronomique*, 414.
2. Flandrin, *Arranging the Meal*, 121–22; Davidson, *The Oxford Companion to Food*, 247.
3. Flandrin, *Arranging the Meal*, 104.
4. A favorite shape for dessert dishes during the Victorian era, a tazza is a high, saucerlike dish mounted on a stem.
5. Davidson, *The Oxford Companion to Food*, 248; Beeton, *Mrs. Beeton's Dictionary of Every-Day Cookery*, 102.
6. Davidson, *The Oxford Companion to Food*, 247.
7. Whitehead, *The Steward's Handbook and Guide to Party Catering*, 49.
8. Williams, *Savory Suppers and Fashionable Feasts*, 109, 272.
9. Beeton, *Mrs. Beeton's Dictionary of Every-Day Cookery*, 101–2; Cole, *The American Fruit Book*, ix.
10. De Voe, *The Market Assistant*, 366–67.
11. Parkinson, *American Dishes at the Centennial*, 16.
12. Williams, *Savory Suppers and Fashionable Feasts*, 173.
13. Leslie, *Seventy-Five Receipts for Pastry, Cakes and Sweetmeats*, 85–90.
14. An enameled iron kettle used specifically for preserving fruits.
15. Leslie, *Seventy-Five Receipts for Pastry, Cakes and Sweetmeats*, 85–90; Williams, *Savory Suppers and Fashionable Feasts*, 276–77.
16. Williams, *Savory Suppers and Fashionable Feasts*, 275.
17. Smith, *The Oxford Companion to American Food and Drink*, 368; Williams, *Food in the United States, 1820s–1890*, 78.
18. Williams, *Food in the United States, 1820s–1890*, 78.
19. Whitehead, *The Steward's Handbook and Guide to Party Catering*, 299.
20. Whitehead, *The Steward's Handbook and Guide to Party Catering*, 299.
21. Parkinson, *The Complete Confectioner*, 48–50.
22. Leslie, *Miss Leslie's Lady's New Receipt-book*, 183.
23. Parkinson, "A Brief account of the principal Herbs, Roots, Barks, Woods, Seeds, Gums, Fruits, Nuts, Flowers, Blossoms, etc. used in Confectionery, Cookery and Pharmaceutical Confects," *Confectioners' Journal*, April 1875, vol. 1, no. 5, 17.
24. Parkinson, "Answers to Correspondents," *Confectioners' Journal*, November 1880, vol. 8, 22; Parkinson, *American Dishes at the Centennial*, 14.
25. Lukacs, *Inventing Wine*, 58.
26. Ripley, and Dana, eds. "Rhenish Wines." *The New American Cyclopaedia*, 43. Between 1806 and 1866 the Duchy of Nassau was an independent German state, located in what are now the German states of Rhineland-Palatinate and Hesse.

27. Baedeker, *A Handbook for Travellers on the Rhine from Holland to Switzerland,* xxiii–xxiv, 142; Stevenson, *The Sotheby's Wine Encyclopedia,* 344.
28. Baedeker, *A Handbook for Travellers on the Rhine from Holland to Switzerland,* xxiv.
29. Stevenson, *The Sotheby's Wine Encyclopedia,* 70.
30. Coates, *The Wines of Bordeaux: Vintages and Tasting Notes 1952–2003,* 191–92.
31. Johnson and Robinson, *The Concise World Atlas of Wine,* 52; Cocks, *Bordeaux: Its Wines, and the Claret Country,* 191–95.

Seventeenth Course: Café Noir

1. *Larousse Gastronomique,* 316; Smith, *The Oxford Companion to American Food and Drink,* 136.
2. *Larousse Gastronomique,* 317; Kimball, *Fannie's Last Supper,* 213; Williams, *Savory Suppers and Fashionable Feasts,* 128.
3. Leslie, *Directions for Cookery,* 389–90.
4. A Boston Lady, *The Dessert Book,* 101.
5. A Boston Lady, *The Dessert Book,* 101; Harder, *The Physiology of Taste: Harder's Book of Practical American Cookery,* 118.
6. Leslie, *Directions for Cookery,* 390.
7. Walsh, *Coffee: Its History, Classification and Description,* 241.
8. Walsh, *Coffee: Its History, Classification and Description,* 268.
9. Harder, *The Physiology of Taste: Harder's Book of Practical American Cookery,* 118; Williams, *Savory Suppers and Fashionable Feasts,* 128.
10. Pendergrast, *Uncommon Grounds: The History of Coffee and How It Transformed Our World,* 6–13.
11. Diamond, *Mrs. Goodfellow,* 66; Ukers, *All About Coffee,* 115.
12. Diamond, *Mrs. Goodfellow,* 71; Ukers, *All About Coffee,* 118.
13. Machray, "Liqueur Sir?" *Ludgate Monthly,* November 1897 to April 1898, 256.
14. Thudichum and Dupre, *A Treatise on the Origin, Nature, and Varieties of Wine: Being a Complete Manual of Viticulture and Oenology,* 613.
15. Thomson, "Maraschino Liqueur Is a Secret Weapon for Your Liquor Cabinet," *Huffington Post,* April 11, 2012.
16. *British Quarterly Review,* January and April 1859, 64.
17. Dallas and Kettner, *Kettner's Book of the Table,* 290.
18. Stewart, *The Drunken Botanist,* 288; Genuine Curaçao Liqueur website—www.curacaoliqueur.com/history.
19. Goodholme, *Goodholme's Domestic Cyclopaedia of Practical Information,* 134.
20. *Larousse Gastronomique,* 386.

An Ovation

1. "Parkinson's Refreshment Saloon," *Sunday Dispatch,* September 2, 1855.
2. "Divorce Case." *Public Ledger,* May 6, 1842; Philadelphia, Pennsylvania Death

Certificates Index, 1803–1915, Ancestry.com; 1880 United States Federal Census Index, Ancestry.com; U.S. Find a Grave Index, 1600s–Current, Ancestry.com.

3. "Seen and Heard in Many Places," *Times of Philadelphia*, June 10, 1897, 4; Kynett, *For Better or For Worse?*, 98.

4. "Parkinson's Philadelphia Ice Cream in New York," *New York Times*, May 25, 1863.

5. Parkinson, *American Dishes at the Centennial*, 20.

6. *Confectioner's Journal*, November 1875, vol. 2, no. 12, 16.

7. Parkinson, *American Dishes at the Centennial*, 8; Hines, Marshall, and Weaver, *The Larder Invaded*, 29.

8. Hines, Marshall, and Weaver, *The Larder Invaded*, 31; Quinzio and Quinzio, *Of Sugar and Snow*, 120–21.

9. Mott, *A History of American Magazines, 1865–1885*, 100.

10. Lobel, *Urban Appetites*, 106; Andrews, "Delmonico's," *American Heritage*, August–September 1980, 7.

11. Lagasse, *Emeril's Delmonico: A Restaurant with a Past*, xiii; Delmonico's Restaurant Group website, www.delmonicosrestaurantgroup.com.

12. Samuel H. Williamson, "Seven Ways to Compute the Relative Value of a U.S. Dollar Amount, 1774 to present," MeasuringWorth, 2015. See also "An Invitation," note 13, above.

13. A present-day shopping list from the Philadelphia region could re-create some but not all of Parkinson's dishes. All prices were obtained in May 2015. All total prices are a rough estimate of what would be needed to feed thirty guests.

Seafood: East Point oysters from Cape May, NJ, are $8.99 the half dozen for a price of $269.70 at Nassau Street Seafood & Produce Company in Princeton, NJ. Although Wholey's Market in Pittsburgh listed the price for six pounds of fresh wild-caught boneless turtle meat at $108 (plus $15 shipping), it was out of stock in May 2015, and the website advised calling the store for availability. Farmed Atlantic salmon is available for $6.99/pound, or roughly $130–140 for two whole salmon at Wan's Seafood, Reading Terminal Market, Philadelphia.

Game and meat: D'Artagnan (http://www.dartagnan.com/) has (frozen) wild turkey (5 to 7 pounds) for $78.99, squab (16 to 18 ounces) for $25.99 and (frozen) veal sweetbreads for $41.99 a pound. Griggstown Farms in Princeton, NJ, has poussin for $9.75 each and four-packs of quail for $18 each. Ely Farm Products in Newtown, PA, has boneless beef chuck roast for $5.99 a pound.

Vegetables and fruits: Cauliflower are $4.99 each, celery $3.49/bunch, and Woodstock Farms organic raw whole almonds are $7.99 for a 7.5 ounce package at Door to Door Organics (https://tristate.doortodoororganics.com/). Navel oranges are $3 for four and Medjool dates are $5.99 a pound at McCaffrey's Supermarket in Yardley, PA.

Desserts and sweets: Pastries were priced at Miel Patisserie & Café, in Philadelphia: A macaroon tower with fifty macaroons costs $120 and a croquem-bouche (a decorative cone-shaped tower made out of small pastry puffs and threaded with caramel to make it crisp) is $160 (both range in price depending on the size), a lemon tart is $24 and a marjolaine (a rich cake consisting of multiple layers of nut-flavored meringue, pastry cream, and a hint of chocolate) is $27.50. Cherry drops and lemon drops are $9 a pound at Shane Confectionery in Philadelphia.

Dairy and baking items: For the caramel ice cream, Kreider Farms heavy cream is $3.99 a quart, Nature's Yoke organic cage-free eggs are $3.99 a dozen, lemons are three for $1.99 and Domino superfine sugar is $2.79 for a 12-ounce package—all at McCaffrey's Supermarket in Yardley, PA.

Beverages: Pierre Ferrand Dry Curaçao (750ml) is $31.99 at K&D Wines and Spirits, NY. Royal Tokaji—Aszú Red Label 5 Puttonyos 2008 for the Sorbets au vin de Tokia is $46.99 a bottle at Joe Canal's Discount Liquor Outlet in Lawrenceville, NJ. Two pounds of French roast coffee is $23 at Equal Exchange (http://equalexchange.coop/products/coffee).

14. Parkinson, *American Dishes at the Centennial*, 27. For all of these conversions, it is important to bear in mind that while we can obtain a "real price," it is instructive to compare the relative value of a converted price; that is, $6 in 1851 is equivalent to an income value of about $2,800 today. Samuel H. Williamson, "Seven Ways to Compute the Relative Value of a U.S. Dollar Amount, 1774 to present," MeasuringWorth, 2015.

15. Interview with Paul Lukacs, September 2013.

16. Lukacs, Paul. *Inventing Wine*, 127; Interview with Paul Lukacs, September 2013.

17. Interview with Paul Lukacs, September 2013; Smith, *The Oxford Companion to American Food and Drink*, 626.

18. Twilley, "The Impossibility of Historical Flavour," *Edible Geography*, January 1, 2013; Goode and Harrop, *Authentic Wine*, 42–43.

19. Interview with Paul Lukacs, September 2013.

20. A single bottle of a 2010 vintage Riesling from the same Rheningau vineyard estates as the wine served during Parkinson's third course sold for £4,577 ($7,000) in 2014. "From an £8,000 French red to a German Riesling at £4,500: The 10 most expensive bottles of wine in the world revealed," *Daily Mail*, November 10, 2014.

BIBLIOGRAPHY

PUBLISHED SOURCES

America's Forgotten History: Surprising Stories and Shocking Facts About Our Past. Pleasantville, NY: Reader's Digest Association, 2010.

Anderson, E. N. *Food of China.* New Haven, CT: Yale University Press, 1988.

Anderson, Lisa. "Talking Turkey About the REAL 1st Thanksgiving." *Chicago Tribune,* November 19, 2006.

Andrews, Peter. "Delmonico's," *American Heritage.* August/September 1980, vol. 31, no. 5, 7.

Aresty, Esther B. *The Delectable Past: The Joys of the Table—From Rome to the Renaissance, From Queen Elizabeth I to Mrs. Beeton.* London: G. Allen & Unwin, 1965.

Aron, Jean-Paul. *The Art of Eating in France: Manners and Menus in the Nineteenth Century.* New York: Harper & Row, 1975.

The Art of Confectionery. Boston: J. E. Tilton and Company, 1865.

"The Art of Dining," *Harper's,* 1876, vol. 52.

Ashton-Alcox, Kathryn. "Bang for the Buck: Shell Planting in the Delaware Bay." *Estuary News,* Winter 2010, vol. 20, no. 2, 5–7.

Baedeker, Karl. *A Handbook for Travellers on the Rhine from Holland to Switzerland.* Coblenz: Karl Baedeker, 1864.

Banfield, Thomas Charles. *Industry of the Rhine . . . Embracing a View of the Social Condition of the Rural [& Manufacturing] Population of that District, Volumes 1–2.* London: Charles Knight & Co., 1846.

Beard, James. *James Beard's American Cookery*. Boston: Little, Brown, 1972.

———. *James Beard's New Fish Cookery*. New York: Hachette, 1976.

Beeton, Isabella Mary. *The Book of Household Management*. London: S. O. Beeton, 1861.

———. *Mrs. Beeton's Cookery Book and Household Guide*. London: Ward, Lock & Co., 1898.

———. *Mrs. Beeton's Dictionary of Every-day Cookery*. London: S. O. Beeton, 1865.

Belden, Louise Conway. *The Festive Traditon*. New York: W. W. Norton, 1983.

Blot, Pierre. *Hand-book of Practical Cookery, for Ladies and Professional Cooks*. New York: D. Appleton, 1867.

———. *What to Eat, and How to Cook It: Containing Over One Thousand Receipts*. New York: D. Appleton, 1863.

Bode, Willi. *European Gastronomy*. London: Grub Street, 2000.

A Boston Lady. *The Dessert Book: A Complete Manual for the Best American and Foreign Authorities*. Boston: J. E. Tilton and Co., 1872.

Boyer, Charles S. An Address Delivered Before the Camden County Historical Society. *Annals of Camden,* No. 3 Old Ferries, Camden, New Jersey. October 11, 1911. Privately printed.

Brewster, David, LL.D., F.R.S. "Herpetology." *Edinburgh Encyclopaedia*, vol. 10. Philadelphia: Joseph and Edward Parker, 1832.

Brillat-Savarin, Jean Anthelme. *A Handbook of Gastronomy*. London: J. C. Nimmo and Bain, 1884.

Brooke, Sir Arthur de Capell. *Sketches in Spain and Morocco, Volume 1*. London: Colburn and Bentley, 1831.

Brown, Henry Collins. *Delmonico's: A Story of Old New York*. New York: Valentine's Manual, 1928.

Burnett, Arlene. "Slow Food: Turtle Soup Is a Throwback to an Earlier Elegant Time." *Pittsburgh Post-Gazette*, June 26, 2008.

Burton, Gideon. *Reminiscences of Gideon Burton*. Cincinnati: Press of George P. Houston, 1895.

"Cabinet Wines." Editorial by Deinhard & Co., *Ridley & Co.'s Monthly Wine and Spirit Trade Circular*, Issue 444, Part 55, Sept. 12, 1885.

Carême, M. A. *Le Pâtissier royal parisien ou Traité élémentaire et pratique de la pâtisserie ancienne et moderne*. Paris: J. G. Dentu, 1815.

————. *The Royal Parisian Pastrycook and Confectioner from the Original of M. A. Carême*. London: F. J. Mason, 1834.

Cassell's Dictionary of Cookery. London: Cassell, Petter, Galpin & Co., 1883.

Chambers, William and Robert, eds. *Chambers's Information for the People*, vol. 1. London: W. & R. Chambers, 1875.

Chapman, Ellwood B. *The Candy-Making Industry in Philadelphia*. Philadelphia: Philadelphia Chamber of Commerce Educational Committee, 1917.

Chesney, Sarah. "The Root of the Matter: Searching for William Hamilton's Greenhouse at The Woodlands Estate, Philadelphia, Pennsylvania." In *Historical Archaeology of the Delaware Valley, 1600–1850*, ed. Richard Veit and David Orr. Knoxville: University of Tennessee Press, 2014.

Choate, Judith and James Canora. *Dining at Delmonico's: The Story of America's Oldest Restaurant*. New York: Stewart, Tabori & Chang, 2008.

Church, J. M. *Bizarre, For Fireside and Wayside*. Philadelphia: Church & Co., vol. 1, April–October 1852.

"City and Business Notices." *Philadelphia Inquirer*, Jan. 1, 1849, 1.

"City Bulletin." *Evening Bulletin*, April 26, 1851.

Coates, Clive. *The Wines of Bordeaux: Vintages and Tasting Notes 1952–2003*. Berkeley: University of California Press, 2004.

"Cochineal and Carmine." *Confectioners' Journal*, April 1875, vol. 1, no. 5, 17.

Cocks, Charles. *Bordeaux: Its Wines, and the Claret Country*. London: Longman, Brown, Green, and Longmans, 1846.

Cocks, Charles and Edouard Feret. *Bordeaux and Its Wines: Classified in Order of Merit*. Paris: G. Masson, 1883.

Cole, Samuel W. *The American Fruit Book: Containing Directions for Raising, Propagating, and Managing Fruit Trees, Shrubs, and Plants; with a Description of the Best Varieties of Fruit, Including New and Valuable Kinds*. Boston: John P. Jewett, 1849.

Confectioners' Journal. Various issues.

Cooke, John Conrade. *Cookery and Confectionary*. London: W. Simpkin, and R. Marshall, 1824.

Cracknell, H. L. and R. J. Kaufmann. *Practical Professional Cookery*. London: Cengage Learning EMEA, 1999.

Crawford, Frances. *French Confectionary Adapted for English Families*. London: Richard Bentley, 1853.

"Créole Recipes." *Table Talk*, vol. 13, February 1898, 71.

Créquy, Renée Caroline de Froulay (Marquise de). *The French Noblesse of the XVIII Century*. Translated by Mrs. Colquhoun Grant from *Les Souvenirs de La Marquise de Créquy*. London: John Murray, 1904.

Dallas, Enaeas Sweetland and Auguste Kettner. *Kettner's Book of the Table* [by E.S. Dallas]. London: Dulau and Co., 1877.

Daniell, Maria. "Spring Meats and Vegetables. How To Buy and Use Them." *American Kitchen*, April 1899, vol. 11, no. 1, 17–19.

David, Elizabeth. *Italian Food*. New York: Penguin Books, 1987.

Davidson, Alan. *The Oxford Companion to Food*. New York: Oxford University Press, 2006.

Davidson, Janet F. and Michael S. Sweeney. *On the Move: Transportation and the American Story*. Washington, DC: National Geographic, 2003.

Day, Ivan. "The Art of Confectionery," in *The Pleasures of the Table. Ritual and Display in the European Dining Room 1600–1900*. York, UK: York Civic Trust, 1997.

De la Reynière, Grimod. *Almanach des Gourmands*. Paris: Mercure de France, 1803.

De Voe, Thomas Farrington. *The Market Assistant: Containing a Brief Description of Every Article of Human Food Sold in the Public Markets of the Cities of New York, Boston, Philadelphia, and Brooklyn*. New York: Hurd and Houghton, 1867.

Di Ionno, Mark. *New Jersey's Coastal Heritage: A Guide*. New Brunswick, NJ: Rutgers University Press, 1997.

Diamond, Becky Libourel. *Mrs. Goodfellow: The Story of America's First Cooking School*. Yardley, PA: Westholme, 2012.

Dickens, Charles. *Dickens's Dictionary of Paris, 1882. An Unconventional Handbook*. London: Macmillan, 1882.

"Divorce Case." *Public Ledger*, May 6, 1842.

Dodgshun, Graham, Michel Peters, and David O'Dea. *Cookery for the Hospitality Industry.* Port Melbourne, Australia: Cambridge University Press, 2011.

Dolby, Richard. *The Cook's Dictionary and House-keeper's Directory: A New Family Manual of Cookery and Confectionery, on a Plan of Ready Reference, Never Hitherto Attempted.* London: Henry Colburn and Richard Bentley, 1830.

Edelmann, Carolyn Foote. "Pirates, Ghosts, and Oysters," *U.S. 1 Newspaper,* August 24, 2005. http://www.princetoninfo.com/index.php/component/us1more/?key=08-24-2005_p_03.

Escoffier, Auguste. *A Guide to Modern Cookery.* London: William Heinemann, 1907.

"Famous Old Caterer Dead." *Philadelphia Times,* May 16, 1895, 2.

Farmer, Fannie Merritt. *The Boston Cooking-school Cook Book.* Boston: Little, Brown, 1912.

Fellows, Charles. *A Selection of Dishes and the Chef's Reminder.* Chicago: Hotel Monthly Press, 1909.

Ferrières, Madeleine. *Sacred Cow, Mad Cow: A History of Food Fears.* New York: Columbia University Press, 2006.

Filippini, Alexander. *One Hundred Ways of Cooking Fish.* New York: Charles L. Webster & Co., 1892.

Filippone, Peggy Trowbridge. "Oyster Varieties: Growing Environment Affects the Flavor of Oysters." *About.com Home Cooking.* http://homecooking.about.com/od/seafood/a/oystervariety.htm.

Fisher, M. F. K. *Consider the Oyster.* New York: North Point Press, 1941.

———. *The Cooking of Provincial France.* New York: Time-Life Books, 1968.

Flanders, Judith. *Inside the Victorian Home: A Portrait of Domestic Life in Victorian England.* New York: W. W. Norton, 2003.

Flandrin, Jean-Louis. *Arranging the Meal: A History of Table Service in France.* Berkeley: University of California Press, 2007.

"Flavors," *Confectioners' Journal,* June 1875, vol. 1, no. 7, 11.

Forney, Tillie May. "Terrapin and Canvas-Back Ducks." *Table Talk,* 1891, vol. 6, 93.

Foster, George G. "Philadelphia in Slices." *New York Tribune*, Dec. 28, 1848. Reprinted in *The Pennsylvania Magazine of History and Biography*, 1969, vol. 93, 56–57.

Freedley, Edwin Troxell. *Philadelphia and Its Manufacturers: A Hand-Book of the Great Manufactories and Representative Mercantile Houses of Philadelphia in 1867.* Philadelphia: E. Young, 1867.

Funderburg, Anne Cooper. *Chocolate, Strawberry and Vanilla: A History of American Ice Cream.* Bowling Green, OH: Bowling Green State University Popular Press, 1995.

Fussell, Betty. *Masters of American Cookery.* Lincoln: University of Nebraska Press, 1983.

Gaskell, George A. *Gaskell's Compendium of Forms: Educational, Social, Legal and Commercial, Embracing a Complete Self-teaching Course in Penmanship and Bookkeeping, and Aid to English Composition.* Chicago: Fairbanks, Palmer & Co., 1881.

Gilbey, Walter Alfred. *Treatise on Wines and Spirits of the Principal Producing Countries.* London: Walter and Alfred Gilbey, 1869.

Gillespie-Peck, Helen. *Winewoman@Bergerac. France.* Cambridgeshire, UK: Melrose Books, 2005.

Gillette, Fanny Lemira. *White House Cook Book: A Selection of Choice Recipes, Original and Selected, During a Period of Forty Years' Practical Housekeeping.* Chicago: L. P. Miller & Co., 1889.

Glasse, Hannah. *The Art of Cookery, Made Plain and Easy.* London: L. Wangford, 1780.

Goode, Jamie and Sam Harrop. *Authentic Wine: Toward Natural and Sustainable Winemaking.* Berkeley: University of California Press, 2011.

Goodholme, Todd S., ed. *Goodholme's Domestic Cyclopaedia of Practical Information.* New York: Charles Scribner's Sons, 1889.

Gouffé, Jules. *The Book of Preserves*, trans. A. Gouffé. London: Spottiswoode & Co., 1871.

———. *The Royal Cookery Book: (Le livre de cuisine).* London: S. Low, son, and Marston, 1869.

"A Grand Dinner." *Andrew County Republican* (Savannah, Missouri), 2 Oct. 1874.

Grossman, Peter Z. *American Express: The Unofficial History of the People who Built the Great Financial Empire.* New York: Crown, 1987.

Hale, Sarah Josepha. *Modern Household Cookery.* London: T. Nelson & Sons, 1854.

———. *Mrs. Hale's New Cook Book: A Practical System for Private Families in Town.* Philadelphia: T. B. Peterson and Brothers, 1857.

Harder, Jules Arthur. *The Physiology of Taste: Harder's Book of Practical American Cookery.* San Francisco: Jules Arthur Harder, 1885.

Hehner, Mike, Chris Dorsey, and Greg Breining, *North American Game Birds.* Minnetonka, MN: Cowles Creative Publishing, 1996.

Henderson, Mary Foote. *Practical Cooking and Dinner Giving: A Treatise Containing Practical Instructions in Cooking, in the Combination and Serving of Dishes, and in the Fashionable Modes of Entertaining at Breakfast, Lunch, and Dinner.* New York: Harper & Brothers, 1881.

Henry, Ray. "Ga. Blueberry Knocks Peach Off Top Of Fruit Pile." Associated Press, July 22, 2013.

Heppe, Kurt. *Explanations of All Terms Used in Coockery [sic], Cellaring and the Preparation of Drinks: Pocket Dictionary.* New York: Kurt Heppe, 1908.

Hérisse, Emilie. *The Art of Pastry Making: According to the French and English Methods Including Cakes, Sweetmeats and Fancy Biscuit Baking, and All Kinds of Confectionery, Plain and Ornamental: a Concise Practical Guide Prepared for the Use of Confectioners, Pastrycooks, and Private Families.* London: Ward, Lock, Bowden, 1893.

Hill, Annabella P. *Mrs. Hill's New Cook Book: Housekeeping Made Easy.* New York: Carleton, 1872.

Hill, Janet McKenzie. *The Book of Entrées: Including Casserole and Planked Dishes.* Boston: Little, Brown, 1911.

Hines, Mary Anne, Gordon M. Marshall, and William Woys Weaver. *The Larder Invaded: Reflections on Three Centuries of Philadelphia Food and Drink: a Joint Exhibition Held 17 November 1986 to 25 April 1987.* Philadelphia: Library Company of Philadelphia and Historical Society of Pennsylvania, 1987.

Hoffecker, Carol E., Richard Waldron, Lorraine E. Williams, and Barbara E. Benson. *New Sweden in America.* Cranbury, NJ: Associated University Presses, 1995.

Holmes, Oliver W. and Peter T. Rohrbach. *Stagecoach East: Stagecoach Days in the East from the Colonial Period to the Civil War.* Washington, D.C.: Smithsonian Institution Press, 1983.

"Home & Garden: Q&A," *New York Times*, August 14, 1985.

Hooker, Richard J. *The Book of Chowder.* Boston: Harvard Common Press, 1978.

"Hot House Grapes." Advertisement in the *Philadelphia Inquirer*, Nov. 11, 1847, 4.

Hovey, Charles Mason. "Notices of some of the Gardens and Nurseries in the neighborhood of New York and Philadelphia taken from Memoranda made in the Month of March last," *American Gardener's*, May 1835.

"How to Make Ice Dishes." *Confectioners' Journal*, May 1880, Vol. VIII, 25.

Ingersoll, Ernest. *The Oyster Industry.* Washington, DC: U.S. Government Printing Office, 1881.

Ingram, George. "Into the Soup: A Rich Snapper Soup Starts with Plenty of Turtle Meat, and Patience." *Philadelphia Inquirer*, April 24, 2002.

Jackson, C. J., editor-in-chief. *Seafood.* New York: Penguin, 2011.

"Jacob Snider, Inventor." *Belgravia*, June 11, 1867, vol. 11, no. 1432, 3.

Jarrin, William Alexis. *The Italian Confectioner.* London: John Harding, 1820.

Johnson, Hugh. *Vintage: The Story of Wine.* New York: Simon and Schuster, 1989.

———. *Wine.* New York: Simon and Schuster, 1966.

Johnson, Hugh and Janis Robinson. *The Concise World Atlas of Wine.* New York: Octopus Publishing, 2009.

Joseph, Robert and Margaret Rand. *KISS Guide to Wine.* London: Dorling Kindersley, 2000.

Kane, Stephanie. "Cape May Oyster Flats." *Grid*, June 14, 2013, http://www.gridphilly.com/grid-magazine/2013/6/14/cape-may-oyster-flats.html.

Katz, Solomon and William Woys Weaver. *Encyclopedia of Food and Culture.* New York: Scribner, 2003.

Kellogg, Day Otis, ed. *The Encyclopaedia Britannica*, Vol. 24. New

York: Werner Co., 1899.

Kenney-Herbert, Arthur Robert. *Sweet Dishes: A Little Treatise on Confectionery and Entremets Sucrés.* Madras: Higginbotham & Co., 1884.

Kiesel, Marcia. "The Surprise of Sauternes." *Food & Wine*, October 1998.

Kimball, Christopher. *Fannie's Last Supper: Re-creating One Amazing Meal from Fannie Farmer's 1896 Cookbook.* New York: Hyperion, 2010.

Kirwan, Andrew Valentine. *Host and Guest, A Book About Dinners.* Bedford, MA: Applewood Books, 2001.

Klopfer, Emil. *Travel, Reminiscences and Experiences.* Alameda, CA: Emil Klopfer, 1894.

Korom, Joseph J. *The American Skyscraper, 1850–1940: A Celebration of Height.* Boston: Branden Books, 2008.

Kurlansky, Mark. *The Big Oyster: History on the Half Shell.* New York: Ballantine Books, 2006.

Kynett, Harold. *For Better or For Worse? Rambles with Progress and Otherwise.* Privately printed, issued by the Kynett family, 1949.

Lagasse, Emeril. *Emeril's Delmonico: A Restaurant with a Past.* New York: HarperCollins, 2005.

Lake, Nancy. *Menus Made Easy; Or, How to Order Dinner and Give the Dishes Their French Names.* London: Frederick Warne & Co., 1903.

Larousse Gastronomique. New York: Clarkson Potter, 2001.

La Varenne, François Pierre. *Le vrai cuisinier François.* 1721.

Lee, Mrs. N. K. M. and Eliza Leslie. *The Cook's Own Book, and Housekeeper's Register.* Boston: Munroe and Francis, 1840.

Leslie, Eliza. *Directions for Cookery, in its Various Branches.* Philadelphia: Carey & Hart, 1844.

Leslie, Eliza. *Miss Leslie's Directions for Cookery.* Philadelphia: Carey & Hart, 1837.

———. *Miss Leslie's Lady's House-book; a Manual of Domestic Economy.* Philadelphia: A. Hart, Late Carey & Hart, 1850.

———. *Miss Leslie's Lady's New Receipt-book.* Philadelphia: A. Hart, Late Carey & Hart, 1850.

———. *Miss Leslie's New Cookery Book.* Philadelphia: T. B. Peterson, 1857.

————. *New Receipts for Cooking.* Philadelphia: T. B. Peterson, 1857.

————. *Seventy-Five Receipts for Pastry, Cakes and Sweetmeats.* Boston: Munroe and Francis, 1828.

Library of Universal Knowledge: A Reprint of the Last (1880) Edinburgh and London Edition of Chambers's Encyclopaedia, With Copious Additions by American Authors. New York: American Book Exchange, 1881.

Lincoln, Mary Johnson. *Mrs. Lincoln's Boston Cook Book: What to Do and What Not to Do in Cooking.* Boston: Little, Brown, 1903.

Littell, E. *Littell's Living Age.* Boston: E. Littell & Co., vol. 31, October, November, December 1851.

Lobel, Cindy R. *Urban Appetites: Food and Culture in Nineteenth-Century New York.* Chicago: University of Chicago Press, 2014.

Lukacs, Paul. *Inventing Wine: A New History of One of the World's Most Ancient Pleasures.* New York: W. W. Norton, 2013.

Machray, Robert. "Liqueur Sir?" *Ludgate Monthly*, vol. 5, November 1897 to April 1898. London: F.V. White & Co., 256.

MacKenzie, Colin. *Mackenzie's Five Thousand Receipts: In All the Useful and Domestic Arts: Constituting a Complete Practical Library Relative to Agriculture, Bees, Bleaching.* Philadelphia: James Kay & Co., 1831.

MacNeil, Karen. *The Wine Bible.* New York: Workman, 2001.

Marshall, Agnes B. *The Book of Ices: Including Cream and Water Ices, Sorbets, Mousses, Iced Soufflés, and Various Iced Dishes, with Names in French and English, and Various Coloured Designs for Ices.* London: Marshall's School of Cookery, 1885.

————. *Mrs. A. B. Marshall's Cookery Book.* London: Marshall's School of Cookery: Simpkin, Marshall, Hamilton, Kent & Co., 1887.

Marshall, Wes. *What's a Wine Lover to Do?* New York: Artisan, 2010.

Mayson, Richard. *Port and the Douro.* Oxford: Infinite Ideas, 2013.

Megargee, Louis N. "Seen and Heard in Many Places." *Philadelphia Times*, May 28, 1897.

————. "Seen and Heard in Many Places." *Philadelphia Times*, June 10, 1897, 4.

Mints, Margaret Louise. *The Great Wilderness.* Millville, NJ: Wheaton Historical Association, 1968.

Mott, Frank. *A History of American Magazines, 1865–1885.* Cambridge, MA: Harvard University Press, 1938.

Murrey, Thomas Jefferson. *The Book of Entrées.* New York: White, Stokes, & Allen, 1886.

————. *Practical Carving.* New York: Frederick A. Stokes, 1887.

"Napolitain' Cake, Historie." *Confectioners' Journal,* February 1875, vol. 1, no. 3, 8.

National Cookery Book Compiled from Original Receipts, For the Women's Centennial Committees of the International Exhibition of 1876. Philadelphia: Henry B. Asmead, 1876.

"Notes from the Watering Places." *New York Herald,* Aug. 2, 1849, no. 5535, 1.

"Old Kriss Kringle's Head-quarters." Advertisement in *North American,* Dec. 30, 1846, vol. 8, no. 2412, 3.

Oliver, Dr. N. T., comp. *Lee's Priceless Recipes: A Valuable Collection of Tried Formulas and Simple Methods.* Chicago: Laird & Lee, 1895.

O'Neill, Molly, ed. *American Food Writing.* New York: Literary Classics of the United States, 2009.

"On Creams." *Confectioners' Journal,* April 1875, vol. 1, no. 5, 17.

"On the Method of Proceeding for the Composition of Ice Creams." *Confectioners' Journal,* June 1876, vol. 2, no. 18, 22.

Owen, Catherine. *Choice Cookery.* New York: Harper & Brothers, 1889.

The Oyster Epicure: A Collation of Authorities on the Gastronomy and Dietetics of the Oyster. New York: White, Stokes & Allen, 1883.

"Oysters! The Bivalves in Philadelphia Where They Come From." *Philadelphia Inquirer,* February 21, 1870, 8.

Page, Karen and Andrew Dorenburg. *The Food Lover's Guide to Wine.* New York: Little, Brown, 2011.

Parker, Robert M. *The Wines of the Rhône Valley.* New York: Simon & Schuster, 1997.

Parkinson, Eleanor. *The Complete Confectioner, Pastry-cook, and Baker.* Philadelphia: Lea and Blanchard, 1844.

Parkinson, James W. "A Brief Account of the Principal Herbs, Roots, Barks, Woods, Seeds, Gums, Fruits, Nuts, Flowers, Blossoms, etc. used in Confectionery, Cookery and Pharmaceutical Confects." *Confectioners' Journal,* April 1875, vol. 1, no. 5, 17.

Parkinson, James W. "A Brief Account of the Principal Herbs, Roots, Barks, Woods, Seeds, Gums, Fruits, Nuts, Flowers, Blossoms, etc. used in Confectionery, Cookery and Pharmaceutical Confects." *Confectioners' Journal*, April 1879, vol. 5, no. 51, 21.

———. *American Dishes at the Centennial*. Philadelphia: King & Baird, 1874.

———. "Ice Cream and Ice Cream Machinery, Ancient and Modern." *Confectioners' Journal*, March 1876, vol. 2, no. 15, 12.

———. "Answers to Correspondents." *Confectioners' Journal*, February 1879, vol. 5, no. 49, 18.

———. "Answers to Correspondents." *Confectioners' Journal*, June 1879, vol. 5, no. 53, 16.

———. "Answers to Correspondents." *Confectioners' Journal*, February 1880, vol. 6, no. 61, 20.

———. "Answers to Correspondents." *Confectioners' Journal*, April 1880, vol. 7, 22.

———. "Answers to Correspondents." *Confectioners' Journal*, November 1880, vol. 8, 22.

———. "Food in Ices." *Confectioners' Journal*, May 1879, vol. 5, no. 52, 14.

———. "Ice Cream." *Confectioners' Journal*, August 1879, vol. 5, no. 55, 22.

———. "Nougat, and its Various Preparations," *Confectioners' Journal*, December 1875, vol. 2, no. 13, 20.

"Parkinson." *Confectioners' Journal*, June 1875, vol. 1, no. 7, 12.

"Parkinson, Provider for Epicures." *Public Ledger*, December 1, 1907.

"Parkinson's Philadelphia Ice Cream in New York." *New York Times*, 25 May 1863, 2.

"Parkinson's Refreshment Saloon." Advertisement in the *Sunday Dispatch*, 2 September 1855.

"Parkinson's Restaurant." *Gleason's Pictorial Drawing-Room Companion*, 28 May 1853, 44–45.

Parloa, Maria. "Everything About the House." *Ladies Home Journal*, November 1891, vol. 8, no. 12, 29.

Party-giving on Every Scale; or the Cost of Entertainments with the Fashionable Modes of Arrangement. London: Frederick Warne and Co., 1880.

Pendergrast, Mark. *Uncommon Grounds: The History of Coffee and How It Transformed Our World*. New York: Basic Books, 1999.

The Penny Magazine of the Society for the Diffusion of Useful Knowledge, vol. 13. London: Charles Knight and Co., 1844.

Pepin, Jacques. "Soup, Beautiful Soup." *New York Times*, March 31, 1991.

Pillsbury, Richard. *From Boarding House to Bistro: The American Restaurant Then and Now*. Boston: Unwin Hyman, 1990.

Prial, Frank J. "In Defense of the Sweet." *New York Times*, November 1, 1987.

Quizno, Jeri. *Of Sugar and Snow: A History of Ice Cream Making*. Berkeley: University of California Press, 2009.

Ranhofer, Charles. *The Epicurean: A Complete Treatise of Analytical and Practical Studies on the Culinary Art, Including Table and Wine Service, how to Prepare and Cook Dishes, Etc., and a Selection of Interesting Bills of Fare of Delmonico's from 1862 to 1894*. New York: Charles Ranhofer, publisher, 1894.

Reardon, Joan. *Oysters: A Culinary Celebration*. New York: Lyons Press, 2000.

Redding, Cyrus. *A History and Description of Modern Wines*. London: Henry G. Bohn, 1851.

———. "The Wines of Germany," *Cozzens' Wine Press*, vols. 1–6, 1855, 114.

"Report of the committee appointed by the Horticultural Society of Pennsylvania for visiting the nurseries and gardens in the vicinity of Philadelphia." July 13, 1830, *The Register of Pennsylvania: devoted to the preservation of facts and documents and every other kind of useful information respecting the state of Pennsylvania*, ed. Samuel Hazard, vol. 7, January to July 1831. Philadelphia: William F. Geddes, printer.

Reynolds, George W. M, ed. "The Rheingau." *The Teetotaler, A Weekly Journal Devoted to Temperance, Literature, and Science*, vols. 1–2, 181–82. London: George Henderson, 1841.

Ripley, George and Charles A. Dana, eds. "Rhenish Wines." *New American Cyclopaedia: A Popular Dictionary of General Knowledge*, vol. 14. New York: D. Appleton, 1862, p. 43.

Ripley, George and Charles A. Dana, eds. "Salmon." *New American Cyclopaedia: A Popular Dictionary of General Knowledge,* vol. 14, 1883.

Ronald, Mary. "Garnishing and Dishing Hot Meats." *Table Talk,* vol. 12, 1897, 120.

Rorer, Sarah Tyson Heston. *Home Candy Making.* Philadelphia: Arnold and Co., 1889.

———. *Mrs. Rorer's New Cook Book: A Manual of Housekeeping.* Philadelphia: Arnold and Co., 1902.

———. *Mrs. Rorer's Philadelphia Cook Book: A Manual of Home Economies.* Philadelphia: Arnold and Co., 1886.

Rothert, Lois Anne. *The Soups of France.* San Francisco: Chronicle Books, 2002.

Rouse, Parke, Jr. *The Great Wagon Road.* New York: McGraw-Hill, 1973.

Rumble, Victoria R. *Soup Through the Ages: A Culinary History With Period Recipes.* Jefferson, NC: McFarland, 2009.

Rundell, Maria Eliza Ketelby. *A New System of Domestic Cookery.* London: R. M'Dermut & D. D. Arden, 1815.

Sala, George Augustus. *The Thorough Good Cook: A Series of Chats on the Culinary Art, and Nine Hundred Recipes.* New York: Brentano's, 1896.

"Salmon." *Stoddart's Encyclopaedia Americana: A Dictionary of Arts, Sciences, and General Literature.* Encyclopaedia Britannica. New York: J. M. Stoddart, 1889.

Sanderson, J. *The Complete Cook: Plain and Practical Directions for Cooking and Housekeeping.* Philadelphia: Lea and Blanchard, 1846.

Scharf, J. Thomas and Thompson Westcott. *History of Philadelphia, 1609–1884,* vol. 2. Philadelphia: L. H. Everts & Co., 1884.

Schwartz, Arthur. *Arthur Schwartz's New York City Food: An Opinionated History and More Than 100 Legendary Recipes.* New York: Stewart, Tabori, and Chang, 2008.

Schweitzer, Teagan. "The Turtles of Philadelphia's Culinary Past." *Expedition,* vol. 51, no. 3, Winter 2009.

Senn, Charles Herman. *The Menu Book.* Food & Cookery Publishing Agency, 1908.

Simon, Andre L. and Robin Howe. *The Dictionary of Gastronomy*. New York: McGraw-Hill, 1970.

Simpson, James. *Creating Wine: The Emergence of a World Industry 1840–1914*. Princeton: Princeton University Press, 2011.

Siskind, Janet. "The Invention of Thanksgiving: A Ritual of American Nationality." *Food in the USA: A Reader*, ed. Carole M. Counihan. New York: Routledge, 2002.

Smith, Andrew F. *Fast Food and Junk Food: An Encyclopedia of What We Love to Eat, Volume 1*. Santa Barbara, CA: ABC-CLIO, 2012.

———, ed. *The Oxford Companion to American Food and Drink*. New York: Oxford University Press, 2007.

———. *Souper Tomatoes: The Story of America's Favorite Food*. New Brunswick, NJ: Rutgers University Press, 2000.

———. *The Turkey: An American Story*. Urbana: University of Illinois Press, 2006.

Soyer, Alexis. *The Modern Housewife; Or, Ménagère: Comprising Nearly One Thousand Receipts*. London: Simpkin, Marshall & Co., 1851.

Staib, Walter. *The City Tavern Cookbook*. Philadelphia: Running Press, 2009.

Stevens, Molly. *All About Roasting: A New Approach to a Classic Art*. New York: W. W. Norton, 2011.

Stevenson, Tom. *The Sotheby's Wine Encyclopedia*. London: Dorling Kindersley, 2007.

Stewart, Amy. *The Drunken Botanist*. Chapel Hill, NC: Algonquin Books, 2013.

Stickney, Robert R. *Aquaculture of the United States: A Historical Survey*. New York: John Wiley & Sons, 1996.

Stimson, Alexander Lovett. *History of the Express Companies: And the Origin of American Railroads*. New York: Baker & Godwin, 1881.

"Strawberries and Cream." *Sunbury American*, April 12, 1851.

Thomas, Lately. *Delmonico's: A Century of Splendor*. Boston: Houghton Mifflin Company, 1967.

Thudichum, John Louis William, M.D. and August Dupre, Ph.D. *A Treatise on the Origin, Nature, and Varieties of Wine: Being a Complete Manual of Viticulture and Oenology*. London: Macmillan, 1872.

Timbs, John, ed. *The Mirror of Literature, Amusement, and Instruction*, Volume 24. J. Limbird, 1834.

"Touches of Old Philadelphia." *Philadelphia Record*, October 5, 1909.

Trubek, Amy B. *Haute Cuisine: How the French Invented the Culinary Profession*. Philadelphia: University of Pennsylvania Press, 2000.

Ude, Louis Eustache. *The French Cook*. London: J. Ebers, 1822.

Ukers, William Harrison. *All About Coffee*. New York: Tea and Coffee Trade Journal Company, 1922.

U.S. Census Bureau. *Report on the Agencies of Transportation in the United States at Tenth Census 1880*.

Visser, Margaret. *The Rituals of Dinner: The Origins, Evolution, Eccentricities, and Meaning of Table Manners*. New York: HarperCollins, 2012.

Von Rumford, Benjamin Graf. *The Complete Works of Count Rumford, Volume 1*. London: Macmillan and Co., 1876.

Walker, Ann and Larry Walker. *To the Heart of Spain: Food and Wine Adventures Beyond the Pyrenees*. Berkeley, CA: Berkeley Hills Books, 1997.

Walsh, Joseph M. *Coffee: Its History, Classification and Description*. Philadelphia: Henry T. Coates & Co., 1894.

Warner, Roger. "Forefathers of the Express." *Express Gazette*, vols. 46–47, 1921, 54–55.

Watson, John F. and Willis P. Hazard. *Annals of Philadelphia and Pennsylvania in the Olden Time*. Philadelphia: Leary, Stuart & Co., 1909.

Weaver, William Woys. *35 Receipts From the Larder Invaded*. Philadelphia: Library Company of Philadelphia and Historical Society of Pennsylvania, 1987.

Weir, Robin and Caroline Weir. *Ice Creams, Sorbets and Gelati: The Definitive Guide*. London: Grub Street, 2010.

Weygandt, Cornelius. *Philadelphia Folks: Ways and Institutions in and About the Quaker City*. New York: D. Appleton-Century, 1938.

White, Jr., John H. *The American Railroad Freight Car*. Baltimore: Johns Hopkins University Press, 1993.

Whitehead, Jessup. *The Steward's Handbook and Guide To Party Catering*. Chicago: J. Anderson & Co., 1889.

Willard, Frances Elizabeth and Mary Ashton Rice Livermore, eds. *A Woman of the Century: Fourteen Hundred-seventy Biographical Sketches Accompanied by Portraits of Leading American Women in All Walks of Life.* Buffalo, NY: Charles Wells Moulton, 1893.

Willcox, James M. *A History of the Philadelphia Savings Fund Society: 1816–1916.* Philadelphia: J. B. Lippincott, 1916.

Williams, Susan. *Food in the United States, 1820s–1890.* Westport, CT: Greenwood Press, 2006.

———. *Savory Suppers and Fashionable Feasts: Dining in Victorian America.* Knoxville: University of Tennessee Press, 1996.

Wilson, Bee. *Consider the Fork: A History of How We Cook and Eat.* New York: Basic Books, 2012.

Wolf, Edwin 2nd. *Philadelphia: Portrait of an American City.* Harrisburg, PA: Stackpole Books, 1975.

Wolf, Edwin 2nd and Marie Elena Korey. *Quarter of a Millennium: The Library Company of Philadelphia, 1731–1981.* Philadelphia: Library Company of Philadelphia, 1981.

Woloson, Wendy A. *Refined Tastes: Sugar, Confectionery, and Consumers in Nineteenth Century America.* Baltimore: Johns Hopkins University Press, 2002.

"The Word Confectionery." *Confectioners' Journal,* Dec. 1874, vol. 1, no. 1, p. 1.

Wright, Clifford A. *The Best Soups in the World.* Hoboken, NJ: John Wiley & Sons, 2010.

Zanger, Mark H. *The American History Cookbook.* Westport, CT: Greenwood, 2003.

ONLINE SOURCES

All Gode Cookery Recipes: Soups and Sauces. Gode Cookery, http://www.godecookery.com/.

Ancestry.com, Philadelphia, Pennsylvania Death Certificates Index, 1803–1915; 1880 United States Federal Census Index, U.S. Find a Grave Index, 1600s–Current.

"Consumer Price Index (Estimate) 1800–," Federal Reserve Bank of Minneapolis, https://www.minneapolisfed.org/community/teaching-aids/cpi-.

Cook, Jerri. "Food and the fast track," *COUNTRYSIDE & Small Stock Journal,* http://www.countrysidemag.com/94-5/food_and_the_fast_track/.

"Cooked Sugar Stages." Joy of Baking Website, http://www.joyofbaking.com/StagesOfCookedSugar.html.

Defenders of Wildlife website, http://www.defenders.org/diamondback-terrapin/what-you-can-do.

Delaware estuary: Oyster Industry—Franklin Institute website—http://www.fi.edu/fellows/fellow7/dec98/history/oyster_history.html.

"French Ice Cream," http://www.foodtimeline.org/foodicecream.html#frenchicecream.

The Genuine Curaçao Liqueur website, http://www.curacaoliqueur.com/history.

"History of the Eastern Oyster" Fact Sheet, Partnership for the Delaware Estuary, Feb. 2002.

"History of the Pressure Cooker," *Miss Vickie's Pressure Cooker Recipes,* http://missvickie.com/.

"How to Experience Cognac," *Le Cognac Website,* http://www.experiencecognac.com/cognacfood.php.

"Ice Cream," Food Timeline, http://www.foodtimeline.org/foodicecream.html#firstchocolate.

"Innovative oyster production takes a big step forward," September 26, 2012, FISHupdate.com. http://www.fishupdate.com/news/archivestory.php/aid/18307/_Innovative_oyster_production_takes_a_big_step_forward.html.

Jacobsen, Rowen. "The Oyster Guide," http://www.oysterguide.com.

Jurafsky, Dan. "Entrée," Language of Food blog http://languageoffood.blogspot.com/2009/08/entree.html, August 15, 2009.

Kloster Eberbach: The Wine Estate of the former Cistercian abbey (Fact Sheet), http://kloster-eberbach.de/fileadmin/media/Weingut/pdf-Dateien_Weingut/Image_brochure_2011.pdf.

"Low Energy Cooking Bygones," http://comestepbackintime.wordpress.com/tag/digester-cookers/.

National Aquarium website, http://www.aqua.org/explore/animals/diamondback-terrapin.

Nelson, Kenneth E. "A Thumbnail History of the Daguerreotype," The Daguerreian Society, 1996, http://daguerre.org/resource/history/history.html.

"Oeil-de-Perdrix," Fine Swiss Wine, http://fineswisswine.ch/neuchatel/oeil-de-perdrix.

Oysters of the Delaware Bay, http://www.cumauriceriver.org.

"Partakers of Our Plenty," Plimoth Plantation website, http://www.plimoth.org/learn/thanksgiving-history/partakers-our-plenty.

"Peaches," GeorgiaInfo—An Online Georgia Almanac, http://georgiainfo.galileo.usg.edu/topics/economy/article/peaches.

"Potage à la Reine: The French origins of a Dutch soup," Coquinaria, http://www.coquinaria.nl/english/recipes/07.2histrecept.htm.

"Precautionary Closure of Shellfish Beds Statewide due to anticipated heavy rainfall from Hurricane Sandy." *New Jersey Department of Environmental Protection Marine Water Monitoring*, October 26, 2012, http://www.nj.gov/dep/bmw/news.html#close102612.

"Purchasing Power of Money in the United States from 1774 to Present," Measuringworth.com, http://www.measuringworth.com/calculators/ppowerus/.

Sauternes Wine Information, Wine Types Wiki website, http://www.winetypeswiki.com/wine/sauternes.

"Snapper Soup," *Eat Your World Website*, http://eatyourworld.com/destinations/united_states/pennsylvania/philadelphia/what_to_eat/snapper_soup.

"Swiss Wine: Oeil de Perdrix," *Rhi's Foodie Life Blog*, June 29, 2014, http://rhisfoodielife.wordpress.com/2014/06/29/swiss-wine-oeil-de-perdrix/.

Tarmy, James. "To Every Wine (Sauternes, Sauternes, Sauternes) There Is a Reason," *Bloomberg*, May 1, 2013, http://www.bloomberg.com/news/2013-05-01/to-every-wine-sauternes-sauternes-sauternes-there-is-a-reason.html.

"Thanksgiving History," Plimoth Plantation website, http://www.plimoth.org/learn/MRL/read/thanksgiving-history.

Thomson, Julie R. "Maraschino Liqueur Is A Secret Weapon For Your Liquor Cabinet," *Huffington Post*, April 11, 2012, http://www.huffingtonpost.com/2013/10/17/maraschino-liqueur_n_1415277.html.

Twilley, Nicola. "The Impossibility of Historical Flavour," *Edible Geography*, January 1, 2013, http://www.ediblegeography.com/the-impossibility-of-historical-flavour/.

U.S. Fish & Wildlife Service, http://www.fws.gov/international/cites/cop16/diamondback-terrapin.html.

ARCHIVAL SOURCES

Advertisement for the Blum Restaurant on Tenth and Market Streets. *Philadelphia Inquirer*, September 19, 1906; vol. 155, no. 81, 6.

Advertisement for "The Green House," from Confectionery Vertical File, courtesy of Library Company, Philadelphia.

Cadwalader Family Papers. Historical Society of Pennsylvania, http://hsp.org/sites/default/files/legacy_files/migrated/findingaid1454cadwaladerpart1.pd.

Parkinson's Restaurant A La Carte. Menu from the International Electrical Exhibition of the Franklin Institute. Philadelphia, 1884. Library Company of Philadelphia, Accession No: 5359.F.

"Salons De Parkinson, Le Quatre Fevrier, 1853," Menu Collection, Library Company of Philadelphia.

Jacob Snider Papers, New York Public Library Rare Books and Manuscripts Division, Accession # *85M21.

ACKNOWLEDGMENTS

Deconstructing a nineteenth-century seventeen-course menu was a daunting task. Luckily I live near two wonderful research repositories with extremely courteous and helpful librarians—the Library Company of Philadelphia and the Historical Society of Pennsylvania. I happily spent hours immersed in the books, files, papers, and images housed at both locations. Connie King, Krystal Appiah, Linda August, Sarah Weatherwax, and Nicole Joniec at the Library Company patiently retrieved my requested items and provided guidance and suggestions regarding additional research possibilities. Lee Arnold and Steve Smith at the Historical Society also helped track down the resources I needed.

Rutgers University is one of the only nearby locations to house multiple copies of *Confectioners' Journal*. Dean Meister, branch manager of the Libraries Annex there, was very helpful in having ready the copies I wanted to view and investigating a query I had later on, thus saving me another trip.

Since this dinner touched on so many different types of food and wine, it was useful to query a variety of experts to get clarification or additional information. The late Lynne Olver, who maintained the website foodtimeline.org, enthusiastically and promptly fielded my questions about a number of food-related topics. Dirk Burhans and Dave Mitchell gave me insight and background regarding the history of Saratoga potatoes—the first "potato chips."

To fully understand the evolution of the Delaware Bay oyster industry and its current situation, I contacted several authorities that were very helpful. Joe Myers of the New Jersey Department of Agriculture kindly explained New Jersey's Aquaculture Development Zone Program. Dave Bushek and Lisa Calvo of the Haskin Shellfish Research Laboratory generously took time out of their busy schedules to show me around their facility and field my questions. Dave also answered and clarified a number of my inquiries later on in the writing process. Donna Moore, Mayor of Commercial Township, New Jersey, offered some meaningful suggestions about where to find information about the history of Port Norris and its role in New Jersey's oyster industry.

Wine and liquors were a very important part of the Thousand Dollar Dinner. The extremely knowledgeable Paul Lukacs graciously answered my inquiries about the vintages that were served that April evening in 1851 and provided specific details about the differences between modern wines and those from the nineteenth century. Wine expert Maureen Petrosky also fielded some questions to help fill in gaps in my research and offered much-appreciated support for the book topic.

I used an extensive number of books and other research materials to develop a thorough understanding of nineteenth-century foods, chefs, dining customs, preparation techniques, the Parkinson and Delmonico families, and the role of Philadelphia at this time in culinary history. Three volumes were especially helpful and always within arm's reach on my desk: *The Oxford Companion to American Food and Drink* edited by Andrew F. Smith, *The Oxford Companion to Food* by Alan Davidson, and *Larousse Gastronomique*.

Many people provided helpful feedback and support while I was working on this book. To all my friends and family who asked how the book was progressing and expressed interest in the topic, many thanks; it means a great deal to me that you care. To my husband and children—my deep love and gratitude for putting up with all my highs and lows during the research and writing process.

I am grateful to have Diane Richardson of the Ebenezer Maxwell Mansion as a friend and mentor. Her thoughtful and insightful comments and positive encouragement of my work always inspires me. I also appreciate the support of Chef Walter Staib of the City Tavern and Molly Yun, marketing and public relations director at Concepts By Staib and their interest in this project. At Westholme Publishing, I would like to thank my copyeditor, Noreen O'Connor-Abel, jacket designer, Trudi Gershenov, and proofreader, Mike Kopf. And last, I couldn't have seen this project through to completion without my publisher, Bruce H. Franklin. His vision helped guide me in chronicling this compelling story.

INDEX

Lightning Source UK Ltd.
Milton Keynes UK
UKOW04f2235100817
307084UK00002B/201/P